CRY FROM THE HIGHEST MOUNTAIN

TESS BURROWS

Foreword by THE DALAI LAMA
Introduction by JOANNA LUMLEY, OBE

20TH ANNIVERSARY EDITION

EYE BOOKS
NON-FICTION

7th Edition
Published by Eye Books Ltd 2018
29A Barrow Street
Much Wenlock
Shropshire
TF13 6EN
eye-books.com

ISBN: 9781785631153

British Library Cataloguing in Publication Data
A catalogue record for this book is available from the British Library

Printed by CPI Group (UK) Ltd, Croydon CR0 4YY

I offer this book with love,
that Tibet
and the Earth
may be free from oppression
and find peace

Contents

Preamble to the 20th anniversary edition

This 20th anniversary edition tells of the beginning of the 'Climb For Tibet' story – my dream, as one small human being, to make the world a better place. This is how our first Peace Climb happened. It nearly cost me my life. But I learned that all the strength I need is there, if I believe in myself.

Armed with this knowledge I kept going. Twenty years on, tens of thousands of individuals of all ages have sent Peace Messages – the little girl who promised not to fight with her brother and changed the atmosphere of her family; the African man who pledged to plant trees which brought food and shelter; and the thousands who sent prayers to help others. This is people power making a difference, at all levels.

These Peace Messages have been carried to far, high spots, and spoken out like Tibetan prayer flags spreading blessings on the wind. I've journeyed extensively across the world with 'Climb For Tibet' team members. We've lit beacons of peace at the North and South Poles, in the Himalayas, the Andes, the Pacific and in Africa, creating a six-pointed star of peace – a grid of light encompassing the planet.

Along the way, over £150,000 has been raised for practical charity projects, for building six Tibetan schools and other humanitarian and environmental ventures – much of this through the sale of my four books. Yes, still there is much work to do. Still the Tibetan people is heavily oppressed. Still there is disrespect for our Earth. Still there are wars. The cry for peace is as urgent as ever. And yet now, as the peace juggernaut revs up, there is a critical mass of people who know we can't turn away from the responsibility of looking after our Earth. My belief is that 'Climb For Tibet' has contributed to turning the corner, and that at last there is enough positivity and love to hold the whole in balance. That the daily diet of horrendous reported news is merely the clearing out of the old. That this is an exciting time to be alive. That we're heading into a time of peace and harmony! We just have to hold our nerve, think of humanity and our Earth as one interconnected entity, and keep working on the love.

The young hero of 'Climb For Tibet', Mig, now lives in New York with his family, running successful clothing stores employing people from the Himalayan region – a far cry from wild mountain slopes. The climb, he says, was his life's most significant milestone, exciting and meaningful, and it has given him the courage to cope with the hardships and challenges that life brings.

I hope you, the reader, may also draw courage and inspiration to face life's ongoing challenges from the pages of this book.

Tess Burrows
November 2018

Foreword

When the Communist Chinese first invaded Tibet more than forty years ago, they talked about peaceful liberation. Instead, we Tibetans have experienced the greatest period of loss and destruction in our history. Hundreds of thousands of people have died, and thousands who had committed no crime other than patriotism have suffered long years of imprisonment. Our monasteries and nunneries, the repositories of our rich and ancient culture, our source of education, have been demolished. Our institutions of government have been set aside, so that the destiny of Tibet and its people is no longer in the hands of Tibetans. Our natural resources, which we used carefully and treated with respect, have been wantonly plundered and the environment spoiled. Even the wild animals who once lived without fear of human beings have been ruthlessly eliminated.

A climate of oppression currently prevails in Tibet. Virtually everything of significance to Tibetans is under attack. At the same time, the people of Tibet are almost powerless to respond. The Chinese authorities brook no opposition to their rule. Protest provokes an invariably harsh reaction. This is where we Tibetans who live in exile have a special responsibility, for we have the freedom to speak up for our brothers and sisters in Tibet. We can make known the reality of life in our homeland. We can help increase awareness of the value of Tibetan culture and the loss to humanity if it should be allowed to disappear.

This book written by Tess Burrows tells the story of 'Climb For Tibet' and seeks to make readers aware of Tibet's indomitable spirit and our undiminished determination, so admirably shown by one young man, Migmar Tsering. It embraces the spirit of compassion, which we Tibetans value so highly, that is to be proclaimed from the mountain in thousands of messages of peace. We Tibetans live in a distant and remote land, but like everyone else we want to live in peace and happiness, and like everyone else we have a right to do so. I hope readers whose interest is stirred by this book may also be inspired to give their support and see their own way forward in love and respect for all beings. Let us all, brothers and sisters of the single human family, live together in peace.

His Holiness the Dalai Lama
Winner of the 1989 Nobel Peace Prize
December 1999

Introduction

Of course it seemed crazy, impossible and over-ambitious: but at the same time Tess Burrows' 'Climb For Tibet' project sounded thrilling, engaging and daring. Could they do it? Or more importantly, could she do it? The expedition would be extremely tough by any standard. And would anyone actually send any prayers? Would the tiny team even reach the summit?

I became a patron on the spot, with great pride and anxiety. There were so many aspects of the trip that intrigued me – a woman of nearly fifty attempting something so dangerous: a unique idea which sounded mad but was to be presented at the Royal Geographical Society; a passionate belief that prayers can change the world; the extraordinary fundraising efforts, all for charity; and the support of the Tibetan community headed by His Holiness the Dalai Lama, who had readily agreed to become the chief patron.

It had everything to make a good story, lecture, book or film – the planning, the ascent, setbacks and triumphs, illustrated by photographs and so forth. But gleaming brightly above all this was the inspiration – if you want something enough, go for it.

This is an enthralling journey of courage and endurance. Now the peaceful crystal shines from Chimborazo. Below it, mankind stands yet again at the crossroads of war and peace, still wondering which path to take...

Joanna Lumley, OBE
May 1999

World map

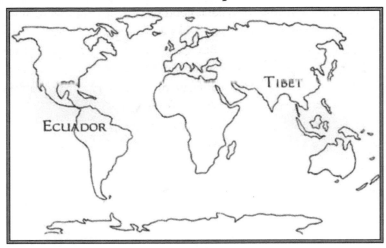

Ecuador

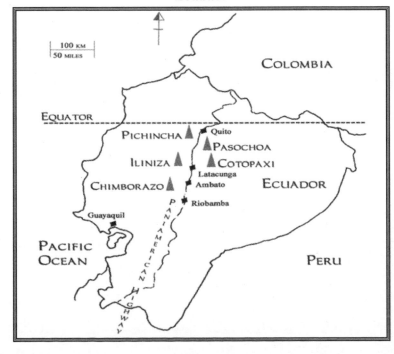

Diagram of the Earth as an oblate spheroid

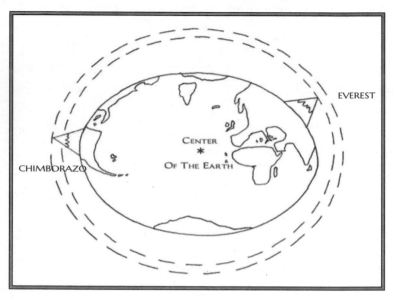

Diagram of heights above sea level

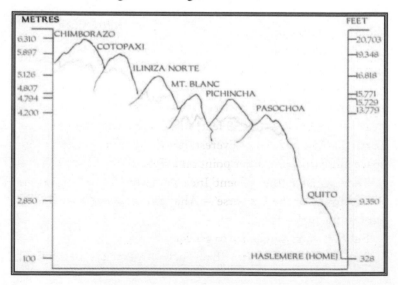

Prologue

If you wanted to express a really important message that would affect the future of humanity, then you could do worse than shout it from the highest mountain.

First, look at the shape of the Earth and see that the point furthest from the centre is in fact not Everest, but a little-known extinct volcano in Ecuador called Chimborazo. Although this mountain is only 6,310 metres (20,703 feet) above sea level, its peak is 2,150 metres (7,059 feet) further from the centre of the Earth than the summit of Everest. It is the bit that sticks out into space more than any other point on Earth.

Then see that the ancient Inca name for Chimborazo was 'Watchtower of the Universe' – Aha! This could be the place to express the highest ideals.

But first you would have to get there.

This book is about just that. Seen through the eyes of the

journey of my body and my spirit, and the window of my heart, it brought me to the realisation that, in the ultimate act of symbolism, in fact the struggle was also to climb my highest mountain within – myself.

And the message from the mountain? Well, this book is about that, too. It's about the deep pain that the Tibetan nation is suffering and has suffered for many decades. It's about the words of the Tibetan spiritual leader, His Holiness the Dalai Lama, who offers humanity a way forward in brotherhood – if only we could listen…

It's about the sheer dedication and love that brought the 'Climb For Tibet' team together and made the climb a reality…

I have a picture carved forever in the temple of my mind: floating whiteness on a sacred mountain; ethereal joy; colourful prayer flags blowing in the wind; a gift for the Earth as blessing for all beings; and a young Tibetan who has just given more of himself than most people would expect to give in many lifetimes. He is lying on his back in the snow, Tibetan flag at his feet. His arms punch the thin air that clasps cruelly at his lungs. Through tears of exhaustion he cries from the depths of his being:

'Peace on Earth'

1 : Born of a dream

6 July 1998 (The Dalai Lama's birthday) – diary extract
I knew I was going to die...even before we reached 6,000 metres. The summit of Chimborazo waited, elusive, shrouded in bright cloud.

Four times I've made the decision not to turn back, when all reason and sense were shouting at me, 'Return alive, go down, now. You're in the final stage of altitude sickness... It's cerebral oedema... The brain is starved of oxygen...swelling and expanding.' Surely my brain is going to explode...too big for my head...trying to get out...like it's on fire. Bits of time are going missing. I must go down quickly...go down.

But the stakes are too high... How can I turn away now? My life is not my own to save... We must reach the summit, that the light may shine for peace... We must reach the summit. We must go on.

My reality is dropping off either side of me... Do not let the body stop... Too much pain to stop... But I want to lie down and die...

13 June 1998

The sun was shining so brilliantly through the small oval window of the aeroplane that I had to shield my eyes to see the curvature of the cotton-wool horizon.

'It's not a commonly known fact that the Earth's not round,' I remarked.

The Dutch businessman in the aisle seat on the KLM flight from Heathrow to Amsterdam turned to look at me. There was just a hint of disdain on his knitted brow. Dressed conventionally, with immaculately combed hair, he gave the impression of being a regular commuter, accustomed to level-headed conversations. He was stuck next to me for the journey.

'Did you say you were going on to Quito?' he enquired politely, as though he was trying to change the subject to something normal that would fit in to a well-structured day. If sensitive, he would have had an impending sense of doom that he was about to be the next victim of a sponsor-collecting attack.

'Yes, we're going to climb the highest mountain in the world.'

'Oh.' There followed a thinking sort of silence. What more could he say, apart from, 'Aren't you on the wrong plane?'

'It's in Ecuador, you know,' I went on.

The stocks and shares section of the newspaper he was reading wavered a little.

'Everyone always thinks it's Everest,' I threw in, trying to pull the carpet from under a nice, safe view of the world.

He finally put his newspaper down, glancing round a little nervously at the other suited businessmen who filled the rest of the plane, all happily studying the daily papers... KOSOVO AWAITS

NATO JETS – THE WORLD'S MAIN MILITARY POWERS SEEK AUTHORITY TO LAUNCH ASSAULTS. FOX HUNTING – THE PEOPLE WILL DECIDE. ERITREAN AIR RAID KILLS FOUR AT AID CENTRE – SCENE OF BITTER FIGHTING. RADIOACTIVITY TESTS GO ON – INDICATIONS OF FIVE TIMES THE ACCEPTED LEVEL. FRENCH PERFUME MAKER SHOT BY ARMED RAIDERS. PENSIONER DIES AFTER ATTACK BY STREET GANG.

'Isn't it Everest?'

'Well,' with familiar enthusiasm and sense of fun at the intrigue it always caused, I started out: 'Everest is of course the highest from sea level, at 8,848 metres or 29,028 feet, but if you measure from the centre of the Earth, then the highest is a mountain near the equator in the Andes of South America.' I could see from the widening of his steely grey eyes that I had his interest now.

'So why…?'

'The Earth's not round. It's an oblate spheroid.'

'Ah.'

'In other words, it's bulgy at the equator, and flattened at the poles.'

'Oh.'

'A learned geographical friend of mine says this is due to what he calls "the pizza effect". Have you ever seen an authentic pizza being made, with the dough spun around? The outer edges of the pizza push out into a yummy bulgy bit. Well, it's the same with the Earth. The spinning on her axis causes a sort of lesser holding on to gravity at the equator than there is at the poles. It's the thing that scientists used to call centrifugal force.'

'So why don't we all learn about that at school?' he asked, his interest building.

'I don't know. Maybe it's because people tend not to stand back and look at the Earth as a whole, or maybe because it's only a small difference we're talking about. If you had a metre and a half globe, then the yummy bulgy bit would only be sticking out about three millimetres.'

I thought about how I had explained it in this way at one of the school assemblies I had spoken to about our project. The youngsters seemed to have understood this well when I demonstrated by spinning a huge old illuminated globe. There were holes in it where the light shone through, and parts of some countries were hanging off. 'Our Earth's falling to bits,' I had said. 'She needs help to be put back together.'

My Dutch friend persisted, 'So what's the difference on the world scale?'

'Well, the oblate-spheroidness,' I replied, enjoying getting my tongue around such a wonderful word, 'can be seen by measuring the diameter of the Earth at the equator, which is roughly 42½ kilometres longer than it is at the poles.'

The puzzled look seemed to imply that this fact had somehow upset his sense of order, that we were spinning through space on a less than perfect planet.

'And the oblate-spheroidness,' I continued, 'means that the summit of the mountain we're going to climb is 2,150 metres – that's more than 7,000 feet – further from the centre of the Earth than the summit of Everest is. It's the bit that sticks out the most.'

'Does this mean that your mountain is the point on the world that's nearest the sun?' he asked.

'No, that honour goes to different places between the tropics every day, owing to the tilt of the Earth and where she is in her orbit. But in fact our mountain is the point nearest the sun on about 15 March and 27 September, near the spring and autumn equinoxes.' Again, I mentally thanked my learned geographical friend for his research.

The conversation was interrupted by the arrival of an air hostess with a plasticated airline snack.

Distracted, my mind wandered back to my Surrey and Hampshire childhood. I was a tomboy of sorts, and never happier than when playing with my older brother, Graham, whom I adored (even though he had tried to discover electricity by plugging me, his baby sister, into the mains). I loved my younger sisters, but the usual pastimes of girls were not for me. Graham and I used to play for hours, creating model towns and animating them with the life of the safe, everyday, suburban world around us.

One day he returned from school, excited by a book he had found... *The New Believe It or Not*, by Ripley, published in 1930. 'Look, Tess, see this page. It says Mount Everest is not the highest mountain in the world, but a mountain in Ecuador is.'

A seed had been sown.

A while later he came home with another significant book, *Banner in the Sky*, by James Ramsay Ullman, a fictitious account of the first climbing of the Matterhorn. It became my favourite book. When I reached the part when the young hero Rudi was unable to climb to the very top of the mountain, I would cry bitter tears until the end of the story and then immediately start again at the beginning. I dreamed of climbing the highest mountain.

But childish dreams get lost in growing up, in pleasing parents and society, and in searching for one's own fulfilment. It was to be more than thirty years before I remembered.

2 : 'Climb For Tibet'

The plane shifted in its temporary orbit and I felt the release of gravity as we started our descent into Schipol airport.

'Come on then, which mountain is it that you're talking about, the one which is the furthest from the centre of the Earth?' pressed the Dutchman amicably.

'It's called Chimborazo.'

'Nice name.'

'And it's actually 6,310 metres above sea level. That's nearly 21,000 feet.'

'Still a hell of a climb then?'

'Yeah, should test us,' I replied, not knowing then quite how true those words were to be.

We were now dropping fast away from the sun towards the cloud cover which blanketed the Earth. Protection or pollution, I wondered, as we banked slightly to enter the greyness, and headed towards modern, industrialised Europe.

'Er, I just happen to have a sponsorship form with me. I was wondering if you would, er, like to sponsor us. It's actually quite an important peace climb and we're raising money to help Tibet and Tibetan refugees.' With a smile I handed my new friend a 'Climb For Tibet' form. It was a thing of beauty, with our logo in the corner, in full colour in honour of the stunning Tibetan flag.

The flag, like so many Tibetan things, is full of meaning. It expresses more than national pride, more even than the hopes of a people now lost but for their spirit, which burns with an unquenchable flame. The white mountain represents the land of snows. The two snow lions embody the dual strength of the Tibetan government: political and spiritual. The wheel denotes harmony. The jewel is wisdom. The yellow sun depicts Tibetan Buddhism radiating out, and the red stripes stand for the six original tribes of Tibet. But the yellow border of Buddhism which encloses the spirit of the nation on three sides is left empty to the right, representing the openness of a land that all are welcome to enter in peace. It is poignant that it was from the east that the invasion came to this once free and beautiful country.

'Do you know what happened in Tibet?' I asked.

'I have the feeling you're about to tell me,' he answered, not unkindly, so I piled in quickly while he was attentive.

'Well, in 1950 the newly formed Chinese communist regime marched in and declared Tibet to be part of China. The peace-loving Tibetans were no match for the Chinese Red Army. They tried for the next few years to work with their invading neighbours, but by 1959 it was clear that negotiations were of no use, and Tibet's young spiritual and temporal leader, His Holiness the fourteenth Dalai Lama, was forced to flee across the Himalayas, only just escaping with his life. The Indian administration generously gave him refuge to establish a government in exile at

Dharamsala in the foothills of Northern India.'

'Is that where he lives now?'

'Yes, from there he's tried for forty years to peacefully regain freedom from oppression for his people. He has had to watch the rape of his homeland, cultural and religious genocide, murder, torture and other horrendous human rights abuses – all in the attempted annihilation of the identity of the Tibetan nation that he represents.'

'But surely he's had help – from the international community, I mean?'

'No, to this day, the governments of the rest of the world have done very little. After all, how did it affect other countries? There was no oil dependency like in Kuwait, it was not on the periphery of the Western world like in Kosovo, there was no direct threat... and trade with China is so important.'

Few who took the time to absorb what we were doing could resist supporting the cause, particularly to spread the knowledge of this injustice.

'Well, of course. I'd be delighted to sponsor you,' the Dutchman responded, reaching for his wallet, and continued, 'Very sad, yes, the situation is very sad. I'm sure many people in my country, too, must be aware, but what is to be done?' He shrugged. A shrug is a small act, just a little raising of the shoulders. It implies a kind of indifference, an attitude of 'Well, what can I do about it? I have my own life to lead and I can't help everyone.' But when you multiply that shrug by millions and even billions around the world, then you have a major shrug problem – a huge lump of indifference towards the inhumanities that are going on in Tibet. We were trying to eat away at that lump.

An Englishman on the other side of the aisle leaned across in front of the obstructing legs of the air hostess who was trying to close overhead compartments and check that all her passengers were safely captive in their seats. Her efficient air said that all was secure, and our everyday lives were not at risk.

'I say, what are you raising money for?' he asked. 'I couldn't help overhearing what you were talking about. I saw the film *Seven Years In Tibet* recently – a superb film. Have you seen it? It portrayed the tragic end to a way of life – maybe the last of its kind – tucked away in the Himalayas, not hurting anyone. It must have been such a beautiful country. You know, the thought of it stirred all my yearnings to be an explorer in the days when an ancient civilisation existed that was unaffected by modern pollution and greed for material things.'

Our project always seemed to attract people who had an interest in the legendary land of Shangri-La.

'I really think Tibetan Buddhism could do so much to help the 'dog eat dog' problems of the world today,' he went on. 'It was a culture where the religion was a way of life, where kindness was more important than money.'

It was the moment to pass him a sponsorship form before he got too carried away with the irrelevance of money.

'Yeah, even though the film's in Hollywood style, it does do a lot to raise awareness of the Tibetan situation and strike a chord with this sort of thinking,' I responded, my mind drifting a little.

The great teacher Sogyal Rinpoche speaks of the Tibetan word for 'body' which is *lü*, meaning 'something you leave behind', like baggage, reminding us that we are only travellers, taking temporary refuge in this body and in this life. He says that in Tibet, people did not distract themselves by spending all their time trying to make their external circumstances more comfortable. They were satisfied if they had enough to eat, clothes on their backs, and a roof over their heads. So, as we obsessively try to improve our conditions – an end in itself and a pointless distraction – he asks, 'Would people in their right mind think of

25

fastidiously redecorating their hotel room every time they check into one?'

I wondered if this belief in reincarnation, and also in karma, the natural law of cause and effect, made it easier to put kindness first, knowing that what you give out always comes back to you at some point. I remembered something my father, Ken, had said. We had been very close, and during the last ten years or so of his life we had the wonderful gift of sharing spiritual discoveries and learning. He had always delighted in the fun and the skill of financial schemes, but one day he had said to his grandchildren, while looking at their school reports: 'It's not being the cleverest in the class that counts. It's being the kindest.' Great sentiments, but very hard to live up to, especially when tired, grumpy and stressed-out.

Undoubtedly, the run up to catching this plane had seen me at my worst. There had been weeks of increasingly frantic and frenetic build-up to 'Climb For Tibet' before our departure, ending with trying to squeeze two months' work into the last couple of days, with almost no sleep. I had never been so stressed, and being kind to those nearest to me – especially to Pete – had gone out of the window. I turned to Pete, sitting beside me – my partner and my gift from the universe. We had worked so hard together to create 'Climb For Tibet.'

'Tell them where the money's going,' he urged with a squeeze of my knee. As always, he was the one with his feet on the ground.

I had a captive audience so I began to explain. 'We're splitting the funds we raise two ways. Fifty per cent is going directly to help refugees who have just escaped across the mountains. They're teenagers and young people in their twenties. Most of them arrive in a pretty bad state, with severe frostbite, malnutrition and clothes in tatters after weeks of foot-slogging by night and hiding from the Chinese patrols in the daytime.'

'Sounds tough.'

'Yeah, and even when they do cross the border, most commonly into Nepal, there's no guarantee that the Nepalese authorities won't send them back. Our refugee camp is in India. It's one of the projects of the Tibet Relief Fund, the charitable arm of the Tibet Society. I asked their director last year what the most needy situation was. He told me the Khanyara Transit School, about 11 kilometres from Dharamsala, was desperate for help. At the moment it's just tin sheds in mud, but they find a haven there, somewhere to sleep, education, clothes and badly needed food.

'More than that, it's spiritual nourishment, as every refugee has a chance to see the Dalai Lama. You probably know, he's frequently described as a "God-King". I once heard a lovely Tibetan singer dedicate a song to him, declaring, "Without him there is no light." That says it all. It's amazing, really, that even after all this time in exile, his life still gives such strength to the Tibetan people…keeps their flame of hope alive.'

'A truly great leader.'

'Definitely. The escapees, though, must find it hard. So often they leave their families in Tibet, and many are still only children who are sent out by their parents to get an education with Tibetan culture and to have freedom.

'You know, we take so much for granted our freedom to say what we believe, to support who we want. Imagine not being able to keep a photo of the Queen, or the Pope, or Elvis, or whoever your star or most revered person is. Imagine being found with a picture on you or in your house, and because of it you're tortured or forced to renounce your support for this person…tortured perhaps in a way that doesn't show, like sticks and electric batons being shoved up personal parts of your body. Then if you still don't renounce this person you're taken off to jail with no fair trial.

27

'Imagine you get angry and shout "Long live the Queen!" or whoever, and you're then tied with your hands behind your back and strung from the ceiling...and left to hang for days, naked.'

Can we imagine?

'Here, let me give you all the cash I've got in sterling,' interjected the Englishman.

'Great, thanks so much,' I smiled, hoping he'd just been to the bank, and carried on. 'The second half of the money we raise actually works for that freedom. It goes to the Free Tibet Campaign. It's an independent British organisation which operates to change the situation and apply pressure at a political level. They do a huge amount to raise awareness through public education and direct action.'

I fished out one of their leaflets to give him: 'Free Tibet Campaign stands for the Tibetans' right to decide their own future, an end to the Chinese occupation of Tibet and the Tibetans' fundamental human rights to be respected.'

He looked perplexed: 'So, you're doing what you can to help Tibet at a practical level, but there's something I don't understand. Why are you carrying out a sponsored climb for Tibet in South America, on the other side of the globe?'

'Because that's where the highest mountain is...the point furthest from the centre of the Earth.'

'Ah, yes,' he responded, with a twinkly sort of a smile.

'Anyway, we can't go waving flags around and supporting Tibetans actually in Tibet, even in the unlikely event of the Chinese giving us permission. It'd bring reprisals on any local

Tibetans who'd even vaguely "collaborated" with us. They'd be called "splittists" from the motherland, part of the "Dalai clique". In all likelihood they'd become political prisoners, be tortured and possibly worse.'

'I feel the problems in Tibet are a microcosm of those of the Earth,' I continued, taking the chance not only to raise awareness for Tibet and tell people what we were doing, but also to put across the wider picture. 'As you said, there is imbalance because greed and power take precedent over caring for other people and the environment on which we all depend. The Earth is crying out in need. Humanity has pushed her beyond what her natural systems can recover from without huge pain to our species. Many people are aware that unless we stop taking now and start giving back, the planet as we know it will not survive.'

'Certainly, and we all hide from this fact, don't we?' agreed the Englishman.

'Yeah, but already there're rumblings and grumblings of the shifts necessary to rebalance it all. Look at all the unusual stuff – droughts, floods, hurricanes and avalanches... The more individuals take responsibility, even in a small way, and work with the Earth, not against her, the more chance there is of survival. That's the only way it'll happen.' I saw kindred understanding in his face. 'We're talking about our own tomorrows.'

One of my yesterdays that had influenced my way of thinking was my time at Edinburgh University. I had been lucky. They were fun and carefree days. A memory of piling people onto an open car (I think the record was sixteen), so we could drive around waving and putting smiles on glum faces, comes to mind.

I also have an enduring academic memory. I was studying ecological science, the first course of its kind in Britain. In the late 1960s no one had heard of ecology – plants and animals in relation to their environment? Interdependence? What's that?

I remember drawing population 'S' curves for animals (plotting changes in numbers against time). The population always intrinsically controls itself when it reaches the top of the 'S'. I felt sure then that human population would eventually be controlled by the levels of pollutants rising to a critical point.

Those were the days of Rachel Carson's *Silent Spring*, a ground-breaking book describing the effects of poisons and disrespect for our environment, and creating for the first time a general awareness that we were messing up the world around us.

We hit the Earth with a thud, as if to confirm that we were all in this 'life boat' together, sailing through space – rocks, soil, water, atmosphere, plants, animals and humans of every race and creed.

'Would you like to sign the pledge on our sponsor form?' I asked both men, not at all sorry that I had been getting stirred up. 'It's like making a commitment to be part of the solution, rather than part of the problem.'

> *As a citizen of the Earth I pledge to take personal action to help the healing of the world, expressing the Tibetan spirit of compassion for all life, non-violence and universal responsibility, for we are all inexorably bound together in a physical, mental and spiritual ecology.*

They signed, with not a hint of Oh-help-I-can't-get-out-of-this-now. I thanked them; every signature was an important part of our mission. The pledge they had signed always rang an urgent bell in my mind, sending it racing back to one day in 1993...

3 : Messages of peace

At this point I would like to have a little aside with my reader. If you're someone who doesn't accept that there is anything beyond the physical, that's OK. You can skip the next few paragraphs – or you could read them and think 'that's a weird bit, she needs burning at the stake' and get on with enjoying the rest of the story.

Most people who haven't had this experience are rightly sceptical. Those who have do not doubt its authenticity, but of course, like many things in life, it sounds weird until you've actually been there and done it – like a coconut might appear to an Eskimo. Sometimes truth is stranger than fiction.

We were a small group gathered in a house for a meeting. Outwardly the building was no different from the others in the street. The plants looked cared-for, the cat fluffy and content. We waited in a darkened room, full of anticipation. Candles were lit and flickered, while a prayer for protection was spoken. My nervousness was calmed by the knowledge that the Tibetans have always consulted the oracle spirit on important matters, such as the confirmation of the reincarnation of the Dalai Lama or his flight out of Tibet. In such an energy of universal purpose, spirits from the world of the non-physical were to speak to us through the body of a trained medium. We were to meet two of the greatest world leaders of the century, both contributors to the freedom of humankind.

Winston Churchill and Mahatma Gandhi had come to tell us that they were trying to help the Earth today from the spirit world, and to emphasise the urgency of finding inner peace. Their ways of speaking carried the quality of their characteristic personalities, but their perceptions and wisdom had expanded to the extent that their words felt like marvellous jewels.

Churchill came through with:

'...Climb for peace, not only peace in the human condition, but also peace in the human spirit... There is one power far greater than the atom bomb, far greater than guns, tanks – whatever armaments you have. It is the power of love and the projection of that love, the essence of which creates, throughout the whole of this planet, a movement of conscious light. How is it expressed? From the highest mountain, the vision is for the eyes, the energy is from the heart... But we must express it in groups so that they and we, united together, project an immense power, and counteract that of the demons, which live in so many hearts and cause so much devastation in this world now...'

The palpable sense of presence changed, and I felt greatly honoured that the body arose and shook hands with me. The touch was gentle and firm.

Gandhi then spoke, and it was as though he were bestowing gifts on us:

> '...What I would say to those who are listening and to those who will read your book in the future is... We do not own anything... we only share it for the duration of our lives, and therefore our responsibility is to return it in good condition for others to enjoy. We must now see ourselves as part of the great global family... We must share in the restoration of all that we have damaged... In the end, if there is no Nature, then we must also die. There is a time lapse left of seven years. If our thinking about caring for the Earth has not changed by then, we will have passed the point of no return. The planet will start to become barren and will die.'

This warning of Gandhi's above all else I have not been able to forget. But I hope and believe that in this critical time, the love and compassion will be powerful enough.

There was one more vital thing to do before we were all disgorged into the busy international terminal. Perhaps it was the most valuable of all – an incentive to open to love and compassion.

'Would you like to fill in the "message from the mountain" box on the form?' I persisted. 'It's giving us your personal message in support of Tibet and Earth peace. By using the words "Earth peace" we are including the harmony of the natural systems of the Earth as well as that of humanity, rather than 'world peace', which tends to mean only the peace of people.

'We ask, too, that the messages be in the Tibetan spirit. That is, an expression of the ideals of the Dalai Lama – compassion for all life, non-violence and universal responsibility.

'We'll read them all out from the mountain. It's a bit like the age-old Tibetan tradition of flying prayer flags from the highest place possible – you would have seen them in the film. Their bright colours represent the elemental make-up of all things. There's blue for sky, white for cloud, red for fire, green for pure life-stream and yellow for earth. They're imbued with mantras and messages of peace, and then the wind-horse carries them far and wide to invoke blessings and wellbeing to all. That's what our messages will do, too. So far we've collected nearly a thousand.'

'What a super idea,' came the English reply. 'It's as though all those people supporting you are actually being part of the climb, and making its effect much more powerful.'

It was even more than that. As with my understanding behind the signing of the pledge, an individual who finds peace changes the peace of the Earth. It's an expression of the law of interdependence. Furthermore, if a person produces a thought and turns it into something 'concrete' by writing it down, then it will help manifest the physical actuality of that thought. The path of creation leads from intention, through the mind, into matter – from the intangible to the physical. So the focus of many peace messages coming together will help create the reality on a larger scale…like many sparks coming together to generate a light.

The Englishman considered briefly, and with a flourish of his gold pen gave us:

May the Tibetan light shine across the world in peace for all nations and for all beings.

34

With happy compliance the Dutchman carefully wrote:

Earth get Love Energy.

'Thank you,' I beamed. 'They're really beautiful messages.'

I was sure such messages had far-reaching effects at the mind level, particularly those from children, as they were shaping the future and helping spread awareness of the importance of caring for the Earth. Happily, many young people today do seem to understand the responsibility every one of us bears.

One of my favourite messages was from a pretty eleven-year-old girl, Siobhan. One day I had been talking with her mother, who confided in me, 'I can't understand it. She and her brother have always ended up fighting when they've been left alone. It's been a real problem. Now, suddenly. they're getting on so well together.'

I had looked up Siobhan's peace message. It announced:

I will be loads and loads less annoying to my brother.

Her mother and I had been stunned by the simplicity and expanding beautiful effect of one little girl's personal change.

Another message that I particularly liked had been from a young Tibetan, Dugdak, who declared with great courage:

Peace to the young people of Tibet and peace to the young people of China.

Here was a touch of the spiritual power of the Dalai Lama's teachings. There can be little more humbling than the example he sets. After having to stand by for nearly fifty years, watching China brutally invade his country, destroy the unique culture and ruthlessly carry out the genocide of his people, he still says 'We must love and respect our Chinese brothers and sisters.'

Sometimes in my life when things upset me – relatively tiny things, even though they may seem huge at the time – I think of these words, and the great strength of them helps me try to convert anger into compassion.

He also says, 'Maybe sometimes your children teach you patience, but always your enemy will teach you tolerance. So your enemy is really your teacher. If you have respect for your enemy instead of anger, your compassion will develop. That type of compassion is real compassion, which is based upon sound beliefs.'

I felt honoured to be setting out to express these highest of ideals from the highest of mountains; it gave a sense of sacredness to the whole event, an opening up to higher aspiration. Indeed, as the ancient Inca name for Chimborazo was 'Watchtower of the Universe,' it seemed entirely fitting that we were planning to place a Tibetan sentinel up there.

I was moved to re-read the precious peace message the Dalai Lama had sent to us:

I am pleased to offer my prayers to 'Climb For Tibet' and all that it touches. The determination of the climbers to undertake a difficult task to highlight a humanitarian problem is indeed inspiring.

The non-violent Tibetan struggle for freedom has gained us the sympathy and admiration of the international community. Through our non-violent freedom struggle we are also setting an example and thus contributing to the promotion of a global political culture of non-violence, compassion and dialogue.

'C'mon, Tess. Let's go.'

Pete was trying to stir me into action. We were last off the plane. As always, I was daydreaming and slow to get myself together. I am often distracted by thoughts of the moment and by reading words that seem to compel me to them, but it must be annoying to have to wait for me all the time. I would always tell Pete that our souls had been drawn to each other to learn the things they needed to learn, and that he was learning patience, and I was a very good teacher.

After fond goodbyes to those whose lives we had touched, there was pressure for us all to leave the plane and rush on with our seemingly agitated existence.

Amsterdam's international terminal, Schipol, was efficient and shiny clean, with state-of-the-art technology. It took us half an hour to walk from one end of the airport to the other. Smart shops abounded, filled with goodies to tempt currency away from the myriad passers-by. The latter's energies mingled: some radiated happiness, others sadness, excitement, annoyance, frustration, tiredness, scheming, anticipation; loving thoughts that brushed against resentment; joy against fear. All colours, languages, ways of life and ideologies were there; those who liked bread without butter, those who had never had to fight for their bread and those who knew what it was like not to have any bread at all. I wondered how many ever thought, 'We're all one species, citizens of one world, part of one life force, yet with what currency are we paying the Earth for all this fantastic convenience? How are Earth Peace shares doing on the stockmarket?'

There was no denying it; we were inextricably part of the

problem, as once again we defied gravity and took to the skies. Just for a moment I imagined we were flying in the belly of a huge white *garuda*, the mythical half-bird of ancient Tibetan teachings who symbolises the perfection of our primordial nature, and whose job it is to devour disease and pollution in our world...

By now the sun's rays were diffused through Earth's atmosphere, creating a pretty, salmon-pink glow, and changing man's grimy, smoke-filled habitat into a thing of gentle beauty. Finally, all that was left were twinkly lights of civilisation reflecting the distant stars, as we followed the sun southwest across the Atlantic.

I settled back and took Pete's hand, always steadying for me, and tried to relax, for the first time in many days. We could do no more frenzied preparation for 'Climb For Tibet.' The adventure had begun. For now at least there was time to reflect.

I felt positive and happy about gathering sponsorship, pledges and messages, but I had questions. There was a mountain to climb. My climbing ability was not particularly good. How would I manage over 6,000 metres? The highest I had ever been before was about 4,600 metres – a failed attempt on Mt Blanc where I had been forced to turn back close to the summit when my companion became hypothermic. How would the rest of the team cope? What could I do about my own inner peace, which I was struggling with, and which so often eluded me? I had read many times that inner peace produces world peace. I so wanted to get it right. Could something on this trip help me to find it? And why had my soul been drawn towards this pilgrimage?

4 : Tibet calling

How easy it was to be at 10,000 metres in the pressurised cabin. There was nothing to it. We had just walked in and sat down. The space was soft and cocoon-like, and there was no cause for stress. This was the gap in time between the page of preparation and the page of enactment. Turn the page slowly, I thought; we need these gaps. Too often we rush through the book of life with no time to take stock, to work out why things happen, what we have learned, where we are going and whether we are on the right path. Perhaps taking time just to 'be' is even more important.

I thought lovingly of my eldest son, Paul, who is a master at this. The world tries to push him into physical achievements – you must do this, you must do that – while he just floats serenely, smiling peacefully. Sometimes I find strength in just standing by him, bathing in his aura. If I tune into his energy, it helps me find answers and calmness. The levels where we help each other don't always have to be physical, or even conscious, although intention is a powerful part of the mind force.

The engines droned, producing a soporific effect on all of us up there, suspended in time. The dry air had that typical airline cologne smell that suggests endless recycling. The lighting was dimmed, inviting sleep, but my mind was in turmoil. It was far too excited and over-tired to switch off.

Pete and I were the advance party. Our job was to establish a base in Quito, sort out communications, research some training peaks, reconnoitre the mountain and generally find out how things work in Ecuador, a remote South American country of which little seemed to be known in Britain. We did not even know if there would be much English spoken. Our Spanish was non-existent, although I had spent a little time in Mexico City in my student days, but I had got by more on smiles than on language skills. Opening a book on how to speak Spanish was yet another job that had not happened before leaving. I would clutch a dictionary for the next month, but a smile may still be the best of all travel accessories. I opened my little phrase book... 'Have you got these shoes in black?' 'That's a funny noise.' 'Where is the bullring?' Hmm. Better hope we'd muddle through somehow, since none of the four of us had any Spanish to speak of.

I looked forward to GT and Mig arriving a few days later to complete the team. This delay meant they were risking being less well acclimatised than we hoped to be; they would not have time to accustom their bodies gradually to the high altitude, but their life commitments did not permit them this luxury.

As an eminent conductor and composer, Graham Treacher, known as GT, was busy with performances. He had found our 'Climb For Tibet' advertisement in the Alpine Club newsletter and, with strong Buddhist and climbing interests going back to his teens, had known at once that he must try to be part of our outlandish way of helping the Earth. It had felt right for us to welcome him. He had had considerable mountaineering experience in many of the world's principal ranges, notably putting up first ascents high in the Tien Shan and in Arctic Norway. He had expressed doubts on his fitness, however, which was cause for concern because of his age. At sixty-five he was the 'old boy' of the team. How would he now perform at altitude? But he was warm and lovely, with a great sense of humour, and everyone adored him.

Migmar was twenty-one years old and a student at the London School of Fashion. He was also a staunch and active member of the Tibetan community in Britain, battling to help his country and his people. He was attending a huge Freedom for Tibet charity concert in Washington, USA, and promoting T-shirts which he had designed. He would also have been visiting members of his family lucky enough to have been given refugee residence in New York. He was thrilled at the impending arrival there of a new Tibetan baby – his sister's.

I had met Mig in 1991 while working for the charity, Climb For The World, on behalf of the United Nations. We had had an international event at which representatives of all continents carried parts of the UN 'flags of all nations' flag to come together symbolically on the summit of the Eiger in Switzerland, portraying 'One World.' We had needed to choose two young teenagers to take part. They were to be a Tibetan and a Nepalese from the Pestalozzi International Children's Village near Battle, West Sussex, in Britain. This was where Mig had been living since he had been brought over from his Tibetan settlement in southern India at the age of nine. He was disappointed not to have been chosen on that occasion, but his day was to come. He had always taken seriously the responsibility that came with the chance he had been given of a good Western education and the opportunities it opened up to help his people. He was full of determination and energy, and frustrated at the lack of progress towards freeing his country.

'I want some action!' he had declared to Pete and myself one day, while lunching on soup and momos at the Tibetan restaurant in London.

'OK,' we had responded, 'we'll give you some action. Come and climb our highest mountain with us.'

He had replied simply, 'All right, I will.'

It was this character trait of actually going ahead and doing things that he talked about, grabbing life with both hands and driving himself with great purpose, that endeared him to so many people. He was handsome, friendly and outgoing, but there was one big worry: he had never climbed before.

Can the belief that you are able do something outweigh all the drawbacks? The intention of the mind helps manifest at a physical level, but what percentage of the total picture is this? Does it depend on the strength of the belief?

Certainly, the belief in a cause and the fact that one is helping others, or the Earth, makes a difference. When I did a parachute jump for charity in 1989 I had been in a state of complete and utter terror. My face had gone grey. Everything in me was shouting 'Don't move!' It was only the thought of others depending on me that had propelled me to that open door to throw myself out.

I also knew that visualising an end result strengthens a commitment to overcome physical limitations. In 1994 my youngest son Mark and I undertook to cycle from John O'Groats to Land's End, raising charity funds and collecting pledges from people to 'not use their cars.' We had barely cycled on roads before. I was actually frightened of traffic, especially at roundabouts, and we were heavily laden with camping gear. The first day we had managed all of eight kilometres. For the next month we struggled, cursed and cried along the 1,600 kilometres, but every day Mark would call out, 'Mum, have you seen us there?' Then we would picture ourselves arriving at Land's End. When we did arrive, without even having had to change a tyre, it was largely due to the determination and mindfulness of my amazing thirteen-year-old son, who had hung onto the fact that we had seen ourselves there. At some level we knew we had already arrived.

Curled up on the plane high over the Atlantic, I felt pangs in my gut as I thought of him and my other two sons. The mother-child bond was so intense I always hated leaving them. I could relate well to the Tibetan Buddhist word for the most compassionate love, which translates as that of 'mother sentient beings'. This refers to the fact that over lifetimes we have all been mothers, which helps us to resonate with this type of love for our offspring. I drew comfort from remembering how accepting my children are of my need to do wild and dangerous things. At least, I reflected, we are all very good at 'tuning in' over a distance to each other's presence and protecting each other with 'white light' – call it love, prayer, healing energy or what you will. The idea of this protective force always gives a safe feeling, and directing it to surround a loved one helps us to feel we are doing something positive to help, rather than creating negative energy by sending fear or worry. This is just another aspect of the power of thought to create our own reality – quantum physics at its best, perhaps.

I thought of some of the events in my life, which were like signposts along the silver cord of purpose, as if an unseen force were asserting, 'You will help the Earth.' Yet it was also part of me that was telling me to find my passion, to listen to myself, to find where I feel most alive, to reach for the moment that cries loudly from the heart, 'This is what I was born for.' If you get the path right, it will flow easily and all the hard work will not be in vain. If you don't bother, there will be snarl-ups or, worse still, boredom.

So why was I now giving so much for Tibet? Where was this stirring coming from? Which signposts had I followed to bring me along this path?

Curiously, I can remember very little Tibetan influence. It was something that was always just there, something I was drawn to. But when I was twelve, I saw an exhibition. There were long tables laid with a feast for the eyes – strange pictures and brocades of the brightest colours, exotic statues, unfamiliar musical instruments, shining jewellery and mementoes of a culture completely foreign to my experience. The exciting scene was mingled with tales of sadness, and something there moved me. There was a feeling of empathy. This was the first time I remember feeling a surprisingly physical reaction, an inexplicable pain in my heart.

Why did it hurt me? It always did whenever I heard about torture, murder and other atrocities. There are so many causes that need help in every corner of the world, but some touch much more deeply than others, and I had always reacted to the story of Tibet with a pain in the heart area, as though it were happening to me.

Then one night I had a revelation. I was reading quietly, just before going to sleep, when I saw a crystal-clear mind picture, combined with the energy sensing that is the way I tend to see things. I saw Tibet. It was gently cradled by the Himalayan Mountains. Out of the mists rose the Potala Palace, ancient fortress of light, representing all that is Tibet – wisdom, knowledge and high spirituality – radiating out like a sun to all corners of the globe. In that moment I understood why all the terrible things had happened to Tibet. I was being shown the overall picture. High in the mountains a level of spirituality had been reached that needed to be shared with the world. Truly, it was being forced out, like ripe seeds from a seed capsule.

I knew then that someday, somehow, I would work for Tibet.

5 : Tibetan heartache

It was a poignant wake-up call to my psyche when I discovered that a Tibetan couple, Pala and Amala, were actually living in my hometown. I remember well the day they told me their story.

Migmar was with me and we had gone to pick them up from their small council flat to bring them to my home for supper. There were pretty flowers outside their house, contributing to the gentle and happy nature of the neighbourhood. With typical Tibetan hospitality they pressed us to come in for a cup of tea. They always offered any food they could, although they had little money. I knew from previous visits that they sat in their one main room, bright and colourful with Tibetan carpets, thangkas and pictures of the Dalai Lama, with rugs over their knees to keep warm, as they quietly meditated or read Tibetan prayers.

Pala was sixty-two and Amala sixty-one, but they seemed older. Four decades as refugees had taken their toll, and life had been hard. Pala had trouble with his back and suffered ill health, but although his round, brown face often looked troubled and lost, it lit up with a devastating smile when he enjoyed simple pleasures like watching a child or talking to a cat, and his eyes held the cheekiest sparkle. Amala was more earnest. The name she went by means 'mother' in Tibetan, and it was maternal energy that she oozed, always caring and concerned for others. She was small in stature and still pretty, but her sweetness and warmth seemed to give her great strength. They did not use their real names. Maybe this was part of the cloak of protection that covered their heart pain.

We arrived at my semi-detached redbrick cottage on the outskirts of Haslemere. It is leafy, commuter-to-London country, typically risk-free and British.

'Very good house, very good house,' enthused Pala, smiling in his broken English, which was charming but sometimes hard to understand.

'Just like a Tibeti house,' was Amala's instant impression. For some reason I really liked that comment. It was something about the synchronicity of different cultures, thousands of kilometres apart and in different time frames. Had I been in a similar environment lifetimes away, somewhere on the four winds?

'Why is it like a Tibetan house?' I asked.

She pointed at all the wood and rocks, and Mig interpreted the word 'natural.' At least they'll feel at home, I thought to myself happily. We ate supper and their initial reticence gradually turned into a torrent of Tibetan tales as they poured out their lives.

'I'll try to translate,' said Mig, manfully.

Their early years in Tibet had been spent around Gyantse, about four days travel by horse southwest from the capital, Lhasa. It was here that, in 1904, the adventurer, Younghusband, having decided to invade Tibet on behalf of the British Empire, had met with Tibetan resistance, leading to heavy loss of life. He subsequently became great friends with the thirteenth Dalai Lama, and there have been good relations between the two countries ever since.

Pala and Amala were married at the young ages of seventeen and sixteen, as was the custom. A year later they had a beautiful little girl, Chime. They lived with Pala's parents until he took a job as a civil servant and they moved to Shekar, a small village about ten days by horse from Lhasa. Their life was contented. Pala was twenty-two, a young man just starting out.

I saw him glance tenderly at Amala. It was clear they had been very much in love.

The invasion of 1949/50 had not affected them in their rural area to any large extent; the Chinese 'reforms' had been concentrated in the east. But after 1959, Tibet would never be the same again. On fearsome wings the Chinese military 'machine' moved west, faster than a horse could travel. No warning went before them. Into Shekar came the soldiers. They forced the monks and nuns out of their monasteries at machine-gun point, tied their hands behind their backs and put them on trucks. They ordered everyone to get out of the government building where Pala was working, and took control. The first load of workers had their hands tied and were pushed onto trucks. Amala and Chime were with Pala. They clung to him and cried so much that a sympathetic Chinese soldier said 'OK, you can go on the next load, but you really have to go then.'

Pala's tone of voice became very definite as he directed his Tibetan words to Mig. He remembers very clearly making his decision. He had no way of knowing that Lhasa had been taken over by the Chinese army and that the Dalai Lama had fled. He did not know about the desecration of all the monasteries, nor about the murders, the torture, the rape or the impending starvation. He just saw all his friends being forced into trucks with their hands tied. He did know, however, that they were to be driven to Shigatse, the second biggest city in Tibet, famous not only for the Tashilumpo monastery, seat of the Panchen Lama, but also for the large high-security jail. The Chinese soldiers told him, 'The Dalai Lama has been taken by thieves. The Potala Palace has been crushed.'

Pala knew his future looked very bleak, and decided he was going to escape. There were soldiers everywhere, but he had been lucky enough to have arranged a meeting place with Amala before they were separated. He was locked in under house arrest. While the Chinese slept he opened the window, and with his heart in his mouth, slid out into the waiting night. The landing was soft but smelly.

His eyes danced with mirth in the telling, for he had fallen into a ditch full of yak dung.

At the appointed meeting place there were Amala and Chime, and very fortuitously Thupten, a friend of theirs who had also decided to escape. He was a trader and therefore accustomed to travelling through the mountains and to finding the route to India, albeit normally by horse or yak.

As the crow flies, the border with Nepal and Chomolungma, the mighty Everest, is only 180 kilometres away, but their route was to take them around mountains, over passes and across steep and difficult terrain to Sikkim, the Indian 'arm' sandwiched between Bhutan and Nepal. They walked and scrambled at night and hid up behind rocks in the day. At least it was March and spring was on the way, but the nights were icy cold.

After ten days and nights they reached Khambazong and

then a further five nights found them approaching the village of Lachen, just as the sun was coming up. This was a mistake. A patrol of fifteen Chinese soldiers was on the look-out for escapees, in particular a high nun, head of the Sakya nunnery. The little group was spotted and caught.

Amala leaned forward, speaking intently to stress how completely terrified she had been.

She had been shaking all over. She had never been so scared. They were taken back to Khambazong by truck and interrogated. What were they doing? Why were they near the border? They told the soldiers that they must have taken the wrong road, that they were trying to get to Shigatse. The soldiers seemed convinced, gave them tea and *tsampa*, and said that they would be taken to Shigatse by truck. Chime was crying and distressed, upset at the machine-guns, the harshness of the Chinese men of war and the atmosphere of fear. So Amala begged the soldiers 'Please let us go by ourselves.' Pala pleaded too, saying, 'I'll sign you a letter stating that we are definitely going to Shigatse,' and in the end the Chinese let them go. The following morning, in full view of all the soldiers, they were shown the road to Shigatse. Looking like a group of peasants, they hoped little importance had been attached to them, but they hid in the mountains for two days and nights, fearful for their lives.

At this point Amala recalls a heart-breaking dilemma. All her family were living in Shigatse – her father, mother, brothers and sisters. She really wanted to go to Shigatse. In the disagreement that ensued, Pala, feeling that perhaps the Dalai Lama had escaped, remembers saying, 'Well, I'm going to India, and I'm taking Chime with me.' Their fate today would have in all likelihood have been tragic had they changed their resolve at this point: Pala was sure he would have been killed.

So they turned south again, even more stealthily. Moving at

night helped them against the bitter temperature, but Chime was exhausted, and carrying her was not easy. Local people, a mixture of Tibetans and Sikkims, assisted from time to time with food and water, and once, for a little way, the loan of a donkey.

Eventually they again reached Lachen, again at sunrise, alarmingly. Fear seeped through them – fear born of the uncertainty of their own fate coupled with the brutal certainty that their country was in the cruel grip of a foreign power. As they neared a little stupa in sight of Sikkim, they stopped at its colourful fluttering prayer flags to offer blessings on the wind-horse, but they had one over-riding memory of a less compassionate moment. Thupten, answering a call of nature, sneered with loud disdain, 'Well, you Chinese, eat this!'

Mig, caught up in the relating of the story, relaxed into a heap of giggles at Pala's recollection. He did not know then that many Tibetans had had to search for food in their jailers' excrement.

So they crossed the border to safety, and to a refugee life of exile and further uncertainty. For the self-reliant Tibetan, having to accept aid was particularly hard. Helping travellers and those around them was natural, but there had never before been poverty in Tibet. Now, as thousands followed the Dalai Lama into exile, the tide of homelessness was beginning.

Pala and Amala settled into the job of breaking stones for roads for the Indian government, until, after ten years, Amala became too ill to go on, and they moved to Simla, where they worked for Save The Children. From there they were chosen to look after Tibetan refugee children, and were sent to Wales, in Britain, as house-parents. Chime, to their dismay, had to stay in India.

I sensed deep sadness as Pala said he believed they were the lucky ones. No one else had escaped from their village. They had had to leave everything. Amala said she was particularly upset at leaving all her beautiful jewellery – important to a Tibetan girl – but more than anything, they were troubled at leaving their families, whom they would never see again. There was no way to contact them to find out how they were until more Tibetans escaped, bringing the news that gradually filtered through to them over the years. They had never even said goodbye...

Mig and I were keen for them to talk about their families, but even after all this time they found it distressing. They looked down and spoke quietly. There was much they did not know. Pala learned that his brother had been shot in the uprising in Lhasa about the time of his own escape. Amala discovered that her brother had been imprisoned without charge for fifteen years, and that her father had died in jail. It seemed that, crazed by starvation, he had eaten the flesh of a long-dead dog and was poisoned. She believed the rest of her family to be living in Lhasa, sweeping the streets in desperately poor conditions, second-class citizens in their own country. Those who did what the Chinese wanted had suffered less. The extent of the courage of those who, with typical Tibetan loyalty, did not, may never be known.

Many with longer and more arduous winter journeys out of the country did not make it. One refugee told me her younger sister had died in her arms during their escape attempt.

We drove Pala and Amala home. It was late, long past their bedtime. Despite their poor health, they would rise at 4.30 am to meditate and to go to work early; they cleaned houses for a living.

They were the lucky ones.

I was touched by the experience of Pala and Amala. It had brought home to me not only that it was real people's lives that were being shattered, but also that the Chinese are of course real people, too. Twice in Pala and Amala's story the Chinese soldiers showed sympathy and compassion. In spite of all the atrocities, can we see life from the Chinese soldiers' point of view? Can we put ourselves in their shoes? They believed they were liberating Tibet from serfdom and an antiquated way of life. They had been brainwashed to inflict suffering. The State was telling them what to do and how to think. Killing was their job. They were used to the cruelty and low regard for human and animal life.

The Dalai Lama says we must love and respect our Chinese brothers and sisters, and that ultimately all people seek happiness. At an individual level, in spite of the unbelievably horrific tales of brutality, can we reach for that level of compassion?

How lovely it was to have some time to let my thoughts roam the skies. I pondered on compassion. Given the Tibetan Buddhist belief in reincarnation, how would it have been if, in their last life, one of the Chinese soldiers had been a Tibetan and Pala had been a Chinese soldier? Maybe he owed him one. What if the roles were to be reversed in the next life? Is it not wise, taking a wider view of many lifetimes, to err on the side of compassion? The taking-it-in-turns aspect is analogous to climbing with someone on a rope. First, you hold the other climber's life in your hands by belaying the rope safely, then it is the other climber's turn to hold your life in the same way. It is definitely in your interest to be compassionate and hold the other's fall. Indeed, it is a natural impulse, for when the two of you are tied together, you need to act as one entity for survival.

What if I chose to come back next time as a tortured and unjustly imprisoned Tibetan so my soul could learn the lessons this entailed? What if my karma dictated that this should be so?

Oh help, I thought. Worse still, what if I came back as a torturer? My case for compassion was growing. If I were able to stand back and view events over many lifetimes, then the things I had thought to be bad would not seem so, for they would have purpose. I would have drawn them so that my soul could grow towards enlightenment (or whatever terminology one wants to use for the highest energy state.) In the process, as the Dalai Lama says, my enemies would be teaching me and giving me opportunities to progress. What if there were a great queue of souls waiting to incarnate into human bodies because of this staggering scope for advancement? Should I not make the most of my chances? As the saying goes, 'Every trouble is a gift from God.'

So if I choose to be compassionate in a troubled situation, my soul is likely to grow and my karma is likely to come back at me with better things. Surely, though, this will only work if it is genuine compassion – a real desire for others to be free from suffering – and the intention in my mind is coming from unconditional love. OK, I thought, good ideals, but when caught in typical emotion-ridden problems on a day-to-day basis, I often forget totally about compassion, and wallow in my anger, hurt, frustration, or whatever emotion seems to be taking an airing. Then my inner peace goes out of the window. As an unenlightened being, how can I stand back and rise above emotions at these times?

Maybe the knowledge that we are all part of one energy helps. Scientists say that many studies are complicated by the energy of the observer affecting that of the observed, making it impossible to look at anything completely separately. We are all interdependent. But while my intellectual understanding is that nothing is in isolation, I find it hard to really feel this at a deep level, as the bit that identifies as me doesn't always like to think that it is part of somebody or something else.

I like the picture of everything in the universe as 'energy soup'.

This may not relate well to school physics, but I understand that the building blocks of all things are dynamic energy particles, which are vibrating at different frequencies, with dense stuff such as rock appearing to be more stable than ethereal substances like thought. All these building blocks emit 'energy waves', which intermingle and act on everything else they come in contact with, so I see everything that happens as the result of the sum total of these different forces acting on it. Bumping into the person you were anyway hoping to meet may not be such a random coincidence. Or, thinking unkind thoughts about your neighbour could lead to his dog being sick on your sitting room carpet.

Given that we are all irrevocably interconnected as part of the same universal energy system, and thus every single happening makes a difference, to some extent, to everything else, it would seem very negative to give out uncompassionate thoughts or actions to another part of the universe. It would at some point come back to the giver in a sort of knock-on effect, like ripples in a circular pond. Equally, imagine how powerful genuine loving compassionate thoughts and actions can be. My belief is that these high-vibration thoughts are imbued with divine energy, thus magnifying their effect manifold.

I find it helpful to equate this universal energy system with the human body. Suppose you have a big toe that has gone septic and is giving you a lot of pain. Do you become angry and try to get rid of the toe? No. (well, probably not). In the long run you need to be able to stay on your feet, and every part of your body is necessary. Therefore, the only answer is to heal it. In these terms, thinking of the body of humanity, I can understand better the Dalai Lama's wonderful, humbling response to the pain of the Chinese situation – to heal with love and compassion.

My thought processes, like the aircraft, purred on and on into the night. The hours came and went. The flight was thirteen hours. I began longing for somewhere to run, greenery and a place where my spirits could soar and I could feel free. I stirred restlessly and tried to stretch. Pete dozed to my right. He was always able to sleep anywhere. My neighbour on the left turned to me from the book she was reading. She was reading in English, though she looked South American. Perhaps she would like to chat?

'It shouldn't be too long before we land to refuel in Aruba,' she smiled, maternally. Only the slightest hint of an accent. She had the air of being a regular traveller on this route. 'Will this be your first time in Ecuador?'

'Mm,' I nodded.

'Holiday?'

'No, we're going to climb a mountain.'

'Ah, lovely. There are many beautiful ones there.' She glanced at my bare feet and I got the distinct impression she felt climbers should always be prepared, with their boots on ready. 'You're going to need some good boots,' she advised.

Some people are funny, I thought, though if KLM hadn't generously upped our weight allowance, I may well have been wearing my boots.

'It's a sponsored climb,' I went on, 'to raise funds and awareness for Tibet...'

'Why do you want to help the Tibetans?' she interrupted.

'Probably because I was a Tibetan in my previous life,' I replied, watching her face carefully.

She laughed condescendingly. 'How quaint.'

Help, I thought, remembering that some religions think believing in more than one incarnation is an anathema that stops you getting to heaven. 'The Dalai Lama says religions are like the spokes on the wheel of life – all vital, but different.'

She looked at me rather blankly.

How can I get out of this, I wondered, without offending the first South American I had met...? 'Different ways of thinking are like different paths up a mountain. We're all aiming for the same high spot...'

Her look said that for her it was a question of right and wrong.

'Truth's a funny thing isn't it? We all have to work out our own,' I mumbled, as she suddenly took off to the loo.

'Oh dear,' I thought. 'She thinks I'm bonkers – win some, lose some.' I resolved to be more sensitive, and ask her about the weather later. Wooh! I could have shocked her a whole lot more. There were all my experiences with conscious dreaming, going back into previous lives, theories on Atlantis – how my incarnations there meant I was now part of a group who, having made a big mess with technology then, was determined to help humans to get it right this time. I remembered some of the stages on the path of my learning – scepticism, fun, disbelief, excitement – and reminded myself that just because reincarnation fits into my beliefs, and those of the authors of countless books I had read over the years, that didn't make it fit with other peoples.' In fact the belief systems of over half the world did not accept it. I wondered though, why all the references to reincarnation were taken out of the Bible at the Fifth Ecumenical Council meeting in 553 AD in Constantinople. At least all religions accept the continuance of the human spirit.

Perhaps if I had known then that I was on the way to test out my own expectations in this regard I would have been less critical.

6 : A glimpse of our goal

As if in a fleeting dream, we touched down at Aruba, a Caribbean island off Venezuela. There was little reality to it. A wall of heat met us at the aircraft door, the sticky atmosphere across the tarmac was thick with the sweet scent of frangipani and hibiscus, while palm trees rustled and waved in the ocean breeze. I breathed deeply. Dark, smiley, island people herded us in and out of the terminal building. My mind gently absorbed the contrast thrust upon it. We had left a now alien, grey, Western world, rushing about with high technology, where money is king and achievement his consort, while here, a mere hallucination away, I guessed daily lives were governed by the sun, the sea, tourism and debt. The difference in cultures serves only to highlight the strength in diversity of the human species, but would we of Earth's family in the end understand that each member of every nation has the same desire for happiness, the same need for inner peace?

Back on the plane I continued my search for some inner peace of my own, a little stilling of the mind. I really wanted to relax. I knew good meditative methods for achieving this, though I usually tend not to bother enough with the mechanics, and rush through all the preliminary stages. I start off by tensing every part of my body bit by bit, holding it for a few seconds, then letting it go in an exaggerated way. It helps to have a lead-in thought like, 'I now let go of all my tension,' and then see or sense it going out of my body with the mind's eye. I find that to visualise an actual shape or colour as a rubbish-removal vehicle helps. So to get rid of tension, fear, anger or whatever, I would see it as a red blob in part of my body and visualise it blowing up or dissolving. These are mind games, but useful nonetheless.

Breathing is my next stage. I try to slow everything down by concentrating on the breath. This focus fields wandering thoughts. I count to ten breathing in, hold for a count of four, count to ten breathing out, hold for a count of four, then start the cycle again. Gradually elongating the counts helps the process. Then more mind play – on every in-breath I imagine bringing in love, white light, healing energy and all manner of positive good stuff, and on every out-breath I let go of everything negative that the body doesn't want.

Sometimes I use a cleansing routine, working with the body's seven main energy centres, the chakras, each with its associated hue of the rainbow. I do this by simply imagining the body swimming through water of red, then orange...yellow... green... blue...indigo...violet and then into white light, while holding the intention of releasing blockages and renewing harmony.

Then I like to rest in a special healing place deep in my mind. Usually it is a rock cave full of crystals, luminescent, magical. It could be a clear mountain pool, a forest glade, or anywhere that expresses beauty and peace.

Normally, at this stage, I can meet with my personal healing guides. I know they have been with me at least since my awareness started to open up a few years ago, about the time I started devouring spiritual books in a search for knowledge on how to guide my children. I sense them always to the right side of my body. I know them only as 'Large' and 'Small' and they are always there for me. They give me advice, particularly about my health, or they zap me with necessary energy for needy spots. However, they only come if I ask for help, and very often I do not ask.

Spatially, around my body, I know there are other forms of assistance, offering answers to problems, understanding, love and access to the divine energy. I know where the doors are, so why do I so rarely find the time to sit quietly and open them?

Often I find more motivation in trying to help others than in getting lost in my own problems. So, once in a deeply relaxed and cleansed state, it is a good moment to offer myself up as a channel. The method I like to use is to picture white light becoming available to me from the divine energy. I am then acting as a transformer, converting energy to a vibration usable at a physical level by directing the stream of light to where there is healing needed – near or far, loved one or stranger, animal or human, illness or sadness. I can only send healing energy and love, which is then one of the forces acting on any situation. I cannot decide how anything should be, such as whether a sick person should live or die. That is up to each individual soul's game-of-life plan. Purposeful prayer is a fine line between the state of ignoring and interference. The power is there – call it God, the divine, love, the universe, the highest energy, life, or whatever terminology is the least baffling or touches the aspect of the moment. It can be directed by the loving intention of the mind for the greater good. It just has to be asked for.

Assisting others in this way also helps oneself in a sort of divine viscosity, but today, although my state of mind was calming down, I did not seem to want to concentrate on any of the wonderful forms of self help. I was still carrying the tension in my back. If all else fails, I thought, resort to the other excellent method of bringing about relaxation and stress release – a neck and shoulder massage from Pete.

Pete was always there for me. How lucky I was to have someone who had taken on not only me and my way of thinking, which had been so different from his own, but also my dream – so totally.

The love of Pete's life had always been climbing, from rock climbing in Britain to all the major mountains of the European Alps. He was a highly experienced mountaineer. He was also a workaholic, exceptionally full of drive and energy, and had done very well working for an insurance company for thirty-four years. Taking the opportunity for early retirement at the age of fifty, he had taken on a few charity events and was busy becoming a ski instructor while waiting for life to offer him ideas on what to do with the next fifty years.

Well, life offered him me when we were introduced at the Argentière camp site in the French Alps on an Alpine Club meet. I had heard about six events he was doing for charity in that one year to celebrate the big five O. None was easy: skiing 130 kilometres across the Haute Route of Europe; running the London Marathon; windsurfing 42 kilometres across Lake Coniston; a triathlon of a 160-kilometre cycle, 3-kilometre swim and 42-kilometre run; the130-kilometre South Downs Way run; and the climbing of Switzerland's tallest mountain. Here be

Superman. Also, he too had recently cycled from Land's End to John O'Groats.

I admired his energy and commitment and, knowing how hard it is to raise interest and sponsorship and actually collect the money, I wanted to offer him a contribution.

My first impressions were of a tall, fit, fine-looking, rather hairy Viking, wearing sunny, colourful gear and exuding joie de vivre and confidence. He seemed to be someone who loved people, running things, achieving things and doing things for others. He oozed strength and dependability. Later I also discovered the unerringly kind and gentle nature of his heart.

'Hi, pleased to meet you.'

The handshake was warm and eminently friendly.

'How would you like to come and climb the highest mountain in the world with me?' I had given no thought to the words. They had just come out, so I went on, 'It's Chimborazo, in Ecuador.'

He gave me a quizzical look. 'That's ridiculous. It's definitely Everest.'

'No, it's Chimborazo. It's the point furthest from the centre of the Earth. The world's not round, it's an oblate spheroid, so everything on the equator sticks out more. That makes Chimborazo the highest mountain.'

'What height above sea level?'

'It's not much more than 6,000 metres, that's less than 21,000 feet. Compared to Everest it's meant to be quite an easy climb.'

'Fill me in on the details.'

Of course I had no details beyond the sense that this was the right thing to do. It was an illustration of the balance of our future partnership; he, left-brain-dominated, logical and practical; me, right-brain-dominated, intuitive and motivated by inspiration.

'It seems we both like raising charity funds by doing tough and interesting events,' I chatted.

'Yeah, people think you're mad, but you can do some useful stuff.' His eyes sparkled at the fun of his challenges.

I was struck by the easy, fraternal energy between us. It transpired he was almost an astral twin with my brother Graham. Their births were only a couple of days apart.

We became part of the same team, setting off with the aim of climbing Mt Blanc, sneaking into the ladies' loo at 3,800 metres at the top of the Aiguille du Midi téléphérique to 'sleep' there before the start at midnight – all part of the ambience of mountaineering.

It was nine months before we got together on a ski-mountaineering trip, and finally organised a meeting about Chimborazo. That was when the dream began to become a reality.

Then came the fateful day when he felt he had to decide. On one side were his wife and four children, whom he loved dearly, a fine home, a life's work and all that went with it, strongly weighted with the desire not to hurt his family. On the other side was setting out into the unknown, risking everything, with a new relationship, and a new challenge that was beginning to tug at him. The decision tore him in two. He could not be true to himself and be faithful to both. There was no easy way out. There would be heartbreak and anguish whichever way he went.

He chose the open door. The sacrifices were enormous and the pain intense for all concerned... I believe only his inner self with its life perspective knew if he had chosen the right path for his greatest soul growth. For each soul, in cooperation with those around it, organises its own challenges to overcome, for the purpose of gathering the strengths it needs along the way.

I glanced at him lovingly. 'Thanks for the massage, my Viking warrior, fighting for peace.' Was that a contradiction in terms? After all, peace is a state of being; fighting a state of action.

'Come on then, let's go into battle and collect some more sponsorship money and messages. People look a bit more responsive now. You take that aisle, I'll take this one.'

The plane was coming alive again and the oh-help-how-can-I-eat-at-this-time-of-day breakfast had just been cleared away. There was the faint magenta stirring of dawn somewhere over the South American continent.

'Did you know that it was considered right for Viking men to have more than one wife, and right for Tibetan women to have more than one husband?' I asked, unsuccessfully trying to draw him into conversation rather than action. Maybe, I mused, the words 'right' and 'wrong' should really be replaced by 'feels right for me in my present situation' or 'is morally wrong for me as dictated by the society in which I now live.'

I was reminded of the time we had been having a meal at a Chinese restaurant and Pete had bravely produced our form, bright with the Tibetan flag, and asked the Chinese proprietor for sponsorship. He, not surprisingly, had not given us any money, but rather than throw us out, had engaged us in deep conversation as to why Tibet was part of China. He stressed that Tibetans had been living in the dark ages, under a cruel feudal system, that the Chinese had done them a great service by bringing liberation and modernisation. China had therefore been right to invade.

Had the Chinese soldiers been told it was the right thing to do all those times they forced Tibetan children to shoot their own parents? Were they wrong to allow the basic compassion of human nature to surface, as in the helping of Pala and Amala?

The question of the morality of right or wrong was here something totally dictated by the point of view of the evaluator.

Yet I felt this should not stop us, or anyone, fighting for what we believe to be important. But if people passionately believe this, and are on opposing sides, then war will result. Is that a reason for keeping quiet and doing nothing? Maybe it works if one holds in one's mind the intention of doing things for the greater good of all. The flip side of this are the many historical examples of passionate religious beliefs leading to crusades of death and destruction. The answer often cited is that the world would come together with a united government and sort out its problems if we were aggressively threatened from outside – perhaps overrun by little green Martians. Yet this could bring an added risk of expanding the use of violence and war as a way of solving a crisis, created again by differing values of what is right and wrong, and allow it to adversely touch other parts of the universe.

Surely the answer is to implode, to come back down to the individual who says no I cannot judge others but, yes, this is what I myself believe to be right or wrong. If I live by this code I shall have my own inner peace, therefore I cannot be at war with anyone around me. In fact I shall be giving off inner peace energy, which will affect all those around me in a powerful, beneficial way. As an individual I *can* make a difference.

This is reiterated by the Dalai Lama's definition of non-violence, which refers not only to the physical level, but also to our thoughts and our essential inner beingness, which are tools for giving off this energy of peace and harmony.

It is of course one thing to say and quite another to do when confronted by the battles of life, but we could set out aiming for the highest ideals. And if enough people tried...

I set to work with the forms. The girls in the next row looked English.

'Excuse me, we're collecting messages for a peace climb in Ecuador. Would you like to contribute? We're asking that they be in the Tibetan spirit of non-violence, compassion for all life and universal responsibility...'

'Oh lovely, that sounds interesting. Let's have a look.'

They thought long and hard and then wrote:

Peace for all mankind.

Let the violence of the past give way to understanding in the present, that peace be of the future.

I pray that we may all expand our love for one another, for our Mother Earth and for God, and that our voices may be heard.

The Indian guy behind returned his form with:

The peace in our hearts is the essence of our souls.

The Scottish businessman said:

Let us look after the Tibetans and all people of the world. Everyone is precious.

The Ecuadorian student scribbled:

Love our beautiful Earth.

I thought I'd try again with my South American neighbour, who was smiling at me nervously. I handed her a form.

'So, what do you think the weather will be like in Quito?'

She looked relieved. 'Ah, now, I can tell you all about that. There is a wonderfully happy climate there. The dry season has just started so it should be sunny all the time.'

Surely, I thought, she must work for the tourist board. The only bit out of the travel guidebook that I could remember was that the predictable thing about the weather was its unpredictability... but I kept quiet.

'It should be about 15° Centigrade when we get there at about nine o'clock in the morning.' She continued, 'The temperature is always pleasant. It rarely gets above 21° or below 7°; but you must remember that it's over 2,850 metres, that's 9,000 feet, above sea level and the radiation is very intense. Now, you must use sun cream all the time and wear a hat. Do you have one?'

'Um...I'm not sure that I do.'

'Most Ecuadorians wear one, though not so much in the city as in the rural areas. You can buy them on most of the street stalls and there are markets everywhere.'

I looked forward to sampling some of the local wares, though I had a strong suspicion I would be getting whisked off up a training mountain before I had time to catch my breath. There was a lot of work to do... Maybe after the climb...

'And another thing, the altitude will make you feel very bad. For at least two days you will be nauseous, breathing will be harder and you will probably have headaches. You must take it easy for a bit until your body begins to adapt. Oh, and drink lots of water. It helps, as does coca tea.'

'Thank you, yes, that reminds me...' I searched in my bag for my little case of homeopathic remedies and pulled out the coca phial, taking one of the little white pills. The body needs all the help it can get, I thought, offering one to Pete, too, but he refused. He was taking Diamox, the standard climbers' altitude remedy.

Also it was time to take my homeopathic 'vaccinations'. There was one that covered tetanus, typhoid, polio, hepatitis and yellow fever and there was the malaria one – time, too, for cocculus, which helps with jetlag. I felt these treatments work with the body rather than giving it more foreign substances to fight against. I had, in the last month, searched out a handful of doctors to discuss the homeopathic protection method. Points of view differed widely, but the majority opinion had been that, although they felt obliged to recommend the standard injections, they themselves would prefer to use this holistic approach.

Back in my bag I came across Yannick. I brought him out and played peek-a-boo with the little child with big brown eyes who was peering over the seat in front of me. People think Yannick is a teddy bear, I suppose because he's round and cuddly; others rudely think he's a duck – I have never understood why; and some dismiss him altogether, probably because he's pink and purple, but he's very definitely a penguin.

This colouring incidentally matches my rucksack, on which he always travels, tied on behind a spare karabiner. Yannick is a particularly smart and well-trained penguin. In fact he's had a lot more adventures than most penguins. He's bounded out of a plane at 600 metres, floated down a river in a climbing helmet, jumped from a helicopter to a mountain top skiing wildly down virgin snow, posed on many a hard-won summit, rock-climbed, ice-climbed, ski-mountaineered, flown from tall pinnacles, spent the night on a sea-stack, on major summits and in a snow-cave. The greatest indignity is repeated swimming lessons in the washing machine and I can barely mention the times he's had to double up as a rugby ball.

I gave him a cuddle. He makes a wonderful pillow.

'You're too attached to Yannick,' Pete commented.

'I am not!'

'You should have left him behind. There were more important things to bring than ducks,' he taunted.

'You're just jealous,' I retorted. I had nearly left Yannick behind in the panic to pack and get to the airport. That would have been awful, like leaving part of me behind. Hmm, I thought, maybe I am too attached. We cannot be happy with anything or anyone if we are attached because then we have fear that we might lose it or them, and that produces a need and then we start manoeuvring to keep that need satisfied. It's possessive love, not unconditional love. If you really love something, set it free. If it really loves you it will come back to you.

So often we deny others that freedom, that space where they need to be, in which to discover their true self, to learn and to grow their soul. The love and respect the Dalai Lama says we should have for our enemies is maybe what we should be cultivating for those close to us too. To respect another's soul by giving it freedom from attachment is hard, because the fear for oneself sneaks in, but perhaps it is as important as love. Maybe that's part of what converts possessive love to unconditional love. How we love is so important.

Wooh! I thought, it's complicated loving penguins.

Thoughts are powerful. They create reality, and love is the most powerful force of all, except that sometimes it seems to act like a sort of glue, and messes up non-attachment.

I enjoy trying to work at some of the Buddhist principles,

though I am not a Buddhist per se. But it usually serves to highlight how far away I am from enlightenment, which seems so unattainable. I find it easier to think in terms of baby blobs of enlightenment that will gradually strengthen, expand and grow up. These could be sparked by moments of love, such as a flash of understanding towards an upsetting neighbour with different beliefs. I glanced warmly to my left...

The cabin was suddenly flooded with sunlight as the promise of a new day hit the plane.

'Good Morning, South America,' I said, eagerly.

Smiles in anticipation of landing and the end of a long journey appeared on tired faces all around. I dug out my sunglasses, and longed to be sitting next to the window to see my first glimpse of Ecuador, though, as we veered left and started our descent through bumpy, thick cloud, the brightness left us and visibility was dramatically reduced.

'What's the name of this place?' I asked my neighbour, who happily still seemed keen to talk.

'This is Guayaquil. We won't be allowed off the plane here, as it's a very brief stop. It's the largest city in Ecuador, right at sea level, a very busy port. This is where most of the trade happens.'

'Bananas?' I enquired hopefully. My body was already in withdrawal, missing its usual dose of breakfast fruit.

'Yes, though oil is now a far more important export.'

'Where does it all go to?'

'The US is the biggest trading partner, but I believe much of the income earned goes to pay off the interest on the national debt rather than alleviate the massive poverty of the country.'

'World imbalances.' I had a feeling there would be many moments of Western guilt as one of the 'haves' in a country of 'have-nots.'

'Mm, and also imbalances within Ecuador. There are a few

very rich…'

'Is inflation still very bad?'

'Yes, about fifty per cent per annum, though it had been up to a hundred per cent. You must be sure to keep your money in US dollars and just change into *sucres* when needed.'

'Thank you. OK.'

'And you shouldn't carry much cash, there are *bandidos* everywhere.'

'Do you mean bandits? Oh help!' But she couldn't dampen my enthusiasm.

The wheels touched down on Ecuadorian soil. Wow! We were here…in a far country of mystery, gold, rainforest, mountains strange animals, panpipes and ponchos. By dint of the equator passing through its heart and the soaring of the Andean volcanoes towards the sky, we were to be the latter-day explorers of its treasures. The adrenaline stirred in excitement at the adventure, the unknown and the new experiences to come.

It was just another international airport through the open doors of the plane, but this was the legendary Ecuador, tantalising us with dreams of Incas and Spanish conquistadors…

Then, like a sidewinder snake briefly touching down on hot sand, our flight lifted off again. We were on the last leg, with only thirty minutes to go until Quito…flying obliquely into the early morning sun.

The energy on the plane was restless. There was much moving about and chatting and ladies queuing for the put-yourself-back-together-again loo. At last we were so nearly there.

Something in the far reaches of my tired, befuddled head was calling. What was it? There was something I was not doing. And then it dawned on me… Chimborazo… We must be flying near Chimborazo… Quick, the map… Where is it? Things all over the place… Yannick…wash-kit…papers…chaos… There… Open up… Yes, of course, it should be coming up to our southeast on the right-hand side of the plane. It must be there, but I'm stuck in the middle seats, far from the window…

Pete, video camera at the ready, chatted up the air hostess.

'Tess, it's brilliant. The flight crew is going to let me film from the cockpit. Isn't that fantastic? But apparently it's very rarely visible, and they think there's too much cloud cover. We might be lucky. C'mon, get with it. Get your camera out.'

I scrambled through my gear to find my loyal little Leica CL, which had never let me down. Grabbing it, I staggered into the aisle. I had to find somewhere I could get close to a window. Peering across the three-deep seats I could just see the shape of an isolated peak rising from the swirling clouds. Could it be Chimborazo? No… But it has to be… No, it can't be…But the map…

Pete dashed back down the aisle. 'That's it. It's really it. I'm going to the cockpit.'

My heart was racing. Wow! I wasn't prepared for this encounter… I had to find a window. I rushing up and down, headless chicken-style. The right-hand seats all seemed to be occupied, at the back by the galley the window was thick with people looking out, the window in the middle was also taken and the wing was masking the view from the only other one.

Oh no…to come this far and not be able to see it properly… I darted up to the front, through the curtains into the first class area. Here was a chance. One of the large double seats had only one person sitting there, next to the window. He was a smartly dressed rather swarthy-looking businessman, quietly reading a magazine – at least it was quietly until he was startled to find himself with a peculiar, agitated woman lying across his knees.

'Excuse me, excuse me… I just have to photograph.' I had my camera up against the window and was snapping away a reel of film. I desperately wished I had brought my long lens, and promised never to go anywhere again without it.

'That's our mountain. We're going to climb it. It's the highest mountain in the world.'

The astonished businessman was wriggling uncomfortably beneath me, but I couldn't tell from his grunts whether he spoke English or not.

'I'm so sorry to disturb you. It's so important.'

I placed my hand on the thick, plastic 'glass'. It was hard to the touch. It was real. It held, as though invented by my own personal mind screen, the most exciting panorama I had ever seen.

The KLM insignia on the wing strut and the gaping circular hole of one engine with its silver halo gave the scene perspective. In the foreground, not cold enough to warrant the far blanket of cloud, was a tumble of steep ridges, valleys and round volcanic craters, playing with the dark shadows. The colour was as indigo as the sixth chakra. These were the bastions of the Andes, running north-south for the length of South America. They served merely as moats for the fortress that arose majestically out of the sea of white cloud just tinged with the last pink of low dawn light. Then, as I watched, its personal cover moved and a dazzling snowy summit revealed itself to me. Everything else was dwarfed into insignificance. Even the horizon seemed to fall away in supplication.

Far out!

Chimborazo – oh, mighty Chimborazo, Watchtower of the Universe, are you really there? I felt deeply humbled at the silence of the reply as my mind sensed rays of light from the magnificent peak spreading out around the world. I recognised then the enormity of the job we had been asked to do, and the focus of energy and love for the Earth that would be required. Please give us the strength to help us achieve our goal, I prayed, and let us follow our pilgrim path with joy. We must not fail.

I had seen my mountain. We had met. It was no longer a dream. I wanted to talk to Pete about it, but my eyes were too heavy. As though all the tension, all the wound-upness had been waiting for this moment, it was now safe to let go. For the first time since leaving home, just minutes before touching down in Quito, I finally slept.

I woke with a start as landing rubber met runway, but instead of the expected roar of braking, we floated back up into the air and came crashing down very heavily in a jarring bounce effect. There was a flash of fear from passengers around, but all I could sleepily manage was, 'Aha, we've made it over the equator!'

It was with genuine warmth that my neighbour and I said goodbye. We had survived the initial misunderstanding by tiptoeing around issues of differing beliefs. She set off down the plane and turned back. 'Good luck with the mountain, and by the way, do be careful not to drink tap water, and only eat fruit and vegetables that have been washed with bottled or boiled water.'

I smiled at her concern. 'Bless you for your help... Bye.' I never did discover what job she did.

'Here, you've got to fill in your immigration card,' urged Pete. It was not as easy as it sounded.

'What do you think the purpose of our visit is? It's not a holiday or business.' I wrote 'Peace business.'

'And this bit – "What articles are you carrying"...?' I wrote 'Personal effects, climbing equipment and messages to the Earth.'

I decided not to put 'a spoon bent with the strength of world peace coming down,' nor 'a magic ring to bring back snow from the summit to ensure our safe return,' nor did I write 'an unbelievably powerful crystal programmed by masters from the other side to help lighten shadows on the Earth.'

7 : Star signs

Quito, at 2,850 metres, stands in the ranks of the world's highest capital cities, alongside Lhasa and La Paz, at around 3,650 metres. The sense of altitude was elating, and enhanced by a warm and friendly feeling of informality. We had the tarmac to ourselves as we wandered away from the plane, not quite sure which of the airport doors to head for. I sighed in contentment and breathed in deeply. The rarefied air was bright and surprisingly clear. It almost tasted good.

We appeared to be in a wide, densely populated valley with enticing, chocolate-coloured mountains to the east and west. I had read that one could actually see snow-topped volcanoes from the city, but today, like most days, distant cloud covered the anticipated vistas along the high valley which runs north-south with the Andean range for the length of Ecuador. Quito nestles naturally into this, the famous 'Avenue of the Volcanoes,' so named in 1802 by the German explorer, Humboldt. The conurbation sprawls for nearly 17 kilometres and is 4 kilometres wide, with a fast-growing population of some 1.2 million. Most of the 11 million Ecuadorians live either here in the Sierra or in the sizzling heat of the coastal plain. To the east is the sparsely populated Amazon region of tropical rainforest, the Oriente, and far to the west is that jewel of eco-tourism, the Galapagos Islands. I longed to explore all of the wonderful diversity of the country.

No one seemed to mind whether we queued to have our passports stamped or not. In the event, we did.

'*Buenos días*,' I smiled, with a very English accent, giving my passport to the immigration official who was attempting to look stern by peering down at me through his glasses. It wasn't until we were trying to leave Ecuador again that I realised he had not actually stamped my passport at all, so the emigration official did not believe I had officially come into the country.

Paying US$1 each for baggage carts we wheeled our luggage to the front of the building to be set upon by the reception committee of locals out to get money from unsuspecting new arrivals '*Dinero*!', 'Dollars!', 'Taxi', '*Dinero*!' There was one scruffy, sad-faced lady in a long, grubby skirt with a tiny baby and an outstretched hand. I gave her a $1 note. It upset me that not a flicker of warmth entered her expression, as though she thought I was being mean – more likely it showed the harshness of her existence. Further open hands appeared.

'C'mon, let's get in this taxi before we get mobbed,' pressed Pete, chucking our mountain of bags bulging with ropes, ice axes and other climbing equipment into the boot and back seat of the nearest bright yellow vehicle, fending off the bewildering demands and requests for employment. Diving into the front seat beside the driver I thrust him the address of the hotel. 'Café Cultura, *por favor*.' Ah well, I thought, as we sped off, that's the sum total of my Spanish. From here on in I'll be making it up – but I didn't work out what to say next, nor did I notice the new country passing by, I just kept seeing the face of that mother with her outstretched hand.

I had been unprepared for the begging. I would have taken it as a matter of course in Asian countries, but why had I not realised that so many South Americans are poor? I had not known then that eighty per cent of Ecuadorians live below the poverty line, whatever that is, and that there is fifty per cent unemployment. Maybe it's only in the Western world that we don't confront real need in such an obvious way. However, being removed from it, in our comfortable lives of 'havingness', only brings with it the responsibility of helping the world balance out – of helping bring harmony. Perhaps many of humanity's problems are caused by this imbalance. Perhaps, I pondered, China would not have felt the need to invade Tibet, which it still calls 'Western Treasure House', if it had had enough timber, minerals and space for its people.

I was shocked, though, when the taxi driver charged us double what the guidebook had given as the going rate.

The Café Cultura hotel danced with the energy of bygone colonial days. There were Spanish archways and whitewashed walls reflecting the sun's intensity, cool stone slabs underfoot, grand, well-used fireplaces, hanging dried flowers intermingled with tropical plants of intriguing colours, textures and sizes, and a welcoming smell of coffee. Our room was dark, slightly musty, and washed in a warm rust-brown, stencilled with voluptuous bodies in action, ghosts of gracious living.

I sat on the large, wooden bed among our half-unpacked bags, trying not to fall asleep. My eyes rested on the rickety, old, carved chest alongside. It displayed a single glass ashtray in the shape of a star. A six-pointed star.

76

Until a few days ago a star had been just a star. Now it mattered how many points it had. This had all come about when a parcel had dropped through my letterbox among all the sponsorship forms, cheques, enquiries and cards of good wishes. It was just a normal, brown, padded, post-office bag, but it had held something extraordinary. Well-wrapped in popping plastic protection was a quartz crystal, only about five centimetres long but perfectly balanced. A clear masculine pointy end reflected light via the precise symmetry of its sides. The smoky female end was milky and mysterious. Unwrapping it I had held it in the palm of my hand and stared at it, mesmerised. It had felt almost sacrilege to touch it, for it carried a sense of unfamiliar and awesome power.

Written on a card were these words:

Channelled by Ivy Smith
Dear Tess,

Souls have been chosen within your earthly world to carry the light into many remote places. To the mountains that groan for the pain of humanity. You will carry this light, the divine presence will fill the crystal heart and the pureness of this love will be received by those who live in shadow. Blessed are the souls who, by the effort and the purpose of their lives, bring the light to others. Your purpose and your dedication will expand throughout the world. The crystal will become a signal, constant in its flow, for many masters have gathered in the spiritual world including myself, Advarr, forming the energy of a star vehicle of pure light. Your imagery as you hold the crystal should be the star. Blessings to you as you journey with heart full, mind open to receive, and each step becomes a prayer.

Master Advarr

My body had gone cold, as though an unseen force were walking up and down it. I had been stunned by the implications. We had to undertake to put this crystal on the summit of Chimborazo. Wooh!

Then, two days after, during the frantic preparations to leave, I'd had a phone call from Beverley. He is a mysterious friend who always appears when there is a need, helps and then disappears, like a celestial messenger.

'Hey, Tess. Good luck with the climb. This is my message from the mountain. It's in two parts:

We hold in the healing light of the Christ star (in the universal sense) His Holiness the Dalai Lama – Tenzin Gyatso – Ocean of Wisdom – and the true leaders and people of Tibet.

We hold in the clear light of love and forgiving compassion the leaders and people of China.'

I had copied his message down over the phone, and then he had said in soft words that imparted loving wisdom, 'I have taken council. Mountains have guardian angels. You should recognise and respect this. Ask to be shown the gateways to the approach. Prepare the way sensing the light from the heart of the angel. Feel the loving presence. Know also that your head rests on the heart of your own angel, who is in the same light. An angel is a thought of God. Go in willingness, humility and gratitude. And always aim for the highest in your own heart.'

While I was trying to absorb this, he continued, 'Oh, and you should visualise a six-pointed star.'

Why, I had wondered, further astounded into silence, was he asking me to visualise a six-pointed star? He did, I knew, assist with the healing work at the White Eagle Lodge, which was symbolically represented by a six-pointed star.

'It manifests harmony. It cannot be off balance whichever way up it is.'

What deep synchronicity, I had marvelled, was producing the need to tell me to visualise a six-pointed star after the directive from Advarr? There had been no question in my mind that the two requests were connected. It was all very intriguing and strange. It was also beautiful. Maybe there were six spiritual masters working on this.

It had been the beginning of a feeling that I was a pawn in a huge game. There was so much going on out there that I just didn't know about, so much I didn't understand; and yet I had absorbed the sense that it was important, and that my job was a vital part of a mission that was affecting everyone and everything.

Now, here in Quito, to see the ashtray was a jolt for me, saying 'Don't forget your quest. You're on the right path.'

I delved into the things-for-the-summit bag and laid the objects out on the bed. It was an extraordinary and precious collection.

I had protected the crystal in a tiny maroon velvet drawstring bag. Taking it out I placed it on top and stroked it gingerly, as though making friends with a once-wild animal. It seemed to glow gently in the dimness of the hotel room. I resolved to carry it in the spirit of love and harmony.

Next to it lay the ring, designed to be worn on the climb. It held a two centimetres-long rectangular box, fashioned carefully and exquisitely in copper. The lid opened to reveal a small cavity. I read the letter that accompanied it:

...I also enclose a ring I have made with a Tibetan 'OM' on the front. I hope it will bring you good luck. Inside the ring is a message for you, Pete, Migmar and GT. If possible you should open the ring at the top of the mountain. Also if possible you should fill the box on the ring with a grain of rock, snow or air from the top of Chimborazo and bring it back to me. This way you are obliged to come back safely.

Know that our thoughts are with you on the way down the mountain as well as up.

Love Bill

The beautiful words produced a lump in my throat, as the poignancy of our mission lay heavy on me. Bill was the close friend of my son Paul. He cared deeply about the Earth and about what we were doing. To me he was a representative of my children's generation. We were working that there should be an Earth in harmony for their future...

This was Bill's message from the mountain:

Them can chain me – them can beat me
Them can take me thing – them can stop me sing
Them can mute me – them can shoot me
Them can steal me friend – them can send me dividend
Them can rape me – them can reshape me

Them can bar me light – them can delay me flight
Them can tax me – them can ajax me
Them can kill me body – them can screw me mind
But
Them can't kill I
And – them can't stop me loving them.

Then there was the birdseed – a little cellophane package bulging with yummy-looking, different-coloured seeds. It had been sent by Lawley, father of my children. Though we were no longer married, we were still very close and supportive of each other. During one long phone conversation I had told him about Vanya Kewley's book, *Tibet, Behind the Ice Curtain*, in which she, as a brave journalist, investigates eyewitness accounts of the Tibetan holocaust.

She had written of how, on inquiring why she had neither seen nor heard any birds during her extensive journeys through Tibet, she had discovered that Chairman Mao of China had ordered that all birds, being parasitic to society, be exterminated. To add to this grave injustice to the Earth, one of the methods by which this perverted deed was carried out was to force Tibetan children to do it, using fear as a tool to achieve such abhorrent things.

Lawley, as a forester who has worked with nature all his life, very sensitive to its design and handsomeness, and with a great love of the wilderness, had been deeply touched by this account. He had asked that the birdseed be distributed on the winds from the highest place, in honour and memory of all the birds that had been killed – along with his lovely message from the mountain:

Tsinghai Plateau
Kisses the sky
Feathered lovers

No longer fly
Nestlings cuddled
Their forest lair
Once nature's belfry
No longer there
Ghosts soar now
Above the peaks
Ghosts of birds that
Never speak
A vision, veiled with
Tears, an old heart weeps
And weeps, prepared on
Borrowed wings to fly
For the whole world
Remains silent
As brave birds die.

The next item was a tiny parcel from Candy, my friend from up the lane. She had been keen to join us on the venture but had not wanted to leave her lifelong pal, an old retriever, Tarka. She had thoughtfully offered to stay behind and assist in the manning of the 'Climb For Tibet' home base along with my kind neighbour, Mary. But two weeks before our departure, Tarka had become sick and died. In letting go of this dear and special bond, Candy had written on our form, 'I enclose a small amount of Tarka's fur as the essence of pure love to be scattered across the planet from the Watchtower…so love may blossom' with the message:

Oh, Great Mother Earth, we salute you!
  From this, the Watchtower of the Universe, may a small seed of understanding sprout and grow so that we may truly realise that we are one, and that we may transcend our fears

and judgements, pain and separation and all that cripples the world...and know the perfection around us.

Loads of love to Tess, Pete, GT and Migmar. Well done! Now get down safely! xxxx

Alongside was the small tape-recorder she had lent us, with which to play a very special tape. It had been made by a talented friend, Gandiva Lorcan, a sacred sound percussionist, using Tibetan singing bowls, gongs and conch horns. I gazed at the case, wonderfully decorated with pictures of stars and planets and a magical Buddha hologram that reflected light in all colours. He had given us the tape to play these amazing stirring sounds from the mountain, for the healing of the Earth. His message was lovingly written on the case:

Much strength – bravo! Yes! – Harmony – courage – love and peace – respect – beauty – love – joy – brill! – OM MANI PADME HUM.

And then there were Uri's gifts. Again, there had been a phone call out of the blue in that busy week before we had left home.

'Are you going to make it?' came a distinctive and positive voice down the line.

'Er...yes', I replied, cautiously.

'You know that you are going to make it without any shadow of a doubt?'

'Yes, definitely... Who is this?'

'It's Uri Geller here.'

It had been exciting to have his interest. I have long been a fan of his. A couple of years previously I had attended one of his talks. He had spoken of holding seeds in the palm of his hand and using mind power to cause them to germinate, of using his psychic powers to aid police work and of coaching footballers in the art of using the mind. He had demonstrated by holding up a key and asking the 300 people in the audience to concentrate on bending it. It had bent double. But most clearly I recalled his eagerness at the potential of using many minds to bring about world peace.

He is renowned for bending spoons with his mind. I have watched carefully as his fingers, barely touching, stroke the neck of a spoon, which bends mysteriously and carries on bending when he is no longer close to it. This draws people's attention so the can then come in with his real work: promoting peace.

It had been arranged that Uri should come on board as one of the patrons of 'Climb For Tibet'. He sent us all copies of his *Little Book of Mind-Power*, asking us to take one copy to the summit, along with a spoon which was to be bent for us. Wooh! I thought, is it right to go littering a mountaintop with so much stuff? It wasn't until much later that I was to be shown the vital significance.

I felt the cold normality of the crazy-shaped spoon, and augured with the little orange book, which was full of inspiring quotes. It opened at the page with one from Shakti Gawain:

In order to cause a shadow to disappear you must shine light on it.

This is the quote we use on all our 'Climb For Tibet' papers. Yeah, that figures, I thought… Synchronicity with Uri… Just tiny signals that all was flowing well along the path.

I smiled at all the items I was guarding, thinking no necromancer ever had such an opportunity to cast so many good spells. In the spinning of time, the different colours and structures of matter, sent in the intention of love and healing, would blend into a blaze of white light…

We went out to explore the city. As it was Sunday, there were few people about, giving an unnatural, hollow feeling to the streets. There was an empty-looking Chinese restaurant across the narrow road, other hotels and private houses on either side, all with tough, lockable gates and impenetrable walls barring access from the street. They were all softened with masses of beautiful flowers, large-leafed tropical plants, palm trees and even the lovely tumbling jacaranda, so the harshness of mistrust was soon forgotten. There was a random spaciousness that lacked the order of a European city. Half-finished buildings mingled with all types of shops, cafés, banks, hotels, residential dwellings, tourist agencies, empty street-trader stalls and welcome green parks. Rubbish was a frequent decoration, but one of the main differences from our own towns was the ubiquitous state of disrepair of the pavements and roads, all full of lumps and holes.

We were in what is known as the 'new' area of Quito, sprawling north from the 'old' part, which is more colonial, cobbled, churched, crowded and impoverished. The city is a melding of ancient cultures. The Incas had overrun the original Native American Indians in the early 1400s. They were craftsmen of gold, silver and fine cloth, and skilled engineers, creating roads, bridges and remarkable constructions using large blocks of stone. Quito had been the Inca capital in the region until 1553, when the Spanish conquistadors and their horses moved in, claiming vast tracts of South America for their European king. Ecuador finally gained full independence in 1830. Today, the 'new' area is heavily coloured by world trade, especially with the US, so burger bars and specialist restaurants abound, and smart shops aimed at tourists nestle alongside tiny stalls cooking sweetcorn or sellers offering only chewing gum and matches.

We managed to find one shop that was open close to our hotel, a little emporium packed with enticing tourist goodies of wonderful colours and textures. It was run by a warm, friendly Ecuadorian, with whom we had fun trying to communicate. He showed us hats, ponchos, rugs and pretty woollen clothes, jewellery, trinkets and silver items, bags, pots and ornaments, wonderfully carved and brightly painted wooden figures and plates, and all manner of Andean goods. I was tempted to start buying gifts immediately, but settled for a lovely chess set for Pete's impending birthday. The pieces were carved from plant ivory, tagua, which is a kind of coconut shell. Buying products made from the tagua palm nut is an excellent way of supporting a sustainable harvest that leaves the tree standing, thus helping preserve the threatened but vital 'lungs of our planet', the rainforest.

It was not until we were leaving the shop that I noticed a glass jewellery cabinet and glanced in at the display. There, gazing back at me was a necklace. It was the deep blue of lapis lazuli, flecked with unique swirl markings and encased in a superbly crafted silver six-pointed star. I was riveted. I knew that this was the star I was meant to be visualising, and that I had been guided to it. Ten minutes without it was enough. As soon as we reached the hotel, we turned around and went straight back to the shop. Pete bought it for me as an early birthday present, and I have worn it ever since.

Things felt good...and the path led enticingly over the horizon...

8 : Fitness to the fore

A new day in South America was trying to coax us out of our much-needed fourteen-hour sleep. We breakfasted on plane leftovers and smuggled-in English fare. Tea was made on our little gas canister stove. No irate Ecuadorian maid came charging in with hands held high in horror at the smoke and bubbling steam coming forth from our room, so we figured it was all right to do so.

Making friends with our water filter was quite another matter. We had to devise the best method of operation. It was a two-person job (at least). One had to hold the input end of the lively hosepipe underwater, in this case in the basin. The other had to be ready with bottles to catch all the pure water coming out of the other end, before it could spurt out all over the room. In the middle, at least three hands were needed to hold the main filter and move the pump up and down. With the use of knees, towels and cooperation we eventually succeeded in producing some drinking water.

We knew however that we had to be careful to use only filtered water for everything, even to brush our teeth. Our fitness programme was too important to jeopardise with a dose of the 'runs'. We had to keep our bodies going with the right fuel and exercise. Mine was only reasonably fit. I had not been able to live up to the superman training programme that Pete had devised. I had managed fairly well to fit into each week two jogging sessions of thirty minutes, two or three swims of forty minutes, a ski on the plastic slope, two climbing sessions on the wall, five yoga sessions, a sauna, and even to sneak in two games of tennis, which was not really considered aerobic enough. But I was unable to increase my work output by running faster or swimming more lengths. Pete had told me, 'You'll never get up Chimborazo if you don't do more.' If I pushed myself further, however, I tended to get injuries and strains, and I did not want to risk being forced to stop exercising completely. That would have been worse, especially as I have the sort of body that objects if it has a day without some sort of movement, either by seizing up or by letting the mind go soggy. So my fitness training had always been a bit like Buddhism – trying to find the middle way; doing enough but not too much.

Pete's own build-up training had always been impressive. He would ask me out on a date: 'Fancy a nice day out? Let's do a twenty-mile run.'

Food knowledge had been much more my cup of tea. After many years of studying the best nutrition for my children, I find myself very sensitive to what my body feels good on. It likes bananas, lots of bananas. Eating twelve in a morning is not unusual. Maybe there was some sort of karmic debt payback in finding myself in a country that is the world's biggest banana exporter, and where one can buy a bunch of fifty bananas for less than the price of an English nail.

Ideally, I like as much fruit as possible early in the day. Then I go for salads, steamed vegetables, eggs, some dairy protein, nuts, seeds, pulses, and wholemeal rice, bread and pasta. I try to stick with simple organic wholefoods wherever possible; no fat, no sugar, no chemicals, no tea, no coffee, no alcohol…at least, that was until Pete and I met and made an agreement. He would become vegetarian and I would become alcoholic. He kept his part of the bargain and gave up meat. I immediately took up having two small beers per year and little sips of wine – but it's not always easy to keep to.

I know I feel better not mixing carbohydrates and protein in one meal as it simplifies the digestion, making more energy available. I also know I feel more alive without wheat and dairy products, although I don't often stick to that one. If I want to feel great I have a day on just fruit. It's a tough discipline, but it helps detoxify. Strictly it should be without bananas, but bananas keep me going.

If I want to get the best out of my middle-aged body-machine, I find I have to work hard caring for it. I have to keep out the ubiquitous rubbish, I have not to overfeed it, or everything slows down and goes soggy, and I have to put in the most real and live foods and supplements I can find. Everyone is different. In contrast to mine, Pete's body seems to be fit whatever he puts in it, even Mars Bars and custard.

What to eat seems to be a battle between putting into one's system that which will give the body optimum aliveness and energy, and that which 'civilisation' throws at one in a convenient form, made to look and taste yummy. Sadly, these two aspects are usually in conflict. So diets strictly adhered to at home are much harder to maintain when one is out and about. It needs foresight.

My time as a mother has given me the habit of carrying healthy snacks to keep children happy, so I tend to keep supplies of apples, dates, seeds, nuts, oatcakes and, of course, bananas with me at all times. We had been able to bring with us useful quantities of these (even dried bananas). This enabled us to maintain a reasonably similar diet to that of our lead-up training programme. Our goal was important. We were going to be asking our bodies to go to their limits, so we had had to increase our fitness levels. Now, our muscles would have to be maintained with protein, fuelled with carbohydrates and kept in good working order with vegetables. The latter, I knew from experience, would be the hardest to find in a safe, edible form. My friends were used to me pacing up and down restaurants growling with salad-withdrawal symptoms. I wondered how it would be now in Ecuador.

'Right! Let's go!' Pete as always was ready to go out long before I was. 'We've got a long list of things to do today.'

My body groaned quietly. Why was he always so efficient and full of energy? I was feeling very lethargic in spite of the long sleep, and would have happily spent the day curled up reading a book. I was not thinking very clearly and had a bit of a headache.

'Everyone says you should spend the first day here resting and getting used to being at nearly 3,000 metres,' I tried, knowing full well what the response would be.

'Well, I feel quite normal, and anyway it's absolutely essential that we climb something tomorrow. We've got to start the acclimatisation programme. I think we should head in the direction of the volcano Pichincha, with two summits at 4,700 and 4,794 metres. It would be great to go high, but let's see how far we can get. It's really close by, right on the western outskirts of the city, but we've got to find out how to get there.'

I had to admit that, so far, I had not been feeling breathless at all. The books said we probably would do at this altitude. The reduced oxygen here from the lower pressure meant that we should be breathing nearly fifty per cent more often to obtain the same amount of oxygen as we had been used to at home, close to sea level. We had to give our bodies time to increase the red corpuscle count and make biochemical changes in the blood to be able to absorb the oxygen necessary to function at normal capacity. It would take months for complete acclimatisation, but generally it seemed to be accepted that over a period of at least two weeks, with gradual increase in altitude exposure, it was safe for climbers to be at 6,000 metres. The maxim is 'ascend at 300-500 metres per day.' In practice many mountaineers exceed this, for their lives are too busy, and they have too many mountaineering ambitions, to keep to the optimum rate. Pete and I had three weeks to acclimatise, Mig and GT rather less, but we thought this would be fine. The plan was to spend time at the Quito altitude, and progressively go up higher and higher mountains. This would work the body with walking and climbing, while it was making the necessary physiological changes to be ready for the 6,310 metres push on Chimborazo.

I wondered if Mig would carry any genetic adaptations to altitude. Although he had never lived at any height other than near sea level, his parents had escaped out of Tibet and all his forebears had lived above 3,500 metres there. Certainly the descendants of the high-living Inca Indians have enlarged lung capacities. Time would tell.

It was not possible to know for sure how well or how badly any of us would cope. The acclimatisation process is unique to each individual and each occasion. Fitness, surprisingly, does not seem to be relevant. GT had climbed previously at 6,000 metres in the Tien Shan with no altitude problems. Similarly, Pete had scaled all the major European Alps to 4,800 metres. I had experienced no adverse effects at 3,500 metres while men around me were on their knees, vomiting and with excruciating headaches. I had suggested at the time that I was not suffering because of being female, a theory that had not gone down at all well.

I did know that if we got the preparations wrong it would not be much fun. People die. Climbing too high too fast leads to Acute Mountain Sickness or *soroche*, as it is known in the Andes. It manifests as dizziness, headaches, shortness of breath, nausea, vomiting, fatigue, insomnia, dehydration, loss of appetite and periods of not breathing during sleep. This progresses to High Altitude Pulmonary Oedema, which is fluid collecting in the lungs, and High Altitude Cerebral Oedema which is fluid accumulating in the brain. Both of these conditions demand an immediate descent to lower altitude for survival.

We could help keep altitude sickness at bay by taking things gently – some hope! We could drink a lot of water – but I did not yet know the word for 'loo' in Spanish. We could take Diamox, which acidifies the blood, thus increasing respiration – although side effects include tingling extremities and even more trips to the loo – and we could also take coca. The coca plant has been widely cultivated in the Andes for 4,000 years. The leaves are chewed and coca tea, or *maté*, is drunk. This wards off the effects of altitude, hunger and fatigue. It also relieves pain. By its use in sacred ritual it has long been an important part of the spiritual life of the Andean peoples, who now find their livelihood threatened by the plan to eradicate its growth – the 'civilised' Western world derived cocaine from it and put it to 'good abuse'.

I decided not to take any Diamox, but took my homeopathic coca pill and dragged my complaining body out. To have the best chance of getting up Chimborazo we had to take every opportunity to adapt to the rarefied air, so I reluctantly agreed that we should plan to go up something the next day. Anyway, it would be Pete's birthday, so what better way to celebrate it than by climbing a mountain?

We headed into the hustle and bustle of the now-busy Monday morning streets. The exhaust pollution in the air was noticeably bad, and on the main arteries every other vehicle seemed to be a bus belching huge black smoke signals. The clamour of the engines and the frequent horns of the rattling old taxis added to the hassle of trying to find our way around, but everyone we communicated with in trial Spanish words, gesticulations and smiles was friendly and helpful. Surprisingly, a few people even understood English, and we would occasionally hear American pop songs wafting out from some of the cafés. The sun shone down with a perfect T-shirt temperature and I soon felt at ease.

We found the South American Explorers Club on Jorge Washington Street. The whitewashed colonial façade displayed the colourful Ecuadorian flag, blowing proudly in the breeze. At its heart was the national crest. It depicted Mount Chimborazo. Standing guard was the Andean condor, wings outstretched. The striped background was of yellow for sunshine, corn and wealth; blue for rivers, sea and air; and red for the blood of patriots who fought for freedom and justice. Just for a moment my hand went to the Tibetan flag on the 'Climb For Tibet' T-shirt that I was wearing. The colours were similar, but the Tibetan blood that had been spilled had not brought about freedom and justice. I prayed that it would not have been spilled in vain. I prayed that the courage of the Tibetans, and their long patient battle in the spirit of non-violence, would result in wider, more lasting freedom and justice for the world.

The South American Explorers Club is a wonderful haven for travellers. It offers all sorts of advice and local information, books, tea, mail, message collection, email and fax facilities, although we never did coincide with an occasion when the latter was actually working. We fired copious questions at Roger and Sheila, the warm, multilingual North Americans who ran the club... Places to stay?... How to travel around?... Mountains to climb?... Money to change?... Where to find food?... What are the best type of bananas to buy?... Where to see condors?... When will it rain?... What to do about taxi rip-off syndrome?... Do the Indian men here really drink kerosene to kill the germs inside?... What is the significance of the Incas eating guinea pigs?... Is Chimborazo in good condition?

Yes, Pichincha would be an excellent mountain to climb for early acclimatisation...thought to be the first major peak in the world to be climbed by a European (the Spaniard, Ortiguera, in 1582)... The summits are Rucu Pichincha, meaning 'old boiling mountain,' and Guagua Pichincha, meaning 'baby boiling mountain'... Opinions vary as to their actual heights... Nice and close to Quito, only 10 kilometres or so... Yes, fine for a day trip... Ask a taxi to drop you off at Cruz Loma... *No problemo*... Have a nice day... and whatever you do don't go on foot up the first bit, it's far too dangerous... Our thoughts went to rock-fall and other climbing hazards, but no... It was rape, *bandidos* and rabid dogs...

We walked the streets of the city, a little taken aback by the rawness of the Ecuadorian way of life, and the feeling that we were in a Wild West movie that underlay the smart tourist façade. The guide book warned us to watch out for strangers offering biscuits that have been injected with horse tranquillisers and be wary of robbers who like to give rucksacks the slit-open-with-razor-blade treatment. I felt that if it was possible to keep a high vibration by holding love not fear in our hearts, then no harm would be attracted to us, so I did not worry. After all, we were giving out the energy of the intention of a peace climb to help the Earth, and we were carrying many loving messages, so surely all would be well.

I thought of the beautiful understanding that my father had given to me a few weeks after he had passed out of his body. I had felt we were communicating at a mind to mind level. You could say it was my imagination, but I had sensed and seen him as he had been in the prime of his life, with dark hair at about twenty-five years of age. He had been with his mother, my grandmother. They had been laughing and joyous. He had explained that he could now be involved in our world, and in guiding loved ones, not so much by seeing what we are doing but by seeing the energy we are giving off. Thus it is not what we do or say that matters, so much as what we feel about it, what thoughts we have and what we hold in our hearts. These determine the vibration of the energy we give off. He could see the emanations from trees and animals, and especially from all of us. So he knew if we were feeling love in our hearts and thinking loving thoughts. This view from a different reality had been scary, in that it took away the apparent privacy of individuality, but its perception had been a precious gift for me. I knew I forgot it all too easily. Now, remembering it gave me comfort and strength.

Outside the money exchange agency there was a security policeman with a huge rifle. He looked barely sixteen years old. Inside we changed travellers cheques in US dollars into hundreds of thousands of *sucres*. It would be easy to become a millionaire, but we were careful not to have too much inflation-loving local currency. Anyway, it seemed possible to pay all large bills in US dollars.

Our new-found wealth seemed to draw those in need. On the busy Avenida Amazonas, lined with enticing shops and extravagantly displayed market stalls, Pete suddenly found himself with a hitchhiker. A tiny girl in a baggy pink top and a long skirt above dirty bare feet had grabbed one of his hands with both of hers and would not let go. She looked about three years old. Her mother, who was sitting on the pavement training her little one to attract attention and beg for money, was encouraging her 'Vas! Vas!' It took *mucho dinero* for Pete to be able to extract his hand.

A long walk through parks lined with palms and araucarias and a circular road up a hill made us catch our breath just a little and slow down. At the top was the only place in the country that sold large-scale maps, Instituto Geographico Militar – *Unidos por la ciencia y el espíritu para el progreso del Ecuador*. We reluctantly left our passports at the gate with armed soldiers and emerged nearly two hours later with a 1:50,000 map of Chimborazo and a 1:25,000 of the Quito area. Neither turned out to be detailed or accurate enough for the kind of let's-not-get-lost use we had in mind – but there was a good view of the city from the hill.

On the way down we stopped at the smallest of shops, about half a metre wide, decorated with cheerful bunting. It was selling bright yellow homemade-type confectionery, and apples and plums. The sweets might have worked as unusual paperweights to take home, but we decided to go for bags of the fruit, which we longingly carried back to be washed in our water filter production line.

Visiting eco-tour operators, finding butane camping-gaz cylinders, unsuccessful attempts at finding fax machines and telephones, and being postman for friends in England, finally left even Pete tired and hungry. We managed to track down 'El Magic Bean', the renowned hangout eating house which advertises 'all vegetables washed in boiled water', and enjoyed, to my great delight, a huge salad, sitting under a lovely hanging vine. We would also have enjoyed the soup if my linguistic abilities had delivered us pea and bean soup instead of pea and ham. I never did discover how to say the word for vegetarian.

Ecuador, you have welcomed us with colour and a smile, I thought, as I crawled wearily into bed that night. Our friend Avril, from Amora International, who were planning to produce a documentary on the climb, had advised us on what to shoot with the video camera. She had said, 'Always look for things that are beautiful.' Yes, *no problemo*, there will be plenty of stuff to film here.

9 : Highs – and lows

It had to be a pre-dawn start, to organise morning tea in bed for the birthday boy. I had wrapped the chess set in an Ecuadorian newspaper, and tied it with deep pink ribbons. These I had borrowed from three special scrolls on their way to Chimborazo. They had been sent with us by our friend Delphine, who had given 'Climb For Tibet' enormous support. In her wise sensitivity to the Tibetan cause, and understanding of the spiritual implications, she had asked that we gather rocks and build three 'stupas' at the gateway to the mountain. These were to be little cairns or monuments, which in the Buddhist tradition are a focus of prayer and pilgrimage. They work as symbols of peace and harmony in the embodiment of the limitless compassion of a pure heart, which is said to be free of the ignorance, attachment and aversion that cause personal and global suffering. They transmit positive energy. Stupas hold great importance.

In each of these was to be buried a scroll, inscribed with a prayer by Kuan Yin, the Chinese Goddess of Ultimate Compassion, and they were then to be activated by speaking peace messages. In this way we would be helping to create the energy of compassion necessary for the climb and its long term effects. The job of the pink ribbons was to tie up with grace the representations of birth.

'Happy Birthday, old boy. Now you're so ancient, maybe it'll slow you down a bit,' I suggested, hopefully.

'C'mon you cheeky thing, get ready. We've got a long climb ahead. I'll organise the taxi to Cruz Loma.'

I gobbled my favourite action breakfast of organic oats, dates, sunflower seeds, soya protein powder, vitamin C and guarana, which is the legendary ground-up seed long used by the Amazon Indians for endurance and clarity of mind. I then threw into a rucksack the essentials – Spanish dictionary, waterproofs, fleece, hat, gloves, water bottles, carbohydrate foods and dried fruit, compass, ski sticks, camera, flag and Yannick the penguin – grabbed my boots and headed out into the waiting day. It did not seem much preparation for a mountain with a summit the height of Mont Blanc but then, I figured, things work differently in South America.

The old yellow taxi seemed particularly rickety as we bounced happily along the Quito streets with the smiley driver chatting away to us. I was enjoying the conversation, but seemed only to understand every tenth word or so. My strange and garbled

Spanish somehow kept the conversation going OK.

It took us a while to become oriented to being in the southern hemisphere, with the sun in the northeast, but after about an hour of driving around we realised that we were going generally south. We had thought that the journey should be about twenty minutes to the west. Enquiries still produced '*Si, si. No problemo*,' so there was nothing for it but to sit back, enjoy the view and wait to see where the driver thought we should be going. This was a technique we became quite good at during our stay in Ecuador.

We left the old part of the city, with its narrow, crowded, cobbled streets, and red-tiled colonial buildings, passing through poverty-stricken residential areas, and took a dirt road uphill. Huge gravel trucks passed us in clouds of dust as the little taxi struggled onwards to a pass and then wound its way down to a small village. Suddenly we had entered an agricultural area that looked as though it had remained unchanged for hundreds of years. There were chickens and dogs and small children playing, but scarcely a suggestion of the modern world.

Our driver, whose name we had learned was Fernando, drove back and forth with much wrong turning and asking of directions from the villagers. This was obviously not a regular taxi route, but he eventually found a rough track going northwest that he seemed happy with. Not so the little car, which spluttered and coughed as the gradient became steeper and steeper, crunching its undercarriage on the rocks that had been piled into the ditches and holes, and skidding on the soft dry sand. Pete's concern over where we were was shifting to the battering the car was taking.

'He's very brave, but it's getting wrecked.'

It was a Lada. Somehow I managed to communicate to Fernando that back home in England I had a Skoda, a near-relation. He beamed and responded with a tirade of expletives.

'We're OK now,' I turned to Pete. 'I think we're life-long

buddies. He's so impressed that I drive a Skoda.'

'He's just being polite,' came the reply, but I felt there was power in a small synchronicity that made friends out of strangers from different worlds. I was reminded of a peace message:

In the communicating of similarities is the finding of harmony between peoples.

We took to pushing up the steepest bits, and resting when there were clouds of steam coming from the engine. It gave us a chance to enjoy the magnificent scenery. We were in verdant farmland. It was mostly patchwork agriculture, small fields, steep and well-terraced. The black and white cattle looked fat and healthy. Young heifers and steers gazed at us through fences made from stakes that were themselves sprouting, such was the fertility of the rich volcanic soil. Sweet little black piglets snuffled around fine horses with intelligent eyes, and large-leafed plants rambled as though with picturesque intent. It was all so prolific and green, reminding me of Queensland, Australia. There were even rows of tall eucalyptus amid spinneys of native forest – all a lovely instance of nature and man working well together.

As we gained more height we could see voluminous cloud formations drifting south to the far distance, joining the alluring, nebulous covers of the Avenue of the Volcanoes. Somewhere down there was Cotopaxi...and beyond that...Chimborazo.

Then came the moment we had been expecting. Fernando declared the rabbit-warren-like track impassable – and his intention to go back down. Pushing and lifting, we helped turn the car around in the narrow space, mindful of the steep precipice on one side. In negotiating the rather more than standard fare, we managed to communicate great thanks to him for his valiant efforts in getting us this far. We even managed to explain that it was Pete's birthday (a difficult concept in sign language), but we were not sure if we had convinced him to try to pick us up later. It was a very remote chance, anyway, that he would actually want to, given the state of his beaten-up little car... We watched forlornly as the yellow city taxi disappeared over the horizon, leaving us alone in thousands of square kilometres of mountain – not quite the one we had planned to climb, but it appeared we had no choice.

Gradually we left the trees behind and the green gave way to the warm and lovely beige of tussock grasses blowing in the gathering wind. This was the beginning of the Andean *páramo*. Ahead of us a dark volcanic plug loomed, drawing us on. Could this be Pichincha after all? No. It had to be Guagua Pichincha, but from the other side.

It took us only three hours to follow the track to 4,500 metres, where there was a locked volcanologists' refuge hut at the base of the tuffaceous cone. We saw no-one except for a man with a shovel and a muddy grey horse, which appeared to be the road maintenance crew.

I felt fine apart from a slight headache that was soon sorted out with guarana, but we were careful to go slowly and steadily and not overexert ourselves. A mere breeze, we concurred, as we were scarcely out of breath. Thank goodness for our fitness. We had spent some time in the Alps a couple of months previously, skiing and ski-mountaineering, and keeping as high as possible for as long as possible. We had even dug a snow hole at 3,000 metres and slept a cold night in it, thinking it to be useful training should we be benighted. It felt as if we had retained some of the acclimatisation gained then.

Suddenly the wind got up and it became really cold. In the lee of the hut we put on all the clothes we had and got moving across the brittle volcanic ash to the rim of the crater. It was only then that I realised how Pichincha had got its name, 'boiling mountain'. It is an active volcano. We had been warned that in 1993 volcanic gases in the crater had overcome a group of people and everyone had died. I understood this then, standing on the edge of the cauldron in the howling wind, with an eerie swirling mist bellowing out, sulphur fumes attacking my nostrils, and peering down into a white nothing which I knew to be 700 metres deep. Momentarily the smoking spectre shifted and I saw tall pyroclastic pinnacles reaching out. I shuddered, not wanting to stay there too long, but caught mesmerised by the stunning scene. Then, turning, I hurried on after Pete up the crater edge to the high point, away from the warm blood of Mother Earth.

Above the summit rock, painted 4,781 metres, we flew the Tibetan flag and, with raised hands palm to palm, chanted 'OM MANI PADME HUM'. This popular blessing, generally translated as 'hail to the jewel in the lotus', invokes the Dalai Lama, the embodiment of compassion. It is always spoken for the wellbeing of all sentient beings. The spirit of Tibet soared on the wild Andean winds and we felt content. Though we had been further and higher than we knew we should have, we had reached our first peak with relative ease and it augured well for the whole venture.

Then down. Ash running was fun in the descent of the first bit, at an angle of about 35°, and we laughed at the exhilaration. Afterwards came the long slog. Down...down...two hours...three hours... four... The soles of my feet hurt intensely and my knees were heavy and crying out with shooting pains. Thank goodness for the ski sticks to take some of the downward pressure. But I was so tired. We were both so very tired (well, Pete was quite tired.) Sometimes I thought I could go no further, and then there was a little burst of renewed energy. The eyes saw so much beauty, but the body pleaded 'Stop! Stop!' knowing there was no choice.

A night out at this altitude with no gear was not something we wanted to contemplate. Perhaps this was a test for our resolve, a practice run to keep the mind focused and gather strength.

In spite of the pain, or just maybe because of it, I felt a sense of being guided, that there was spiritual assistance at hand. This feeling was to remain with me. I wished I had brought the crystal. For some reason I felt it would be easier to access help with it. I decided always to carry it with me in future.

Night fell fast, killing a rose-quartz evening sky. It was 6.30 pm. The suddenness of it surprised us. We had not yet become used to being so close to the equator. Hobbling on through the darkening gloom, we eventually came to a place where we could just make out the first outlying little farmstead of the village. There, next to it, like a vision of an angel, stood a small yellow taxi...and then there was Fernando, rushing out to take our rucksacks. How very sweet it was.

'Someone upstairs is looking after us,' Pete grinned, but I am not sure he thought that later, back at the hotel, when he was raring to go out for the birthday supper he had been looking forward to. Feeling as if I would never walk again, shivering all over and unable to eat, I refused to go. He went out, and returned after a while with a bag of chips.

I knew my system was in a weakened state and had not yet recovered from the stress in the lead-up to coming and the lack of sleep on the flight out, and that I had overdone the altitude adaptation, which had caught up with me. It seemed to be a delayed reaction. I continued to shake, had a raised temperature, felt dizzy and could not sleep all night. Every two hours I took vitamin C and homeopathic belladonna. To this I attributed the fact that the chills had gone in the morning, and that I could climb out of bed. However, we were both unsettled and bad-tempered with each other, and the tiredness meant we were not thinking things through clearly. There was much to discuss, research and decide, which was annoying while we were feeling so grumpy.

We talked a lot about Chimborazo. Pete's main worries were about the practicalities of getting up it and making sure everyone was safe. Being the most experienced member of the team, this responsibility lay heavily on him, particularly regarding the novice, Migmar. I was more concerned with making sure we carried out properly all that we should do for it to be a pilgrimage to the Watchtower of the Universe with the intent of helping Tibet and the Earth. We decided that the two days we had before Mig came would be put to best use by journeying down to the mountain to do a recce.

The main problem before that was to establish a suitable base in Quito, somewhere cheap and able to accommodate the comings and goings of our expanding team. There was also the possibility of a film crew joining us. We wearily traipsed the streets, checking out options until we had narrowed it down to two: one hostel that Pete liked and one that I liked. There seemed to be no compromise to our disagreement.

Eventually we tossed a coin; I won, and Pete graciously conceded defeat. With our accommodation sorted, relations between us eased. By allowing the apparently wider influence of Lady Luck to decide, we had dived into the river of life with all its interacting forces, and were going with the flow, rather than clinging to our own hanging branches. We had moved a little towards trusting that all would be well.

I was really happy with the place that the 'river' had provided for us, the Hostal Posada del Maple. Its quiet little street, Juan Rodriguez, was in the centre of the new area of the city, and stuffed full of pollarded but shady maple trees. There were two delightful courtyards painted in the typical burnt-pink colour, and dripping with lovely ferns and tropical plants. Interesting items of Ecuadorian art abounded and it was run by a charming lady, Manuela, who spoke good English. We arranged to leave some gear there while on the Chimborazo recce.

However, more frustrations were in store for us that thrust us back into a grumpy mood. We had a long list of people in England and the US to get in touch with, not the least of whom were our children. Having tried unsuccessfully the South American Explorers Club and various hotels, we discovered the telecom centre a lengthy walk away. Here we queued, handed over money and were sent to little cubicles in abortive attempts to find overseas lines. It seemed there were blockages everywhere. It was perhaps a good thing we did not know then that communications with the outside world, essential to the running of 'Climb For Tibet', would always be fraught with difficulties. It was as though we were being told, 'Focus on the here…focus on the now… The important thing is that you get up the mountain in the right spirit.'

That thought helped me find some peace. After all, how I felt had to come from me. I could not blame what was going on in the environment around me. If I was giving out churning, soggy, boring vibes, that is what the 'river' would be like. If I was in harmony with myself, I would float in peaceful, loving energy.

I told myself to get a grip. 'You're doing exactly what you want to do with your life. This is exactly where you need to be…'

Back at the Café Cultura for our last night we tried to celebrate the delayed birthday with a nice meal by a welcoming log fire, but with my two sips of wine, I was gone. Sleep, the great healer, took over and finished the work of restoring my equanimity.

10 : The way to Chimborazo

I couldn't wait to be near Chimborazo. We were going to see our special sacred eminence of the Earth. Our feet were actually going to touch the lower reaches of the mountain about which we had talked and dreamed for so long.

We rationalised that it would help us plan the climb itself if we went over to assess things. But it felt as though we were cheating, going too soon. We weren't acclimatised; we didn't have the whole team with us; the time was not yet right. Still, we were being drawn there. We could not keep away… We had to go. And there could be only one first meeting, so this would be it. I would savour this journey.

We rose at 5 am, pumped water for all our bottles, packed up, taxied our spare bags to Posada del Maple and ourselves to Terminal Terrestre de Cumandá, Quito's main bus station. The whole four-hour bus journey to Riobamba, a distance of nearly

200 kilometres, would only be 17,000 *sucres* (about £2 sterling), though this was not the height of luxury.

We drew noisily out of the bus station, emitting smelly black fumes into the early-morning rush hour. The driver went at speed, weaving deftly in and out of pedestrians, languishing, broken-down vehicles, the ubiquitous cracks in the road and other hazards. He stopped frequently and people kept piling on and off with varying, interesting-looking loads. One Quechuan Indian lady, in a red shawl and typical Ecuadorian hat, brought a basket of what could have been washing, and one a little wicker bird cage, cheeping loudly. From the front of the bus emanated a strange sort of wailing. One man was wearing a smart Western-type suit. Everyone was smiling and joking, and an air of contentment seemed to pervade day-to-day business. There was a TV on board, so we went along watching the national pastime – the football.

We sat at the back, thinking the elevated rear seats would offer us the best view (of Ecuador, not the football). Squashed between one that was completely full of holes and one that had collapsed, I settled down to updating my diary, a job which soon became difficult, and then impossible, as the bumps grew in magnitude. I looked up to see my erstwhile imperturbable companion flying through the air, and hitting his head on the roof of the jolting old bus, clearly finding his attempts to get video footage of our journey becoming just as impossible.

A wonderful old Indian man came to sit beside Pete in the collapsing seat. He was of the usual stocky build, with a bright red striped poncho and standard brimmed hat. His face was dark brown and weather-beaten, his nose aquiline and distinguished. There was a simple pride about him that said, 'my race has walked this land for generations'... He stared, fascinated by the hairy beard on this tall stranger. Suddenly he could contain himself no longer. Reaching across the hessian bag of celery that he was holding, he pulled at the tawny hair on Pete's arm. His face lit up in a brilliant smile, which even his brown and broken teeth could not dull. Then he gently stroked his own hairless arm.

Was this another example of the breaking down of barriers between nations?

In the understanding of differences is also the finding of harmony between peoples.

My mind drifted to the Tibetan situation. Maybe, I pondered, even though many Chinese people have themselves been victims, their oppression of Tibetans is a reaction of fear due to not fully understanding the basic difference between the two peoples. A way of life with the top priority being given to the State and its laws is inevitably very different from a way of life that gives this ultimate position to a monk and his teachings.

Better communication should help further this understanding of differences. So, with the explosion of information available through computer technology, which youngsters in particular seem to thrive on, there is hope for the future. If we, the body of humanity, like the world wide web, are one interconnected energy system, then we are partly Chinese. More to the point, we are more than one fifth Chinese. That's quite a lot of body. The more we try to understand the differences of the parts of our body, the more in harmony it will be, and this cuts both ways.

Education for all is therefore critical. However, for Tibetans in Tibet, particularly in rural areas with an eighty per cent illiteracy rate, there is little access to formal education. The monasteries used to be the seats of learning, but the Chinese destroyed virtually all 6,000, and banned many of the religious practices. (Today many have been rebuilt to encourage the tourist dollar). So, for the Tibetan, by deliberate racial discrimination, there is little opportunity for jobs, and consequently food and housing are limited. To make matters worse they are now outnumbered by Han Chinese, who have been moved in.

There must be a way forward, as there can be no way back now to the old ways. There must be a way forward in peace and harmony and understanding. The UN charter states that everyone has the basic right to freedom.

Suddenly pandemonium broke out on the bus. Loud wailing turned to mewing and a little bundle of black and white fur darted fearfully between the doubled-up legs, looking for freedom and safety. Various passengers dived to catch the runaway amid curses and shouts, but to no avail. Then the mewing became louder as our smooth new friend next to Pete calmly grabbed the kitten by the scruff of the neck and delivered him to his owner, who returned him to the bag from which he had escaped. She was also an Ecuadorian Indian in shawl and hat, with big, beautiful earrings and a cracked-teeth smile to match. Peace was restored.

The road to Chimborazo lay due south from Quito along the Pan-American highway, following the Central Valley of the Andes, the 'Avenue of the Volcanoes'. I wished we could see beyond the tantalising cloud cover, but all of Ecuador's mountain jewels remained hidden. Once we had left the city behind, green fields and agriculture were all around us. I gazed on dairy cattle, pigs, plantations of maize, cabbages, potatoes, large glasshouses for market gardening, eucalyptus and pine windbreaks, small flat-roofed dwellings, all with TV aerials and pretty white lilies, larger and more wealthy-looking haciendas and, always, dogs. The lush, fertile farms filled the picturesque landscape as far as the distant black lava of the volcano slopes. Villages clustering along the main highway featured falling-down mud-brick houses, light workshops, piles of old rubber tyres and young men playing volley ball. There were market stalls, fruit and vegetable stands and, for the fast food connoisseur, roast guinea pigs on spits.

Fine churches with beautiful flowerbeds dominated the busy towns. Noisy, colourful street sellers boarded the bus with their bulging baskets while we were caught in traffic. They touted interesting unknown foods, sweets and fried biscuits that we were tempted to try but decided not to risk – particularly the speciality *allullas*, made from flour, pork fat and unpasteurised cheese. Pete did go for a strange orange drink. Buying it was one thing, drinking it while being violently bumped up and down was quite another, as the roads were contenders for the worst-in-the-world award. They were made more interesting by the fact that the craters were deeper at the sides, so there was a natural tendency for drivers from both directions to aim at the same bit of road – the middle.

The bus gained some height, clambering through pine plantations over a pass at 3,500 metres, just as it began to rain, dulling our view further. Then the road dropped and we rattled and bounced down into Latacunga. This town has the rather unlucky distinction of having been totally wiped out by the erupting Cotopaxi three times: in 1742, 1768 and 1877. It says something about the human ability to trust that today it is a bustling well-built centre of 40,000 people, even though Cotopaxi continues to exhibit fumarolic activity.

A swarthy young man with a cigarette boarded, happily the only human smoker we had seen. A woman with a baby wrapped in a bundle got off. The little one had been considerably quieter than the cat. He was probably used to long hours strapped to his mother's back as she hoed the soil, like many we passed by.

Potato crops became more frequent as we moved south, and the land became dryer and dustier. Cactuses abounded and gardens became less frequent. Ambato, the next main town, was wrecked by an earthquake in 1949, but had been beautifully reconstructed with impressive avenues and fine buildings – the joys of renewal.

Climbing steeply out of the town alongside a truck full of complaining chickens, and a sheep riding precariously on the roof of a car, we had a growing sense of anticipation. Somewhere to the west, beyond the terraced slopes, behind a screen of cloud, lay a volcano that had not erupted for 10,000 years – our mountain. I could sense its presence. I anxiously felt the crystal in my pocket. We were getting close.

'The guidebook says there should be great views of Chimborazo from this pass at 3,600 metres.' Pete was eagerly searching the mist. It had started to rain again, and was dull and drab. 'It's more like Scottish climbing weather than the Andes.' Our elevation now was too high for cultivation or pine forests. A scene of blustery tussock grass stretched into the murk.

'There's more wisdom in the unseen,' I quoted, usefully.

The bus took us down and spewed us out at Riobamba. It was near here that, in 1797, a huge landslide had smothered and killed several thousand people. There seemed to be a certain restlessness about the Earth in these parts, as though trying to shake off human habitation. Are we humans just visitors on this planet? Are the forces of nature so strong that we are irrelevant? Or are we so inextricably part of the whole system that the energy we give out, governed somewhat by our thought processes, can make a vital, powerful difference to the world around us?

The Inca people, whose empire dominated the Andes for over a century, frequently made supplications to the gods, in the form of ceremonial rituals, human and animal sacrifices and other offerings. Mountaintop venues were considered particularly sacred. Could our pilgrimage and its offering of peace messages help appease the demons of war, aggression, greed and inhumanity that blow across the Inca Earth Goddess today?

Bidding *adiós* to the bus driver, I asked him where I could deposit our bag of rubbish. He indicated for me to dump it in the road alongside other heaps of trash. I shook my head, saying 'No, no!' He signalled for me to give it to him. I did so. He then dumped it in the road himself. We all live by different values, I thought, but maybe the awareness that all things are interconnected would precipitate more of a sense of caring and responsibility, for then whatever one does to the world one does to oneself, in spite of our isolating barriers.

Our developing linguistic skills were further put to the test as we approached the line of assorted yellow taxis. Eventually we were happy with the negotiated rate of 200,000 *sucres* to the Refugio Hermanos Carrel, and a return the next day. Chimborazo must be one of the easiest high mountains in the world to get to the base of. There cannot be many places where it is possible to take a taxi to 4,800 metres – the height of Mont Blanc.

We sped off west out of Riobamba, by now accustomed to the swerving around the potholes and rocks in the road. I chatted to the friendly taxi driver in my pretend Spanish while Pete tried a seasick video session out of the window. We passed cement works and were approaching an area of pine forest when we were flagged down by the police at a roadblock.

'*Qué pasa?*' I enquired of our driver. By way of a reply he made a sharp movement with his hand as if he was cutting his throat with a knife.

'*Bandidos?*'

'*Si, bandidos!*'

I could not help laughing. Again I felt that sense of unreality, as though I were playing a part in a film. How would it be, I wondered, to consider the whole of life as playing a part in a film? Maybe it would then be possible to laugh at everything upsetting or stressful. Maybe I could then find real inner peace.

We started gaining altitude again, leaving behind an isolated little village, with clusters of whitewashed, flat-roofed houses and curious donkeys. Past drumlin-like hills with clinging patchwork fields, we followed a dirt track, streams of dust following in our wake. We rose above the tree line and the landscape took on a general greyness. Ash was everywhere. By the look of the cutting on the side of the road, there was very little soil for the tussock grass roots to cling to in the bands of differing volcanic material, showing ancient eruptions. This was the Earth's geological map of a time before man believed he ruled the planet.

Then, as I looked out from the dusty window of the taxi up into grey billowing cloud hanging from the roof of the sky, something momentarily shifted. There was a vista of distant snowfields. A dazzling white light shone. My gaze held it…and then it slipped into the oblivion of the unseen. Now there was a presence… right upon us… Wow! We were in the aura of Chimborazo. My relationship with the mountain was about to begin. Like a sexual exchange, would the mingling of auras affect our energetic makeup for time to come? Would there be a letting go?… A surrender?… A giving?… And what trials?… What euphoria?…

The raw beauty of the wild open *páramo* became a loose volcanic plain. If it were not for the low shifting cloud and gathering dust, I felt sure we would be able to see far distant horizons with a sense of the Earth's curvature.

'*Veis allí. Mira!… Vicuñas!*' shouted the driver suddenly, excited to be able to show his tourist guests the sights. No Buckingham Palace, though, could compete with the fascination of viewing our first Andean representatives of the animal kingdom. He pointed

114

to a herd of about ten llama-type creatures, light chocolate brown in colour, grazing close together, looking a bit like baby camels but without the humps. They raised their long necks, unperturbed, as we passed by. I wondered what they could possibly be finding to eat here in this barren desert, at an elevation of 4,000 metres.

I tried to find out more about the *vicuñas* from the driver but the language difference was frustrating. I did know, however, that the local Indians had long found the llama useful, not only for haulage, but also as a butcher's shop, as a fine wool factory, and even for racing. Quite a handy sort of a package, really. These were definitely not llamas, I gathered, but presumably from the same family. I heard the words 'Inca' and *'protección'*. Yes, I figured, many early people had made wise decisions not based on greed, and were in harmony with their environment, knowing that they were part of it.

The way was now seriously rutted. At times it was hard to tell the road from the desert. On looking carefully, the empty windswept wilderness was home to tiny, pretty, yellow flowers, which peeped through the harsh greyness, saying, 'Beauty is always there for the looking'. Meanwhile, a lone bird, which our driver called an 'alcong', soared on a freedom wind, negotiating the mix of flying dust.

We had been skirting around the southern perimeter of the mountain, now we turned steeply northeast towards the base. The rough track wound its way to a solid-looking climbers' hut – the first refuge. On either side, ethereal strands of white cloud drifted in an almost eerie welcome. I wondered if this, like a Tibetan white scarf of greeting and blessing, was the gates of Chimborazo about which Beverley had spoken. I tried to open my heart, to be receptive, to be humble and sensitive to the energies around.

Our driver left us there, at the end of the road, after writing down *'una de la tarde – 13.00 horas'* for the next day's pick-up. Against the two-tone pink-wash wall, which prettily set off the heavily barred windows, peeling tin roof and rusty oil drums, lounged four climbers – two American and two British. They were waiting for their pre-arranged taxi to come to take them down. They had huge rucksacks full of climbing equipment and wore heavy duvet jackets. Their tired but relieved expression and exhausted pose told its own story, but we eagerly exchanged greetings and fell into conversation. There was friendship from the intense common bond of the challenge of the mountain. They had all left the higher refuge in the dark hours of the night for a summit attempt. Two had been forced to turn back early on. Two had made it to the Veintimilla lower summit, and then not been able to negotiate the legendary kilometre of knee-deep and sometimes waist-deep soft snow across to the true summit.

Their gifts to us were peace messages:

The greatest sadness at the end of a life would be not to have reached for the stars.

All men are brothers on a mountain – Let the world be a mountain.

Now is the seed of eternity.

Life is precious. Don't waste it.

Their gift to themselves had been their struggle.

11 : Tantalising taster

From here on up, above the Carrel refuge at 4,800 metres, it was to be the highest that either of us had touched the Earth. We savoured the elation. The sharp cold demanded thermal underwear be put on (where was the girls' changing room?), also thicker trousers, jackets, hats and gloves. This had the useful effect of lightening our loads. We set off, both with a typical element of competitiveness, determined that the altitude was not going to have an adverse affect, and that fitness and strength would override. I found it took more of an effort to breathe in the rarefied air, as though something heavy was sitting on my chest, but I felt OK, and set a slow and steady pace, using ski sticks to help take the strain of the heavy rucksacks.

We had only two hundred metres of elevation to gain to reach the second hut, the Refugio Edward Whymper, somewhere just above us, out of sight. We picked our way steeply up a rough trail across varying sizes of rocks, some of which were a lovely warm rust colour. Suddenly a huge one loomed at us out of the mists like a lost pyramid. On close inspection it proved to be a memorial to eleven French mountaineers who had lost their lives in an avalanche in 1993. A chill went through me that dampened my excited anticipation. This was no walk down a leafy lane.

Three quarters of an hour took us to the Whymper refuge at 5,000 metres, a lofty elevation for any building. Although wrapped in a cloak of ghostly cloud, it looked substantial and welcoming. It was slightly larger than the lower hut, and a few wooden shutters almost gave it a feel of the European Alps. The dusky pink of the walls toned in with the milk chocolate sienna of the surrounding volcanic material, and was warm and friendly. The colour pink, to me, has always expressed universal love and gentleness. Here was a haven of shelter from some of the world's wildest winds and unpredictable storms…a little cradle rocked by Mother Earth.

A cheerful hut warden greeted us in the dark interior, where half a dozen wooden tables and benches clustered around a huge sunken fireplace. There were two small cooking areas with propane gas stoves and pots, pans and utensils which looked as if they had been left there in 1736 by the French who first surveyed the mountain. Upstairs in the sleeping area there were four rooms full of bunk beds, with foam mattresses and space to sleep about fifty friendly sardine bodies. En-suite facilities were sadly lacking, but outside there was a little shed containing a small noisy generator that operated lights for a couple of hours a day, a bucket of ice water fed by a hose that came down from the glacier stream, and two loos. Beside each, if you were lucky, was a pile of newspaper, with a space on the other side for the used variety – nearly all the comforts of home...

We paid the US$10 per night fee for each of us, and as there were still a couple of hours before dusk, wandered slowly across the rocks up the route ahead. Behind the swirling mists lay the southwest face of Chimborazo. We were there – at last. I tried to harmonise my energies with those of the mountain. This is an important thing to do at the start of any meeting, but I felt it was particularly important now. I wanted to come in the right way, so that our pilgrimage would be accepted, and we needed to show respect, and ask permission to climb from the 'spirit' of the mountain. This was just a little sensitivity that many would laugh at, but I had learned about this on a climb back in 1990.

It had been the year when many groups were fighting for the moratorium to ban mining in the Antarctic. We, two companions and myself, had climbed the Old Man of Hoy, Britain's tallest sea stack, in the Orkneys. We had slept on the summit, from where we had hung a huge banner stating 'Save Antarctica'. Much good had come from the venture, and the moratorium had been declared, proving to me that small groups can help effect important changes. After abseiling down, however, I had taken a moment to meditate, and had sensed the disquiet of the strong masculine spirit of the stack, from whom we had not asked permission. Subsequently none of the vital photographs taken by the camera crew had come out. OK, laugh, but I knew that at a non-physical level it was because we had not been sensitive enough to harmonise and ask permission. I have endeavoured to mentally call 'permission to climb' before every climb since.

Chimborazo did not seem to me to be either masculine or feminine. This was unusual; I had not experienced it before. But there was something balanced about the energy. Maybe its ancient sacredness determined this. Maybe it was that this mountain spirit was well advanced, and close to the divine source.

We decided one of the stupas should now be built as a form of supplication to the mountain. I knew this should be carried out with a pure mind, so I asked for help and tried to be receptive. In my head I heard the words I had been told: 'Prepare the way, sensing the light from the heart of the angel of the mountain.' There was a strong feeling of calm presence.

The site held importance, as it was to be our gateway for the ascent. We followed what appeared to be the direct route upwards for about four hundred metres until a little promontory 'felt' like the right place. Here we collected beautiful rocks of differing colours, shapes and sizes from the variety in proximity, and cleared a little round base area, which revealed that beneath all the loose material, the body of Chimborazo was a deep burned volcanic brown. Then, in turn, we spoke from the Chinese writing of Kuan Yin, the Deity of Compassion. We read from the right hand corner:

NÄ MÕ HÄ LÄ DÄ NÕ DÕ LÄ YÄ YÄ...

We then scrolled the prayer, tying it with the pink ribbon, protected it with clear plastic, placed it on a flat stone in the middle of the base and carefully constructed the pyramidal cairn over it. It was about a metre high, and built, we hoped, to withstand the winds of time.

Chimborazo, Watchtower of the Universe, we ask for your blessing on our climb, that it may shine a light in the world, and help Tibet and Earth Peace. May we be open to all that needs to happen. May we return safely.

A sacred mist clung to our hearts in the loud silence.

I gently balanced the crystal on the top of the stupa… It glowed softly…

'Advarr…we have brought your crystal to the mountain…in preparation…'

On saying these words I felt the now familiar cold, tingly feeling go up and down my spine, only this time it was in my legs, too, and the emotion of the moment fed tears to my eyes.

Pete and I hugged – a deep, soul hug. Together we spoke out Delphine's lovely peace message:

I pray with all my heart for Tibet to be free. And may that day herald the freeing of all our hearts into the one and great truth shining down on a liberated world illumined with compassion.
OM MANI PADME HUM…
OM MANI PADME HUM…
OM MANI PADME HUM…

The wind began to rise and howl as we returned to the hut. I was reminded of a saying which sits on my desk at home – *Every stone raised for the Greater Good brings the mountain nearer to perfection.*

Thus was the stupa activated in the birth of a seed of compassion. Thus was our presence on the mountain acknowledged.

Darkness was falling fast. Alongside a handful of other climbers, we needed to cook some supper during the short period of dim lighting. We had powdered soup and Horlicks, and packets of bean mix and rice, chosen for their quick cooking time. It was not very appetising, but we had to get as much liquid as possible into us, as well as stuffing in the carbohydrate. For we were each aware, by unspoken agreement, that the other was hoping to give the mountain a go in the early morning, and if it were possible we would try. We had automatically packed all our climbing equipment in our rucksacks, just in case.

That said, we were supposedly only checking out the route. To go any further would be insane. We were not acclimatised. Five days ago we had been at sea level in England. Our bodies had not had time to adapt to the thin air. But, as every climber knows, there is an irresistible urge to see how far one can go – Mallory's maxim of 'because it's there.' The extent to which it is tempered with suitable caution is a measure of personality. Brave or foolhardy? Wild or wise? Maybe it is a measure of how much an individual's soul desires experiences that give an opportunity to gain strength.

Our guidebook said that the Normal route takes a path left out of the refuge until gaining a prominent scree slope, then follows a huge horizontal snow ramp (El Corredor) to reach the edge of the main Thielman glacier. From there it angles left up a steep snowfield to a pass above a large rocky outcrop known as El Castillo, and then heads northwest up the long ridge, avoiding a large crevasse just beneath the Veintimilla summit before crossing the snow basin to the main summit. Usually the ascent takes eight to ten hours. Allow two to four for the descent. It did not appear to be too desperate a route. Top climbers could even describe it as 'just a walk.' Walking, of course is a purely relative term that I, as an inexpert climber, would probably call a 'dire walk' and a non-climber would definitely call a 'death warrant'.

There was a guide in the hut who spoke some English, so, happily, we were able to discuss the route. He told us that the Normal route was much too dangerous this year due to heavy rock falls in the El Corredor area. Most of the climbs were being undertaken via variations of the Direct route which was considerably harder, tricky to find and, after the rocky part, mostly 45° angled ice. (Pete thought it to be graded between Peu Difficile and Assez Difficile on the Alpine system). The guidebook said that initially the Direct route heads straight up the Thielman glacier and it meets the Normal route where it leaves El Corredor. We then went on to read – 'This route is not recommended since it is subject to avalanches and tends to be heavily crevassed.'

Up until now both of us had felt surprisingly good, and little affected by our altitude of 5,000 metres. Now, suddenly, as we finished eating, it hit us. The Earth started moving up and down uncontrollably. Perhaps aided by an element of apprehension, I felt as though I was about to throw up. There was an intense dizziness that made me feel I was not in charge of my body. It was annoying and slightly frightening. I found that if I sat still with my eyes shut then I could minimise the effect. Then I discovered that I could do things very, very slowly if I did not move my head. I managed to negotiate clearing away the supper and the tricky business of taking out my contact lenses, and staggered up the wooden ladder stairs to the bunks. Lying down felt better, but it was a long time before I could pluck up the courage to sit up and blow out the candle. I felt so bad that I figured I would throw up if I moved. I sucked coca pills miserably in the cold darkness. Even though I had all my climbing gear on, including my jacket, and was in my sleeping bag, my body still seemed icy, and I was shivering heavily. Thoughts jabbed around in my head, taunting sleep. There was an unusual silence coming from Pete's direction, too, so I figured he was not planning a twenty-mile run.

In spite of how we felt, we had still set the alarm for the middle of the night to view the weather and consider climbing. Conditions on the mountain appeared to vary from minute to minute and we knew there was always risk, but somehow I trusted we would be guided to make sound judgements. If the wind was very strong we would not go out, as it would be horrendously wild on the ridge. The alarm went off and I turned my head torch on. It was 11.45 pm. I could hear footsteps going up and down outside – others deciding on the weather. Pete was making negative noises. Three times I asked high inside myself if we should go out. Three times the answer came back 'no'. Still not wanting not to do it, I asked for a sign to confirm this decision. Within a few seconds a fierce and violent wind had sprung up and howled through the little window, rattling it noisily.

Fate, it seemed, with its habit of intervening in the right places, had dictated that on this occasion our efforts were to be saved for the right time. I realised that by wanting to climb before we were acclimatised, we had not shown respect to the mountain. I felt apologetic. Our intended purpose of seeing the hut and the route would be well carried out. All was well. There was, however, a sense of being steered and guided by an external force – external yet internal, a powerful force that was all around but also within. For the rest of the night I dozed fitfully, my stomach still churning, and we did not even try to get up until 8.00 am.

Staggering up, still intensely queasy, I shuffled down the ladder in the huge hut sandals provided and, bleary-eyed, went out of the door into the waiting morning. Brilliant light hit me. It was so bright I had to shade my face with my hands from this wonderful gift of sunshine. The cloud cover had lifted and there before us lay the southwest face of Chimborazo, in all its radiance and splendour. There had been a lot of snow in the night. It was as though fresh cream had been poured from the heavens, flowing through the indigo blue mountain shadows. All around the hut was white. I looked up to the stupa area where we had scrambled across the rocks yesterday, now bespangled with glistening snow. I saw the tongue of the Thielman glacier reaching down, all newly dressed. My searching gaze took me on and up over cliffs and ledges, seracs and crevasses, to the snowfields of the sloping shoulders. Here like the crowning glory of a sage's long white hair, the spindrift blew in great clouds along the ridges… on and on, up and up into the deep cobalt sky…oh, how beautifully… to a rounded summit framed in rising snow and caught in the clutches of the Inca Sun God. Even now this was not the true summit. From our foreshortened vantage spot, the highest point lay beyond…waiting…

The excitement in Pete's eyes mirrored my own as we watched this stunning picture. He, at least, seemed to be feeling better, and was able to take some good video footage, which would be useful to study later and show the others. A couple of French climbers came and stood with us. They pointed out two dots on the mountain – two Swiss guides who had left at the midnight hour when it was slippery and fiercely gusty, with poor visibility. They were now descending and we were able to follow their progress with the loan of binoculars until we could see them with the naked eye. It was good for us to be able to pick out the route, and observing them descend with relative ease made me feel happier about the climb. My worries of the previous night dissolved and my hopes soared again that all would be well. Although those ice slopes did seem horribly steep and, if they did for me, then surely they would for Mig, too.

The shifting wind brought in cloud from the south and it was no longer possible to view our shining volcano. All that tantalising beauty, all that daunting, frightening, alluring being was gone from sight. It was time to turn away and move down to the lower hut for our taxi appointment. I also hoped I would feel less sick down there. Pete felt fine now, but was upset at the loss of his head torch, which was vital equipment that we could not climb without. It seemed to have dematerialised from the pile of gear on his bunk. I told him that misplacing things was a typical Gemini trait but that did not seem to help much.

We were slightly surprised – pleasantly so – to find our taxi driver waiting for us. He took us down, retracing our steps across the desert and grasslands, to find a bus in Riobamba. This time we scored a rather more modern vehicle, the comfort advantages of which were offset by the fact that the driver seemed to have the ambition of reaching Quito in the shortest time possible, even to the extent of leaving the conductor on the roof while he was sorting luggage. Luckily we did want to get back quickly, as we were looking forward to collecting Mig at the airport – and speeding away from the distant, cloud-hugged slopes of Chimborazo, there was only the merest glimpse...

Merest glimpses, though, can stir thought processes. Am I in control of my life? It's exciting. I want to do it. I want to move forward. I can't wait. Yet...it's scary. It's wonderful and scary at the same time. But what if I don't make it home? What about my children? I don't need to conceptualise the 'what ifs' of avalanches, crevasses, falling and disasters at a physical level, as that would be allowing negative energy to take root. However, I know that there is fear – not doubt, fear – hiding somewhere. Is it fear of the unknown? Or fear of coping? Or fear of falling? Or is it only a camouflaged racing of the heart?

Maybe something will happen so I don't have to do it. Maybe if I shut my eyes and forget about it, it will go away. But if I backed out of things in life just because they were scary, then I might get to the end and say, 'I nearly did this and I nearly did that,' instead of 'Wow! that was really living, man! Doing that made me feel really alive – so full of purpose. I know it was where I was meant to be.' If I don't grab it now, then perhaps my soul will have to set up a similar scenario in my next life, wherever that may be, and see if I can be persuaded to go for it then. This is presumably what my soul, hopefully with the assistance of divine energy, has set up for me to do here. It is my part of the river of life. My position of existence has been organised around me as it is. What I do with it …well, that's up to me. Can I go through with it now?

I was facing issues I had swept under the carpet for years and years, due to their scariness. I knew now was the time for exposure because I seemed tied to so much else that was so big and powerful which was carrying me along. There was Pete, whose presence was strong beside me. There were Mig and GT. There were all my loved ones and friends at home. There were all the hundreds of 'Climb For Tibet' supporters. There was the Tibetan nation. There were six billion people, more than one billion of whom were Chinese. There was the Earth. The crystal was throbbing in my pocket and there were spiritual powers that I did not quite understand. Somehow it was all connected. We were all part of one big team, helping each other.

I knew that the time had come to face myself. The moment of truth was approaching.

I was determined to be there.

12 : The Snow Lion Heart

How many Tibetans had previously passed through these arrival portals at Quito airport, I wondered, as we waited among the excited toing and froing of the evening Ecuadorian throng. Nearly everyone was wearing casual Western gear, but there was an air of high spirits and emotion just below the surface which set them apart from an English crowd. There were small, dark-skinned girls, pretty against their bright-coloured hats and jerseys; clamouring men in denim jeans, complaining to nobody in particular about the delayed flight; ladies chatting non-stop to friends; and young boys, noisily creating chaos with a football.

The arrivals lounge appeared to be the pavement outside, and a large barrier marked the area where we were allowed to be. We tied the Tibetan flag onto the bars so that it was the first thing that Migmar the Snow Lion Heart would see as he walked out. Probably no one else would recognise this flag from half a world away, but for Mig it would say 'Welcome. Your nation is special. Today the spirit of Tibet comes to Ecuador, high in the Andes. It is carrying the message of world peace from the Dalai Lama – from Asia, via Europe to South America.' Many stared with interest at it. We just smiled knowingly, unable to express its purpose in Spanish.

A shoeshine boy pestered Pete, who finally submitted. The tiny imp of about eight years old knelt on the pavement and indicated for Pete to place a foot on his small wooden box, where he vehemently polished first one shoe and then the other with his black brush and cloth. Then his handsome little face looked up anxiously at the tall foreigner towering above him and burst into sunshine as he was paid twice the going rate. Not so his friend who was a few years older and seemed to be helping to find customers. His brown face, framed by bushy Afro hair, was sad, and stared at us with large, mournful eyes, which revealed cares far beyond his years.

Suddenly the milling and noise intensified as passengers began pushing their way into the greeting crowd. And then, there was Mig...looking fit and well, walking purposefully and with his usual big, cheeky grin. He carried a borrowed, old, faded red rucksack. It was stuffed to the brim, with a yellow Karrimat down the side. A small bag with 'Tibet' embroidered on it hung from his neck and, typically, while everyone else was covered from the chilly night air with jackets and pullovers, Mig wore a sleeveless fitted shirt which showed off his broad muscular chest to perfection. His left upper arm displayed a tattoo in Tibetan writing, 'OM MANI PADME HUM.'

Grabbing the flag and waving it madly, I was eventually able to thrust it around his neck. There was a faint familiarity about the occasion – something to do with the manner of greeting.

'I wish I had a white scarf to welcome you in the correct Tibetan manner,' I said, wistfully.

He laughed. 'You know, Tess…the flag is even better.'

Our taxi from the airport had a meter this time, which meant that at last we would be charged a reasonable rate without having to haggle. This could be useful if ever we worked out how to spot metered taxis, I thought. It appeared that any make, shape or size of car was allowed to be a taxi, so long as it was yellow.

We drew up outside the little porch of El Hostal Posada del Maple and pressed the bell for someone to open the outer door. Peering through into the interior, we could see warm mid-brown wood, benches and tables, young people chatting, tourist brochures and notices, and a pervading aura of friendliness. It was a traveller's oasis.

'Well, Miggie, this is home,' said Pete, with a paternal arm on his shoulder. 'You'll be sharing a room with GT when he arrives in a couple of days.'

'Cool! Looks great,' Mig smiled.

'Get lots of sleep and keep away from the girls tonight,' Pete continued, with a wink at me. 'It's going to be tough adapting to the altitude.'

'Hey, I'll be just fine. You don't have to worry about me.'

With the confidence of youth and his happy demeanour, Mig tended to accept and adapt to all things that came to him in an easy-going way. As a representative of a refugee nation, this was to his advantage, though underneath I knew he was keen to 'get going,' and that he burned with a fire of determination to do something to help his people. There was so much passion and frustration in the waiting, shackled by the enormity of the task of finding a way to regain Tibet's land, culture and freedom. At a political level the situation seemed hopeless, with the world kow-towing to China, a huge economic market waiting to be exploited, while human rights needs are brushed aside. Now, here, with 'Climb For Tibet,' there was an opportunity to raise his country's profile, to produce funds for those escaped and homeless, and to assist in a non-physical way.

In Britain he had already achieved so much with extraordinary maturity and energy for one so young. He had contributed to the putting together of demonstrations, rallies and events with the Free Tibet Campaign and other organisations. I had watched him at the Wednesday evening demonstrations outside the Chinese Embassy in London. He was always the one to shout the loudest – 'Stop the murder! Stop the torture! Free Tibet! Chinese out!' Surely no one expected the Chinese just to walk out, but by shouting 'Chinese out!' they were expressing all that everyone felt: the anger, disgust and desperation of the Tibetan people.

I had watched him, too, at the rally on 10 March, the anniversary of the Tibetan uprising in Lhasa in 1959 when around 100,000 Tibetans had lost their lives. This is an annual occasion when Tibetans and supporters march through the centre of London, waving banners and flags, stopping traffic and turning heads of hundreds of people, tourists and British alike. I had seen Mig shout with his whole heart and soul, 'Long live the Dalai Lama!' It had stirred me to the core.

I knew many believe there is a natural instinct to show aggression and a desire to fight back. How would you feel if your country had been invaded and ransacked, your culture destroyed, your religion trampled on and your fellow countrymen and women oppressed? It would hurt. Can we imagine how much it would hurt? I believe these hostile feelings are being held in check and transcended by the Tibetan Buddhist spirit of the Dalai Lama, who radiates the light of love and compassion. The high regard in which he and his beliefs are held is the panacea for aggression and fear. This is the strength of the Tibetan people, the reflection of the light that shines into the needy world today.

Now, would Mig, as a totally inexperienced mountaineer, be able to manage the climb to express the Dalai Lama's message of peace, the highest ideal, symbolically from the point furthest from the centre of the Earth? For that matter, would any of us?…

We had only been able to organise one training weekend with all four of us before leaving. This had been in the mountains of North Wales. One day had been spent being interviewed on camera by Chris from Amora, and we had included some rock climbing on Little Tryfan. Pete and I had been happy that Mig and GT had clambered up the 55° rock face and abseiled down with no problems. It had been Mig's only substantial training with a harness, helmet and ropework, and he had managed with tentative ease.

On the second day, Pete had set us a 23-kilometre 'potter,' up and over seven well-nigh 1,000-metre peaks. It was along the Carneddu range, approaching from the north at Aber. We had started fresh and keen in damp early morning mists, delighted in the time to chat, recount our life stories and get to know each other as a team. There was enjoyment in the freedom of the hills, with rucksacks on backs and heavy boots on feet, striding across track, bog and rock. On the first peak we had devised the 'Climb For Tibet' formation. Standing in a circle, palms of hands flat against those on either side, arms high in the air, we chanted 'OM MANI PADME HUM.' The unbroken circle signified unity of purpose. It was team bonding at its best and we conducted the ceremony on every peak thereafter.

The sun shone warmly as the day wore on, turning into a rare gem, with wonderful shimmering views into the far distance. Hoisting the Tibetan flag on a ski stick, Mig carried it aloft, attracting the attention of other hill wanderers, who were then accosted with sponsorship forms. Pete sang 'Onward Christian Soldiers,' prompting a distinct sense of going into battle, with the fine sight of a bare-chested, brown Tibetan bounding from high rock to high rock in the Welsh hills, and the brightly coloured Tibetan flag streaming out above him.

I had hobbled, exhausted with painful feet and knees, into the Ogwen car park with the late afternoon sun, having watched Mig relish the steep descent with leaps and bounds, and GT steadily and rather more sedately scramble down. Turning to Pete (who had to be stopped from doing another seven peaks), I had said, 'Yeah, you're right. We have a great team.'

'Training tomorrow, Miggie, on Pasochoa…up to 4,000 metres!'

The breakfast daily-plan-and-jobs-list took place in the main courtyard of our hostel, with its tropical plants, hanging ferns and lusciously filled terracotta pots. Little tables and chairs gave a sunny, sheltered 'hanging out' spot. I loved it. The Western traveller was well catered for, so we could help ourselves to oats and other cereal and hot drinks, and we were brought freshly blended fruit juices of guava, strawberry and papaya, also rolls and eggs. Mig, being a good Tibetan, always had chilli sauce on his. Breakfast was a happy, sunny time. How lucky we were to have found such a good base at so little cost.

This day was set aside to unpack and settle into our new home, to attempt faxes and phone calls, seek out a supermarket and search for a source of wholemeal bread.

Up above the clothes washing area was a small terrace overlooking the rooftops of Quito, with the roar of traffic and horns wafting up from the streets below. A frangipani-type bush crawled up the white fencing, with bright red flowers. Here I watched a beautiful little humming bird collecting nectar with its long beak. I marvelled at its amazing wing beats, too fast to see, holding its body still in mid-air. Now I knew that we were in the tropics.

By the time the early afternoon cloud came in high above us, I was happily lost in the maze of little streets around the hostel. They were full of boarding houses, small businesses, tourist agencies, shops with intriguing, dark interiors, stalls displaying their wares on the pavement, along with sellers of sweetcorn cobs and roasting meats of indefinable origin and distasteful aroma. I felt hugged by the area in a benign, contented way, and enjoyed the anticipation of what might be round the next corner.

I was trying to find the office of Native Life; a well-respected environmentally and culturally responsible tour company run by Lincoln, who was the boyfriend of Emily, the daughter of a friend in England. We had had a happy breakfast with them one day at Café Cultura and they had been very kind, offering lots of good information and advice (in English!) – stuff like 'the tropical forests of Ecuador hold the greatest diversity of species on Earth'; 'they are being seriously threatened, especially by the oil industry'; 'keep a look out for condors'; 'Chimborazo is no picnic.' Lincoln had once climbed to the Veintimilla summit. It had been 'hellishly hard.'

Now, here, walking along the street was the tall, beautiful Emily.

'Hey there – just who I needed to bump into!' Emily was conducting anthropological research for a postgraduate thesis and, having already spent over a year in the country, was a mine of information. She told me Lincoln was worried about us climbing Chimborazo, and recommended strongly that we take a local guide with us. I promised we would give it some thought. Then I asked her about Pasochoa.

'Make sure you go up via the Fundación Natura Forest Reserve on the northern side of the volcano. It's a national park with an educational and research centre. It contains one of the last remaining areas of native inter-Andean forest, which used to cover the whole of this region. There're trails through it, which you'll love. It's full of wonderful things. Apparently there're more than 120 different species of birds alone. They say there are pumas and I've known friends see condors.'

Wow! I thought, to see a condor would be the crowning gift from the Andes. I remembered the excitement of meeting a wild wedgetail eagle in Australia, and feeling the regal presence of a top bird of prey... 'I'd like to know more about the condor. Are there many around?' I enthused. I knew that he was a character revered in mythology and sacred to the Incas, who believed he carried the sun into the sky each morning. He was considered to be a messenger of the gods. I had also read that the Andean condor's eyes were eaten in the belief of improving human eyesight. He must be a national treasure: even his name translates as 'gold coin.'

135

'Well,' she replied, 'they're seriously threatened, now. I've a friend who might know about the numbers that are left. I'll try to find out for you.'

I thanked Emily and went to scour the guidebooks. Condors are of the vulture order. They are the largest flying land birds on Earth, reaching wingspans of 4 metres. Ancient fossils have been found of over 5 metres. That's a lot of bird. They live mostly on carrion, but also go for other birds and small and sick mammals, including young goats and sheep, which has made them unpopular with the farmers. Of course they can do nothing about man's hunting and poisons, and a pair will only lay one egg every two years. However, they're tough – they can survive for days at a time without eating.

That was more than we could do so, later in the day, with an eye on keeping our stomachs happy, we introduced Mig to the wonders of Quito fruit milkshakes at El Magic Bean, where there was also the added advantage of English language newspapers from the United States. Mig was keen to track down information on Bill Clinton's state visit to China.

'Basically, Clinton is offering the hand of friendship just to be able to stimulate trade,' he said. 'The encouragement of trade will be taken as an endorsement of the horrendous human rights abuses that the Chinese government carries out on Tibetans – and on its own people, too – an endorsement also of the labour camps that many of the goods are made in. If he gives China "preferred nation" status for trade, it'll take away the lever that the rest of the world has to work with to try to get them to make changes – like to boycott goods made in China and not to trade.'

'But surely,' Pete argued, 'encouraging trade is a good thing because it means that the Chinese people, brainwashed through the Communist system, will learn more about the ways of the West, democracy and the truth about the situation in Tibet. Their propaganda machine has totally misled the people, even Chinese children are brought up to believe that the great Chinese motherland had liberated a backward and unhappy Tibet.'

'Well,' replied Mig with a sigh, 'you may be right. But the Americans have so much power. I mean, Clinton could do a lot to help. We all have high hopes that at least he will encourage Jiang Zemin to have a meeting with His Holiness.' He looked fleetingly downhearted.

'It's not always easy to see that things are unfolding as they are meant to be on a wider perspective, is it?' I consoled, remembering my vision of Tibetan spirituality being sent out across the Earth. 'There's an awful lot of individuals and small groups throughout the world exercising their free will and backing the Tibetan cause, though... Look at all the supporters of 'Climb For Tibet.' Surely there must be a collective free will in the consciousness of humanity that is being more and more influenced in this way. Think of all the positive thoughts and prayers that are being sent out. By the way, there's something we need to show you.'

I placed the crystal gently in Mig's open hand without comment. He treated it with great reverence and quietly stared at it for a while, sensing the energy it carried. Then he said, 'You know, I feel all cold and tingly up and down my back.'

I smiled. What strange forces were at work here? I read Advarr's card to him. All three of us felt the heavy responsibility and spiritual power surrounding the whole event.

'It's so important that we get there. Are you afraid of the climbing or the mountain?' I probed Mig.

'Me? To be honest… No,' came the quick reply, and he fingered the small picture of Guru Rinpoche (Padmasambhava) he always wore round his neck. It had belonged to his father, who had died two years previously in India. He chanted his guru's prayer for sacred protection every day:

Hung. Ogyen yulke nub chang tsam pema gyaltser dhongpo la yamste choekyi ngodup nyen pema jing ner shel su ta kor tu khan do mang po kor ge ki je su dha dup kyi chin ki cap chir she su sol guru padma sedhen hung! Om ah hung benza guru padma sedhen hung.

This is a very powerful prayer for all things to do with the self. Mig believes it guides, maintains health, ensures a clear path and keeps away evil spirits. Now, it gave him great inner strength and a feeling of complete safety.

Also on a cord around his neck he wore a tiny red bag given to him by his mother. It held coloured wheat blessed by Nechung, the Oracle, deity of the Dalai Lama. It carried a pervading protective force. There was certainly no need for Mig to be afraid.

I knew better than to ask Pete the same question. With his long experience in the mountains and his practical, feet-on-the-ground character, he would not have any tinge of fear.

But I confessed to my diary that night that the nagging fear in my heart persisted, particularly now I'd seen Chimborazo. I read Uri's positive *Little Book of Mind-Power*, which helped. I cradled the crystal again in my hands and felt the tingly sensation. I knew we had so much help…but I was still frightened.

13 : Condor connection

All our Quito mornings seemed to dawn fair and warm. Pasochoa training day was no exception. We were up early, keen to build up our altitude tolerance and get our bodies moving in a sustained way. Mig was in just-give-me-a-mountain-to-climb mode. Remembering how dozy and weak I had felt on my first day, it seemed remarkable that he was in such good working order. Maybe it was the call of youth, or maybe dynamic masculinity, for Pete, too, hadn't seemed to have suffered much from the altitude, and I had trouble recalling a time when he was not in just-give-me-a-mountain-to-climb mode.

Jorge, who worked at the hostel, had fixed us up with a friendly driver, José, for the 30 kilometres or so journey south, which took us on a route out of the city past colourful, bustling markets. We indulged in a banana stop. Huge yellow mounds of differing varieties greeted us. I was ecstatic.

As we travelled on through the verdant farmland of the Central Valley to the vibration of the jostling engine-drone, the ever-changing shades of green started to look almost unreal. My eyes were seeing but not registering. My conscious practical mind, which does appear occasionally, was saying, 'Make the most of this time sitting in a car... Use it for meditation...active meditation...getting in touch with self...opening up to the help which is available...' My body became heavy and far away...

I am viewing the Earth from a position in space... There is ethereal cloud... I am focusing on Chimborazo... The summit is prominent and holds a huge six-pointed star balancing in a horizontal plate... Light from the star reaches to the base of the mountain and beyond. My personal guides are telling me that the spirit of the mountain is revering a Council of Masters. As I watch the summit decked in the star, a shard of white light comes towards me as though it is summoning us in safety and in purpose. My sense of knowing absorbs that we have been accepted by the spirit of the mountain.

The vision had barely faded, and was still touching me at a heart level, when I sensed a different presence. It was condor. I felt an opening up...a connecting...a bonding... It was as though deep in the melded energies of the universe there was sympathy with us and a touching with love by an animal essence.

The bumpiness of the road increased and the jolting brought my physical awareness back. 'I think we've just had a meeting arranged,' I relayed shakily to the others. 'We're going to see condors today.'

Pete, who was still trying to understand my rather weird way of going about things, but nevertheless seemed to have faith in me, was pleased. 'Well done, Babe.'

Mig turned and, looking over the top of his smart fashion sunglasses smiled, 'Cool!'

I tried to find out more from the driver with my pigeon Spanish. '*José, es condores aqui?*'

'*Si, si,*' came the reply.

'*Donde los condores?*'

José waved his hand about. '*La sierra...*'

Ah, I must have it right. '*Cuántos condores en la sierra?*'

'*Unos cien.*'

'*Solo cien en todas las sierras?*'

'*Si, si.*'

Could he mean there were only a hundred condors left in the whole of the Ecuadorian Andes? The vulnerability of something so special worried me. How quickly in the span of Earth time had they disappeared. The famous English climber, Whymper, had written of them in their droves back in 1880, having seen organised condor hunts using horsemeat for bait.

We passed tough-looking horses along the cobbled track to the Pasochoa Forest Reserve, winding our way through fertile smallholdings. There was something deeply satisfying about the rich, chocolate-brown earth supporting all manner of vegetables and fruit. I recognised sweetcorn, avocado, pumpkin, papaya and oranges. Chickens roamed around each little hacienda with the small children, and usually there was a milking cow and sometimes pigs. Blocks of eucalyptus, some with huge trunks, acted as windbreaks and provided shade, though today the weather was gentle with cloud and drizzly showers and the air was warm and sticky.

'You know, it reminds me so much of India,' said Mig, excitedly. 'It all feels so familiar.'

As the track deteriorated into gravelly ruts, we weren't surprised when José, who was not at all brave, decided to abandon us. We set off to walk the last few kilometres, watched warily by a tan mongrel pretending to sleep on a ramshackle veranda.

Happily, a pickup truck full of youngsters came by and we were crammed into the back amid chatter and laughter, and taken to the entrance of the park. As tourists, we were quite rightly charged 35,000 *sucres* (US$ 7), which was ten times as much as the locals. It was gratifying to see that, in this country full of poverty, high priority was given to maintaining a precious natural reserve, the beauty of which was all around us. At the education centre were boards full of information about the exceptional flora and fauna. I longed to be able to understand more of the information. I presumed the volcanic lava had given rise to all the wonderful profusion that was blossoming, but that the steepness had prevented agriculture taking over in the past. We were, I reminded myself, in one of the few places in the world that is both at a high altitude and almost on the equator. If this was one of the last remaining forests of this type, then there must be a wealth of knowledge and unique species here, which could be useful for medicinal and economic purposes, as well as an important larder for Mother Earth's energy-balancing feeding system. *Un bosque para todos*, one of the signs said – 'a forest for everyone.' I felt lucky to be here.

Initially, coloured arrows guided us along the trails as we picked our way to gain as much height as quickly as possible. From 2,700 metres at the base we were hopeful of gaining the highest part of the rim of the large crater of the volcano at 4,200 metres.

A pretty, bubbling stream talked to us for a while, until we

142

turned south and found ourselves pushing through bamboo forest. The inviting trails zigzagged up with tunnels of hanging branches, and as we climbed we caught glimpses of distant patchwork hills through the thick foliage. I had always thought of bamboo as panda fodder, so I wondered if this was what it was like on the other side of the world, along the slopes of distant Chinese mountains.

After an hour or so, Mig called a halt in a clearing carpeted by pale brown, rustly bamboo leaves. 'To be honest, my boots are killing me, guys,' he grimaced. Inspection revealed raw red blisters, which Pete doctored with plasters. The plastic boots were very old. They had been kindly donated by a Cotswold Camping sales assistant after hearing of Mig's need for equipment (sadly no one had donated us new equipment). He had to get used to plastic boots for taking crampons safely when on snow and ice. But Mig's feet were not at all happy with the idea. They had always preferred wearing sandals. From now on he would always be struggling with painful feet.

Hobbling on, Mig told me how he placed his mind on other things, allowing healing energy to enter, and the pain retreated somewhat. He picked a stout, green bamboo pole to be his companion, and we clambered on to the sound of a symphony of birdcalls and fleeting darts of colour and airborne form.

Gradually inter-Andean forest species took over. There were many podocarps – the only conifer native to the Ecuadorian Andes, mountain palm trees, laurels, ferns, white and purple orchids, and bromeliads – the beautiful staghorns, with long entwining lianas and huge lichens. Some were epiphytes, some saprophytes, but all were species that depended on one another and formed a miraculous interconnected web of life. It was not hard for my heart to feel in tune with the joy that danced all around us.

As we climbed higher, smaller trees took over, and in the diffuse light Mig was intrigued by the covering of tall mosses growing on all the branches. 'Hey, look Pete...these are just like your arms!' he teased. Actually, I was quite fond of Pete's strong forearms but I had to laugh, too, thinking that on some deep level my hairy Viking had rainforest origins, and how the Earth was such a mishmash of the energy of matter thrown together in apparently random harmony.

Suddenly, as though a line had been drawn at 3,500 metres, we reached the upper limit of the forest and came out into bright sunlight. A cool wind played on our faces. We were on steep tussocky grassland interspersed with low billberry and juniper-type bushes. Wonderful views stretched towards Quito. What a beautiful land this was. It wasn't hard to imagine it in the days before human habitation. Nature dominated the picture, from the lush river valleys to the far snow-capped volcanic peaks.

Now I was beginning to feel the lack of oxygen in the air. The find-your-own-way path demanded attention on the acutely angled mud and slippery vegetation. I tried to take a slow but steady pace and practised a few mind affirmations... I am strong... I am fit... I love everything... I have all the energy I need...

Gasping a little and breathing heavily I joined the others at a level grassy knoll. It appeared to be on a spur that ran up to the crater rim. Pines spread out before us to the east. They were a spidery variety, whose three-needled whorls hung like little lanterns, greeting us. It was a lovely spot to munch gratefully on our lunch, (though most of the drinking water supplies seemed to have already fallen victim to the thirst of the youngest member of the team). We enjoyed the wonderful integral bread that we had found. Generally I prefer to nibble most of the time on a climb, and organise my pockets to be full of yummy grazing material, but to have lunch as such means that Pete has to stop for a bit and it's an opportunity for me to rest.

Here, Pete enjoyed filming with the video camera. It was good footage against this background of sweeping mountain landscape. Mig borrowed my penknife and, with great mindfulness, carved 'OM MANI PADME HUM' into the bamboo stick, the pale inner cream of the Tibetan lettering standing out exquisitely against the fresh green.

'I shall inscribe a mantra for every mountain I climb,' he stated, with a purposefulness that expressed the wisdom of generations. 'This stick will be empowered with the energy of meditations and prayer.'

We continued across the sloping ridge of brown, windswept tussock grass. Pete was going well, and moved ahead to check out the route. Mig and I waited at the point where the ridge meets the rim of the crater, with a wonderful view at least 8 kilometres across to the far side. One hundred thousand years ago there would have been an eruption in a cauldron of fuming magma, destroying and transforming the original ancient volcanic cone. Today, from the collapsed side, spread deep green virgin forests, climbing steeply upwards. We sat on the grass, soaking up the beauty and watching the clouds moving over the wide-open sky. Mist swirled into the crater from the west, and then more mist on mist. It was like a canvas being painted, particularly as, to a Tibetan, cloud represents the creative power of the mind.

'Look Tess, there's a fluffy white dragon...and look, there's another that's a fire-dragon. How brilliant! It's so lucky...it's a really good auspicious sign...especially, you know, as I was born in the year of the dragon.'

'Yeah, how lovely.'

Mig turned towards me, but his eyes became transfixed. Following his gaze I caught the scene unfolding behind me. There was a rush of wind…an atmosphere of a sudden presence of power…smell of musty quicksilver. Like a huge angelic shield, two large shiny wings glided towards us, folding as a tail went up in one smooth landing motion… Condor was with us.

He stood awkwardly on large feet with gruesome flesh-tearing talons. His naked head jerked from one side to the other, pink crest flopping, showing off the white ruff of his wrinkled neck and a sharp, curved beak. Just for a second there was eye contact. Then he spread his great wings to the sun…and was gone.

Oh wow! Far out!

For a while we were too stunned almost to breathe. What an appearance!

'Hey Man! That was something!' Mig was the first to speak. 'Did you say that condors were vultures?'

'Same order. His generic name is *vultur gryphus*.'

'You know, in Tibet the vultures are considered sacred. It's because of the sky burials. I've never seen one, but basically human flesh is cut up and fed to the vultures. It's a way of recycling dead bodies in a land where there's a scarcity of burning material for cremation, and little soil for ground burial. The soul has already been blessed and flown, and the body is no longer of any use. It's an important service that the vultures do for man.'

'Sort of like a system of natural harmony?'

'Mm. I mean, Tess, this might sound strange, but when the condor was here…it was as though he knew…'

I nodded. 'You know, the native American Indian brave always had an animal spirit to be his brother.'

'Yeah?'

'Maybe, the condor has come to watch over you and 'Climb For Tibet'.'

'You reckon?'

'Yeah, and he is very like the Tibetan in many ways...'

'Well, he certainly looked like he had a white greeting scarf round his neck.'

'He did. You know, maybe the karma of the Tibetans and the condors has a similar sort of resonance.'

'Yeah, probably.'

'That reminds me of a story, Miggie... The son of a friend of mine went to work in a small town in China. A Tai Chi teacher was very kind to him and gave him some lessons. The teacher was very poor, but when the son offered to pay him he refused, asking instead, 'Please, when you return to the West, please resonate my name with honour.'

'Different values.'

'Yeah, different values. I wonder if he knew of the atrocities caused by his government in the name of the honour of the motherland.'

'Most people in the world don't,' replied Mig. 'I'm sure he wouldn't have known about stuff like the monks being made to shoot their own much-loved teachers...or the forced sterilisations and abortions for the Tibetan women...their babies thrown into dustbins. To take life goes against everything a Tibetan believes...'

'I simply can't see how one human being can treat another like that...'

'Well, dreadful horrors continue to go on... And you know it's worse when it's close to you. My friend Ngawang Choephel is in jail for eighteen years for the crime of studying Tibetan culture. We know of the brutal conditions there, the torture, the beatings, the interrogations... We know he's barely alive...'

I knew it all too well... the sickening feeling hearing about it...

the tears of horror.

'C'mon Miggie. At least we're trying to do something about it. Look, there's Pete waving for us to come up.'

The joy and excitement of meeting the condor mingled with the sadness of the suffering of the Tibetan people, and was stored in our hearts.

Carrying on up the lee side of the crater, through taller and taller grasses, there was the lovely sensation of the wind blowing through ripe corn. Close by, the steep drop into the inside was guarded by a couple of paper-bark trees whose red and yellow bark hung in tatters, standing sentinel over the winds of time.

Ahead was a breast-shaped cliff protecting a patch of dense, scrubby vegetation. It was not the summit but needed to be negotiated if we were to continue. On closer inspection we found that the cliff was very shaly and the main holds were either small loose stones jutting out of mud or unstable looking plants – not a route to inspire delight in a rock climber. Pete just happened to have a rope with him (useful load-carrying training), and being one always to take the risks on these sort of occasions, left his rucksack to haul up later and gingerly led up the face, fingers clinging to loose holds, big boots balancing on pebbles.

'Well done! Impressive Viking stuff,' I called up as he belayed to a rather insubstantial bush where the gradient eased. I tied Mig into the end of the rope and he stashed his stick and slowly and carefully managed to climb up without mishap. I followed in similar vein.

Some serious scrambling later we were pushing our way

through a surprise jungle bash to arrive at the base of the 'nipple'. Peering out from the vegetation, we saw ahead of us solid rock, at last. It was a smooth grey cliff reaching up to a rounded top. It looked possible to take a diagonal line across and then maybe a circular route to the final stance.

Pete set off again with the rope trailing. He managed to gain the traverse with skill, but then seemed to be searching around for some time. Eventually we heard, 'I'm coming down.' To lead up is one thing, to reverse down with no protection quite another. An anxious half an hour later he was back with us, shaking his head.

'It's no good. There's absolutely nothing to belay on to. It needs a longer rope. We can't do it.' There was a sense of disappointment all round, but safety is the number one mountaineering priority.

'Never mind, let's have a look over the crater edge,' said Pete, manoeuvring through the plant growth with care. There, waiting for us, was a perfect ledge with just enough room for a smiley Tibetan, a girl with a penguin on her rucksack and a man with a video camera at the ready. We sat in a line, legs dangling, perched in a high eyrie. The world lay beneath us. Pete put the altimeter around Mig's neck and asked him to practise taking a reading.

'We're at exactly 4,000 metres. Seems a good height.'

As though on cue, the fly-past began. They came out of the sky from the east. Like a squadron of gliders mustering on a warm thermal current, they circled round and round above the Pasochoa summit. There were three of them. One was larger than the others. Each was magnificent, soaring effortlessly on wingspans the size of a car.

'Wonderful!' whispered Mig.

We watched in awe as they widened their circling and flew within the crater. Looking up against the grey clouds we could clearly see their undersides, white tails and black wings silhouetted with characteristic long-feathered hands. As they banked lower, the show changed to a backdrop of deep forest green picking out the white ring of the head and the upper wing feathers reflecting the light. Levelling out at 4,000 metres, they took one graceful sweep in front of us. Our auras reached out and touched.

This beautiful contact and acceptance of us in their territory demanded a response.

I called out: 'Oh Spirit of Condor... We greet thee and ask for blessings on our 'Climb For Tibet'... For you are brothers of Tibet... You are rare... You are special... And you have a need for freedom.

'We combine our energies... And know that we will move forward in freedom... And that the Earth will survive in harmony.'

The meeting was over.

Each in our own thoughts, we started back down, reversing the route. The sun started to sink low in the sky and a cold wind chilled our aching bodies (well, mine was aching). I was grateful to reach the darkening shelter of the forest. I brought out of my rucksack my retractable ski sticks. I find these do make a big difference on a descent. They are meant to take more than ten per cent of the weight off the legs coming down, so, particularly where knees are a problem, they are great.

I was deeply tired, but not down-and-out, as I had been on Pichincha. Pete and Mig seemed disgustingly fresh and lively – as were the mosquitoes. Night fell as we reached the education centre. It was deserted. With difficulty, we found someone who explained the system of buying a card to use the phone to order a pick-up truck to pick us up. We then sat on a step to wait, warmed by the glow of our experiences and entertained in the darkness by the dancing lights of fireflies and the musical accompaniment of crickets playing their harps and rhythmic froggy drums.

Mig had done well, coping with the rigours of his first training day. The rigours of an extraordinary evening were in store for him.

14 : Words from beyond

Two young US backpackers in the hostel kitchen stared at Mig in horror as he made the post-supper tea. It was no ordinary occurrence. He had decided to make Tibetan tea as a treat for us.

'Basically, it is just normal tea with milk and salt and butter,' he explained. 'It should be yak butter to be authentic, but I've only been able to find the cow stuff.'

The backpackers disappeared hurriedly.

We sat down to enjoy the universal pleasure of friends taking tea together. Mig drank his with relish and delight. Pete, as a regular tea drinker, was doing well. Personally, I'm not very keen on butter or milk or salt or even tea, but I struggled through the first few sips with a smile, knowing that it was special. Then I felt I should make my feelings known.

'Mig, I'll do anything for Tibet... Anything that is...except drink Tibetan tea.' I really hoped I hadn't offended him, so I added, 'I'm sure it tastes better with yak butter.'

'Yeah, of course,' he laughed. 'It's a different taste. You know, I think it's the idea of it that takes a bit of getting used to.'

'Mm...maybe... Some things in life seem a bit weird, but I guess you've just got to try them. Let's take our tea upstairs where it's quiet,' I urged. 'I want to play you a tape.'

Here, I would like a little aside with my reader again. There follows a record of more conversations that some find hard to swallow. You might like to jump to the end of the chapter, or you might like to try it. You may become used to the idea...

'OK, Miggie, here we go. A couple of months ago Pete, Delphine and I went to visit the man who is a medium for the spirits of Winston Churchill and Mahatma Gandhi... We sat with them and taped our conversations. It could be useful and interesting for you to hear what they have to say, as we specifically wanted to ask their advice on the Tibet-China state of affairs. It was an incredible experience. They spoke very clearly and characteristically, using the medium's voice box and body. It was the second time I'd been, and at no point during either visit did I have any moment of doubt about the genuineness of the happening. Anyway, this is it. Are you ready?'

Mig listened to the recording of my second encounter with these spirits, enthralled...

Churchill came through first. The medium was sitting back, open-chested with his arms on the chair arms, and spoke in a jovial way:

I'm very happy you're here. I don't get the opportunity very often to come. Indeed, in recent years, I have been quite absent. Hmm, it is a great joy that I'm able to speak and to welcome old friends, hmm, hmm.

I had been thrilled at the opportunity to greet him again. I had explained that we were doing a special climb, to raise awareness and funds for the heavily oppressed Tibetans, and were holding up Tibet as an illustration of working for harmony in the world. We would be honoured to have his opinion.

The response was quick and somewhat grandiose:

I am familiar with the situation. First of all, one has to be realistic; there is no way the Chinese are simply going to abandon Tibet. Therefore, all this anger and all the pressure makes no difference against the Chinese. What you have to do is to shame the Chinese from inside. They're a very honourable nation. They hate being shamed. If you are going to have success, and Tibet is going to renew itself as a spiritual country, it has to be done with the help of the Chinese, and not in opposition. So the Chinese have to realise the desecration of this spiritual country is against their honour...

The Chinese have always in the past believed themselves to be very spiritual, and I believe that once the church in the heart of the people of China has been given some amount of leverage, it will start to grow again. Spiritual things are not the opium of the masses, but the food, the nourishment of the masses. So if you start telling them that what they have done is to destroy thousands of years of spiritual growth, can you not see now how the shame comes in?... When the people start to realise that they have, in a sense, been duped.'

So I had probed as to how we could help the situation with our peace messages.

The messages of peace should not be anti-Chinese, but appealing to the spirit and honour of the Chinese to consider Tibet in a totally different way. To see it all right as a protectorate of China, which is something that you will not change, but to give back the spiritual heart, which Tibet has over thousands of years evolved and held. That's the way I would do it. That, I believe, is the best advice.

Therefore, if you are to pass your messages to the Earth, you must focus them into the consciousness of that particular Earth which at this moment is dominated by Chinese military. There must be a working towards peaceful coexistence whereby the Chinese do not lose face. They hold control of Tibet, but their military machine must be removed from the sacred ground of Tibet. That is the only hope there is. I believe the Dalai Lama considers the same thing, particularly after so many years and with so many nations on this planet doing nothing to assist him.

What you have in Tibet is very disagreeable, very distasteful, like a horse dropping – a very smelly situation. The other governments won't remove it because the horse is more important. The horse is the economic opportunity of the massive continent of China.

I had interjected that, surely, on a worldly basis Tibet holds great importance as a spiritual centre, to which he had replied:

On a spiritual level it's very important, as an economic part of the commercial system for which the world itself applies all its rules, it is insignificant. One day it may be different. I hope so, but that will be one day – not now.

155

So I had asked if he could see from his perspective how things would be in the future.

It is given that all things are like the spokes in a wheel; it depends which spoke you take, to which destiny you will go. We have no control over the destiny of mankind. We can guide you along the way. We can assist you when you stumble, but you have control.

I had been startled to hear little squeaks that seemed to be suspended in the air close by. I was intrigued to find out afterwards that 'spirit noises' are quite common, but not everyone can hear them.

I'm being told my time's up. I've been standing up too long talking. It comes to us all...' There was the sense that he wanted to laugh. Then he became serious again. 'What I would like to say to you is this. Whatever little consciousness you create, when you make it with many people it becomes multiplied thousands of times. Two people together do not make four, they make sixteen. It is an odd thing, but spiritual energy doesn't multiply as you think in arithmetic terms. It has a magnification factor far beyond and no one quite understands why it is able to do this. I believe now it is simply that God touches the essence of man's sworn endeavour, thus releasing it universally into that which is magnificent.

Surely he had been referring to peace-message energy coming together and expanding – how lovely. I had mentally stored his stirring words as he ended with:

I will watch with interest...join you on this great endeavour. Thank you. Good night, God bless you all.

There had been a heavy sigh – a shifting of energies. The entity that was Winston Churchill passed from the body. The atmosphere in the room was thick with spirit. The candlelight wavered and burned low. Quite suddenly, there had been a totally different feel; and we were with the lighter, distinctly Indian presence of Mahatma Gandhi. He had leaned forward, hands clasped in eagerness. I would have liked to have somehow shown respect to the wisdom of the greatest of world leaders, but he went straight in, his voice lilting…mesmerising…

If I am to come and speak to you for a moment it is to express something which I am hearing here. When the British Raj were in India we wanted them to go as friends, not as enemies. When the Chinese leave Tibet they must leave as friends not as enemies. Therefore, if you go forth and you try to rouse human anger against the Chinese you will cause the Tibetans much pain, because the only way is to create peace through friendship… Understand me. So if you're going to do your work, which is most important – and it is good because it is close to my own country and we want to see an opportunity for India to make a bridge back into Tibet – think of this. At the moment there is a wall… It is bad, but if we are really going to be brothers and sisters we need to remove the wall. And the wall that is created is not made politically because there is a war condition, it is made of fear… The Chinese fear. They do not want to leave Tibet because they are frightened what other people will do with Tibet when they have gone. So what they want is to be given the opportunity not to lose face. So if you are going to read messages, why not do it in this way: praise the Chinese for the things they have done, and let them know that if they leave Tibet, they will leave as friends, like the British Raj left India. Forget how they came, look towards how they will go.

The question then had been, what can we praise them for? What good have they done in Tibet?

The Master of Peace, whose life had so inspired the Dalai Lama, replied:

It is not always that what you see, it is that which happens... and what has happened to Tibet is that it has been forced into the present century. In the end no state can rely on a barbarism of spiritual domination which has no grounding with the rest of the world. Before the Chinese went to Tibet no one was allowed in, everyone was a foreigner. If we are going to be brothers and sisters we do not stop them coming into our house. We open our arms and let them sit in our aura. So, if the Chinese have accomplished anything it is to allow the whole world to know about Tibet.

Yes, and now we have all had the pleasure of hearing the Dalai Lama... And the teachings that have come out of Tibet that needed to be heard in the West.

Exactly. The Chinese did go about it the wrong way but it had the right effect. The British Raj came to India to exploit us, but when they went they had shown us how to live in a modern world, because we were many small states not connected together. We were many people ploughing the fields in poverty and being warlike to each other because we did not understand our neighbours. When the British Raj left, India was one country. Now I know you are going to talk about Pakistan.... I am also aware that it was not as it should have been, but it was not the British Raj but the Indian people that caused that disaster, and the reason they caused that disaster was because they had not learned to live with their brothers and sisters. You cannot hold two religions and fight about them. You have to accept your neighbour's religion as he accepts yours, because no one has the truth: not I as a Hindu, not a Muslim, not a Christian, not even a Buddhist, but everyone has a little bit of the truth. And in the end when we can all together merge as one family, then we will understand what this wonderful spiritual experience is all about, because it is given to us in the mystery of God that each of us has a little part, but not the whole.

The spirit requires simplicity and I believe it was true when in your holy book it says you will not go into the kingdom of Heaven unless you are like a child. The child is without wealth because it is born before it can make wealth. It has a simplicity and it has a trust... And I believe the only thing in this world that is to be taught is to trust one another... Because there is enough food to feed everyone, there are enough resources in this world to sustain everyone, and in the end the richest man cannot take a single penny to heaven. In the end, only the spirit lives on and the wealth is lost. We are living in a society of greed and suffering... but it is changing.

I had wanted to ask Gandhi about his words of five years earlier, about the seven years before the Earth could wither and die, but I was apprehensive about what he would say. Was he feeling more optimistic now about the general outlook of humanity towards caring for the Earth?

It is not changing, but now I do not think man will destroy it. I believe that at the last minute there will be a change, but at the moment I am distressed by what I am seeing. I had hoped to speak with you all, many people on the Earth, and change their attitudes. It became clear to me that people often enjoy a conversation which has something unusual about it, but it is not my words that count, it is not me that counts, but my conscious *words into your head that count. Because, like a great electrical wire, it is only when all the little atoms are joined together that the electrical circuit works in harmony. It is only when all the people on the Earth live in harmony with each other that the whole ecology of the Earth motivates itself in harmony with the universe. You cannot take the floor from beneath you without falling. But that is what you are doing at the moment. If I were to be as one negative I would say I cannot see a change, but I am not like that. I believe that God is testing us all. I do not think he would create such beauty for it to be destroyed. And, while he has given us free will, I think he will maintain some control before we are so stupid as to destroy the very essence of what he has given us. These are my thoughts. It is true to say that very little has changed for the better.*

I had asked him then if we could help the peace of the Earth, help with the inspiration. Gandhi had sat back, and the higher pitch of the voice box laughed in such an Indian way:

Are you not already doing it? Are you not going to go and make the messages powerful and therefore internationally heard? Is that not the way of it?

I had smiled, embarrassed at this acknowledgement from the great man, as he continued:

I would be most pleased if I was in a body, and I would climb with you.

Would he do us the honour of giving us a message to speak out from the mountain?

'I offer my prayers to 'Climb For Tibet' and all it touches'

Pala and Amala

Migmar milkshaking

Tess milkshaking

GT and Yannick

Pepé

Pete in the *páramo*

Climb For Tibet team-bonding - *Om mani padme hum*

Reading out peace messages

Tess and Mig with the Tibetan flag

Mig exhausted along the way

Mount Chimborazo – southwest face

Inset: The crystal on a gateway stupa

Mig in *chuba* flying the flag

Umm... It is only when you reach the top of the mountain that you recognise how great is the inheritance our creator has bestowed on us, and then recognise that we are all part of looking after the great gift He has given us, hmm?

I'm telling you, when you take such a venture as yours, it is like the salt march that I did. It is not the salt part that counts, but the effort to get there that is very important. It is the result that comes afterwards. Therefore before I went on the march I made sure all the media knew all about it. I knew the newspapers would report it. I knew I was going to get coverage all the way. You must do the same thing. You must give yourself ample publicity, so it is not simply the climb, but the people who are watching you. And then you will get the greatest response and the greatest success for it, and the success is not simply the climb but that which the climb is symbolic of.

Did this also apply, I had asked, to the six Tibetans whom he must know were currently on hunger strike in Delhi? Surely that was going too far.

Yes... I am well aware, for they are in my own country, but I will tell you I have also been in that particular way many times. How can you change if your heart believes that you are doing the right thing? And if in the end you give up your body, if you truly believe that you will continue to exist after this body has decayed to dust, well then it is the spirit which is most important. Sometimes you can afford to give up the body.

When I died I had my loin cloth and my shoes and I was the happiest person, not the way I went, but I was happy that I had lived the way I had lived. And if I had been in the Raja's palace I would have been unhappy because I would have felt that I had ruined my own spiritual consciousness by accepting treasure on the Earth. Those who have made themselves rich and powerful change completely when they are in spirit, and often question that very aspect of themselves.

When I came into spirit I found a strange circumstance which I had not expected, and you would call it a debating club. We are all here trying to reason why you do the things that you are doing... It is given to us to believe that you are all afraid to understand that you can perfectly and harmoniously live as a spiritual being on the Earth. You hold on to all your possessions as if you never want to leave your physical body. Yet you are like all terms in nature, told from the very moment you have intelligence to understand that you are only here for a short time in this physical form, and when you are told this, is it not sensible to seek the spiritual aspect of yourself? What do people do? They try to shut themselves off from reality and they bathe themselves in treasure. They take drugs, they take drink, they do all these things because they go against their nature, their spiritual nature. That is why you have a world which is going the way it is because people are afraid to recognise themselves.

Why then does nobody seem to learn from past mistakes or past lives or karma?

God never said to you 'I will make you grow.' He simply said 'I will give you the experience from which you can grow.'

And is that why there is so much pain?

No one can be protected from the physical experience, because everyone has freedom to do and be as they wish, and natural law is given that God will not in any way impose His own power. But in all things of the Earth there is one powerful energy, which, if you *trust it and always honour it, will not let you down – and that is love. Nourish the whole world with love and you will receive love back. It is the currency of the spirit. Therefore, if someone is requiring to go through an Earthly experience of a painful nature, it is not simply their physical body which is healing, it is also a giving of love to stimulate the balance, because the physical and the spirit are one. Does that make understanding to you? However, I have been here for nearly fifty years, and I tell you I still do not understand the mystery of creation.*

I had been surprised by this, but, trusting his wise perspective, I had wanted to ask a personal question, not quite able to voice the words.

I can speak to you in this body. I can walk with you without a body, but I cannot talk to you when I have not got a body.

'Well, it's about my father, who died a year and a half ago, and we promised each other we'd keep in touch and I've done nothing as yet to... I'm searching...'

He has visited you though.

There were squeaks of spirit high in the room. Some sort of information service was taking place.

You have had evidence of his connection with you. He left you a message. Now he has gone on to do his own thing in this world here and he is perfectly at peace. But he will not alter anything that you are doing by contacting you, because he wants you to be yourself. You must realise that love is not a selfish act of possessiveness, but a desire like a bird to be free to soar in the sky.

163

Gandhi, the great soul, prepared to take his leave and allow the consciousness of the medium to return to its body:

It has been a delight to me. When you are in spirit you are as one isolated by a dimension which is again a mystery. When you feel the love of people on the Earth and are drawn back through a body to be able to communicate, you realise that you are not simply an observer but still part of the great motion of human tide, evolution moving it, to, I hope, wondrous positions on mountaintops.

The click of the ending tape on the pocket player startled us into the reality of our hostel room... The wooden floor...the yellow walls...the drip of the tap in the shower...

We held with awe a sense of the continuation of the human spirit. This is a concept that Tibetans take for granted, but Mig was still excited.

'That is so brilliant!... You know I'm sure they're right about all that stuff. I must send a copy to an old lama I know in India. He is a huge devotee of Gandhi and the power of the peaceful way he achieved so much in his lifetime... That is just so brilliant!'

I smiled at his excitement and at the honour that I felt had been bestowed upon us to be part of the meeting, but also at the normality with which I now accepted the conversations.

Yes... Mr Gandhi... Yes... We will be a voice for your message... And we most certainly are striving for the mountaintops...

15 : Wondrousity

Gandhi aside, the only other person I've ever known to use the word 'wondrous' was GT. Enthusiastic, intellectually effusive, outgoing and fun, GT expressed the joys of life, and, in keeping with the edict of balance that what one gives out, one attracts, his arrival at the airport was a joyous occasion.

While waiting for his flight to unload, Mig and I held out the colourful Tibetan flag, in the face of staring and bemusement from onlookers in the busy crowd. Pete was practising with the video camera. He filmed the arrival area, where a beautiful Ecuadorian girl was preening herself in the reflective window of an information booth. She might have been upset to know that her private moment was immortalised on celluloid, unaware that all our moments are immortalised in the great scheme of things, with every little thing we do making a difference and creating the blend of eternity.

In a similar expression of grandiose open-mindedness, trying to understand the huge picture of time and space, I always called GT 'Brother of the Universe'. His response to me was 'Sister of the Cosmos'. So I searched my Spanish dictionary for the correct translation to greet him with.

'*Saludos!... Hermano del Universo!*' I shouted, as our fellow adventurer appeared through the mingling passengers. Standing before the crowd, as though at the finale of a performance, was the archetypal conductor: flowing mass of grey hair, flamboyantly gleaming eyes, aquiline nose and distinguished beard. He displayed an air of graciousness, even with the heavy rucksack on his back and faded old climbing boots on his feet. Cheers went up. GT grinned from ear to ear. There must have been something about his presence that caught the excitement of the crowd because everyone started clapping.

'And there you all are,' he beamed. His arms went up above his head, taking the roar of applause in his stride. 'But this is really beyond the call of duty... Isn't it marvellous?... Well... wondrous... This is just wondrous!'

We had been joined by warmth and merriment. There was a satisfaction in his arrival, a bonding in our sense of purpose together in a strange land. Our team was complete.

The sun shone down on our courtyard breakfast, evaporating the night dew. GT enjoyed absorbing the sights, smells and sounds of his new environment – the rawness of the rough brown pots, Spanish chatter, tropical foliage, thin, sweet air, the Inca artefacts, Ecuadorian eggs and coffee, and the friendliness of our hosts.

He looked in remarkably good shape after the long journey, but there was cause for concern, as Pete and I were already nine days ahead of him with the altitude acclimatisation programme. His body had a lot of catching up to do. Pete was particularly worried about his fitness preparation. Although he had been able to have a few days walking in the hills, his time spent waving a baton rhythmically and enthusiastically about was not what Pete would call great training. Maybe a large heart was all it would take. Time would tell.

We all poured out information at him to bring him up to date on the last few days.

'You're going to love it here,' said Mig. 'I feel quite at home already. You know, there's something about the Ecuadorians that's almost Tibetan. They look quite similar. I even saw someone who looked quite like my mother.'

'How very interesting,' replied GT. 'It could be the influence of the early American Indian peoples...with way-back Asian origins...'

'It's the girls that Mig's looking at in particular,' interjected Pete.

'Too right, Pete,' responded Mig, 'but you're OK...you've got your love bird with you...' He looked wistful.

I laughed. 'You'll soon have them falling at your feet, as usual, Miggie. Keep up the training with the flowers.' I was thinking of our trip to Wales, when Pete and GT had been teaching Mig the nuances of English wooing techniques.

'Mm!' came in GT. 'Give flowers...raises the quality of the ambience... Very important.' He smiled and then fished around in his pocket. 'But take a look at this. This is what was given to me on the way to the airport by the lovely young Debbie, who's now my girlfriend.' He held up a handsome piece of deep royal blue stone flecked with pale brown. 'It's lapis lazuli... It's to place and leave on the top of Chimborazo.' He spoke the name of the mountain with a lilting reverence as though he were introducing a piece of music that he had just written, and I caught an edge of the feeling of the importance that this climb carried for him. 'Isn't it wondrous? She also gave me a special cloth on which she's drawn a beautiful Buddhist message of transience... And my little daughter Chloe has done me a quintessential painting to take...so many precious things...'

We studied the stone.

It is said that the healing properties of lapis lazuli were much used in the ancient times of Atlantis, not only to promote good communication with the divine but also to harmonise that which exists in the inner and the symmetry of form of the outer, expanding the essence of brotherhood, cooperation and the ability to produce abundance for all humankind. This was not just any old stone.

I fingered the lapis lazuli star around my neck, and Pete and I exchanged glances.

Synchronicity!

Quite suddenly, Mig moved into overtone chanting mode, producing amazing deep vibrational sounds which changed the atmosphere of the South American courtyard to a far-away Himalayan monastery. We were caught up in its spell...and enchanted.

Now was the time to tell GT of the magic of the crystal, the stunning message from the Master Advarr and our wonderings about the six-pointed star. He listened intently, and slowly read the message aloud, not sure what to make of it: 'Souls have been chosen within your earthly world to carry the light into many remote places. To the mountains... The crystal will become a signal... Many masters have gathered...forming the energy of a star vehicle of pure light... Blessings to you as you journey... This just appeared, eh?' he asked quietly, deep in thought.

I nodded.

He gently handled the crystal, noting its exceptional clarity, and took time to absorb it all. It was strange, but surely…it was wondrous.

There was a moment of silence. Then Pete spoke softly, 'Look up. What can you see above us?'

Above the breakfast table were four hanging baskets, dripping with green ferns. In themselves, apart from their fresh loveliness, there was nothing unusual about them, but then I spotted it: the wire base of each basket was in the shape of a six-pointed star.

Synchronicity?

'Ah, but there's more. Have a look at the replay of the footage of Mig arriving at the airport.' He pulled out the little screen from the video camera and pressed the play button. We all crowded round and watched. There was Mig receiving my welcoming hug with the flag, and above us a bright light dominated the picture. It shone effusively as a six-pointed star.

Synchronicity.

'Wow!' I said excitedly . 'That's excellent! I'm sure these are all little pointers on the way that we're being guided along. I don't think it matters that we don't quite understand how or why. The important thing is that all around the world different groups are being guided to do wonderful work producing little blobs of light, and together they're a powerful force of change for the greater good. I see our 'Climb For Tibet' journey as a quest for one such blob of light.'

'Well, Sister… We'll leave that side of things for you to sort out,' GT smiled.

The spirit of our coming together in aspiration was strengthening. However, if our mission was to be accomplished we had to turn to the nitty-gritty.

16 : Nitty-grittiness

Careful planning was necessary, using Pete's left-brain skills, to allocate the number of days that were available before the climb. This could not be moved from 6 July, the date that we had chosen months ago. It was the Dalai Lama's birthday, a sacred date in the Tibetan calendar, which is celebrated worldwide as a focus on His Holiness and the Tibetan philosophy of peace.

We had to make sure that GT had the chance to acclimatise to the level of the rest of us as rapidly as possible, while we were still advancing in our own programmes. It was also important to enable Mig to gain as much mountaineering experience as possible. It was now 23 June. We had to be on Chimborazo and able to cope over 6,000 metres by at least 4 July. That left only eleven days.

We could squeeze four summits in, with gradual ascending heights. Pasochoa and Pichincha were nearby and revisiting them would save time. Any other mountain needed time to investigate it, organisation to reach it, a day to climb and time to return. My pleas to Pete for rest days fell on deaf ears, or met with a do-you-want-to-climb-Chimborazo-or-not? stare, even with the excuse of fifty postcards to write. Energy had to be carefully rationed. I found that even though I was fairly happy at 2,850 metres now, I went through phases of feeling really tired, with the body reluctantly following dragging feet. This was certainly not going to be a holiday.

Ideally, we wanted to try to climb Cotopaxi, at 5,897 metres, four or five days before summiting Chimborazo, so no acclimatisation would be lost. But then, if we had a really tough time on Cotopaxi, and pushed our energy resources to the limit, the chances were that we would be too tired for the big one. Gaining acclimatisation and fitness were finely balanced with being in the right moment both physically and mentally. We were subject to the vagaries of the weather, notorious for upsetting the finely laid plans of the best mountaineers. Also, we were severely restricted by not knowing how things worked in this country where we couldn't speak the lingo.

We turned for advice to 'Safari', a tourist agency run by an ex-Englishman, David, who was more than happy to share his knowledge and experience with us. He specialised in mountaineering. Yes, he could run the whole thing for us, take us everywhere, feed us, provide guides, every little detail would be taken care of and it would only cost us a few million *sucres* or a four-figure amount in $US. If we had been rich American tourists we might have been happy to hand over the responsibility of everything, but that was certainly not what we wanted. This was the 'Climb For Tibet' expedition.

It started a debate on whether we should think about employing guides on Chimborazo, as had been suggested by

Lincoln. Pete and GT, as experienced mountaineers, were aghast at the thought of even contemplating guides. It was not really climbing a mountain if you follow someone up, are shown the way and are not using all your skills of navigation, strength, bravado, technique and ingenuity. The achievement was not what a 'real' climber would call acceptable, even though they knew that decisions would finally be made on the grounds of safety.

'I say, old boy...what do you think?'

'It's just not proper. Good god, man! We're British!'

Our circumstances were rather special, however. It was absolutely vital that we climb on 6 July, as so many people were involved with us on that day with their own climbs or message readings, although the day before or the day after could perhaps be contemplated if necessitated by bad weather. There was little written about the possible routes up. We had scant knowledge of the area. And most importantly, we had a complete novice with us, and we had to make sure that he, above all, reached the summit.

The debate simmered. The thought of having a guide or guides did not actually bother me, except for the cost (I wasn't very good at non-attachment to money). At US$75 per day plus expenses, a guide was cheaper here than in Europe. But we were all pushing our finances to the limit. 'Climb For Tibet' had already cost us personally huge amounts, and there was no way to get any of our expenses repaid unless the documentary film made a lot of money. That was a very tenuous hope, but a hope, nonetheless.

I was not a good enough climber to mind being 'taken' up a mountain. The only reason I had ever got up a serious mountain was because I had been lucky enough to be with good climbers. Maybe it sometimes helps to have a personality of the happy-to-be-led-female variety (as long as it is in the direction that I want to go).

172

The important thing was the wider picture of what we were doing. If having a guide increased our chances of getting to the summit then that was good. We had to get there. We were going to get there, whatever it took.

I didn't mention it to the others, even to Pete, but I certainly had no intention of going home until we had climbed it.

I knew it would be useful to do some visualisations, as the mental picture contributes to the physical actuality, so I tried envisaging the four of us on the summit. Somehow it seemed forced, and I couldn't quite get into it. I couldn't see us there. I wondered what it was that didn't quite resonate, but I put these thoughts aside to work on all the many things that needed doing at a practical level.

While GT was coping with first-day exhaustion, Mig had important things to do like buying food to cook for us all and viewing the World Cup. I passed the door of the hostel television room and watched him making friends with other football fans from around the world. I saw the 'you're cool' way they smiled at him. He seemed to have an extraordinary ability to communicate at a deep level with people even though he couldn't speak their language. Maybe football, too, was a bit like a language.

Pete and I found ourselves with a vast amount of 'office' work, for which we needed to sort out the communication hassles. Most were to do with organising the documentary film. Amora was associated with the Wisdom TV channel in the US, who had commissioned a cameraman to come to film us. Wonderful, we thought, it's all going to happen, the story of the peace climb will be told to the world, and there will be huge awareness for Tibet.

Abortive attempts at fax, phone and email from all over the city, accompanied by exorbitant costs, not only of money but also of our energy, finally put us in touch with Michael Tobias, from Los Angeles. His credentials told us he was rather more than a cameraman. A seriously fine climber with first ascents to his name on many continents, he had lived and wandered extensively throughout the Himalayas. He was author of twenty or so books and had written and directed over a hundred films, including documentaries about the Dalai Lama, currently with his series on the great spiritual thinkers of the century. His primary activities concerned animal rights, ecology and public policy. We were excited that he sounded such an extraordinarily involved human being on so many fronts. Pete spoke with him on the phone and was hit by his exuberance. 'Fantastic! Whymper's mountain! Humboldt's Ecuador! We can really help Tibet with this. Please, organise accommodation for two assistants and myself and find a local cameraman and sound guy. We need a bus to get us there and food…and a cook…'

Thus started the whirlwind that was to eat into our relatively organised plans.

'Now, I've been told to film a story about three climbers and a monk. Is that right?'

'Ah!' said Pete. "Well, sort of…'

We discussed the roles. The monk had to be Mig (I didn't feel strongly enough about the inkling of a previous lifetime). Tradition had it that one member of every family in Tibet took up robes and moved into a monastery. Since the Chinese invasion it had been almost impossible to uphold this way of life, but Mig had thought about the possibility. He would like to become a monk and sometimes he had yearnings. He could certainly shave his hair off as a symbol of devotion.

'Please don't, Mig,' I tried to dissuade him. 'You've got lovely hair, and anyway you would get really cold up high. Maybe you could just climb in Tibetan national dress with your *chuba* on top of your climbing gear.'

'Well, to be honest, Tess… Yeah… It's more important to

always be happy with what we've got.'

'I'll try not to forget that, Miggie.' Although I was so much older, our relationship felt like that of long-time friends, with a deep respect for each other. He was a typical young man, yet he carried an innate sense of sagacity. I often learned from him.

But we were already becoming influenced by the glamour and potential of a film, rather than concentrating on the business of climbing the mountain. At least it relieved the stress and frustrations of trying to keep in touch with our 'Climb For Tibet' base, and Amora in England and Wisdom in the US.

Pete, as the only technically literate one among us, was allowed to use the hostel computer, but after spending two hours typing long emails he was told they had been lost. There had been a power cut and they probably had not been sent. We might know tomorrow if they had gone. We might not.

The South American Explorers Club fax was still not working, though we found wonderful helpfulness and information there and directions to fax facilities at a nearby hotel. Eventually one went through. 'That will be 160,000 *sucres* (£20), please.'

At the Quito telephone centre I queued for half an hour and, in trying to leave a message for Candy at the home base, had the wonderful surprise of speaking to my son, Mark. He chatted about Paul and himself with all the usual school problems and excitements that made me long to be there. Another life a world away was calling to me. He also relayed the peace message from my middle son, Scott, who was travelling with his girlfriend, somewhere between a beach in Indonesia and a macadamia nut farm in Australia. It indicated the sense of responsibility that many young people feel today:

Travelling around the world across three continents, we see continually the cycles and relationships between all nature and people, and we see how very crucial we are in either tipping or preserving this delicate balance. Universally we must and will take responsibility in every walk of life and stand up for the values and actions that heal our Earth – from environmental devastation and pollution, from extreme poverty, from political violence and genocide... And we must move forward with eternal and essential feelings of compassion and peace.

Scott's intelligent perception, along with his caring-enough-to-bother attitude, enhanced my tender feeling of closeness to him. I thought of the time, two years previously, when we had visited a Tibet art exhibition in London together, and viewed a team of monks constructing an exquisitely lovely Tibetan sand mandala – a sacred circular pattern used to aid meditation.

This one had been dedicated to world peace and harmony. On completion, after weeks of careful labour, it was to be swept up and thrown into the Thames, to symbolise the Buddhist principle of transience; that all things are impermanent. Scott and I had decided, along similar lines, to dedicate a 6,000-piece jigsaw puzzle to harmony. We had enlarged our kitchen table and set about the construction of our own mandala.

After this brief connection with my sons, I was able to float happily around the city, excited by touching in with my mother-child bond, always the most intense influence for me. It made me feel in contact with instinctive, natural systems. Whatever else happened in life, that was always there. There was strength in its purpose and its love. I wondered, though, if I would ever understand how Tibetan mothers must feel, making the heartbreaking decision to send their children secretly across the Himalayas on a harsh and life-threatening journey, to try to reach a strange land wherein they might find freedom, education and a future.

Back at the hostel, in keeping with the priority of keeping our bodies in good working order, Mig cooked up a yummy meal of rice, vegetables and lentils, adding chilli and meat for himself. His carnivorous habits always surprised me, as they seem to go against Buddhist thoughts of reverence, but then Tibetans, like condors, don't usually kill animals, yet will eat the sustenance that life offers by way of survival in a harsh land.

GT voted the meal the best he'd ever tasted, and showed his appreciation by conducting the washing-up symphony with a couple of plates held aloft. 'Crescendo…now pianissimo…'

Pete, in spite of all the many things he had been trying to sort out all day, had found time to search out a lovely bunch of flowers for me, as an expression of love and partnership in our great endeavour. Yes, guys, being given flowers does work. I felt cared for, feminine and special.

Curling up with Pete to go to sleep, I thought, at this moment it's not hard to be happy with what I've got.

It was a joy, too, to return to Pasochoa to show GT its delights. He loved the wondrous sounds of all the birds and the magic of the ancient forest, and was able to feel in tune with the Earth.

But by the time he reached 3,800 metres he was coming up very sluggishly to the grassy knoll near the pine trees where we waited for him.

'I'm so sorry I'm so slow,' he apologised, breathlessly. 'I never used to suffer like this.'

He confessed that never in his life had he bothered with training for a climb. What strength of character he must have, I thought, just to go and carry out a climb without preparation. Was that the old way to do it?

In spite of the focus on our altitude training we all tended to forget that we were nearly as high as the top fifty mountains in Europe, and that we shouldn't expect the body to respond in the normal way. Even superman Pete was breathing heavily, though he wouldn't admit it. I knew because I could hear it on the replay of the video.

That night Mig had a dream about climbing Everest. This said to me that what we were doing was affecting us on all levels... that the anticipation and stress was seeping through our minds while we were trying to cope with all the day-to-day things that needed doing. Would we be able to keep the pressure in check and put it to good use to motivate ourselves?

Jorge usually brought breakfast for us. His sunny demeanour prompted us to smile and joke with him, though none of us had any idea what the other was saying. He was delighted to bring us an early morning visitor. It was Emily, who was going down to the lowlands for a while, but suggested we contact Lincoln's office to get help with our planning. She had also checked out information on the condors for us. There were, according to the last census, believed to be only thirty left in Ecuador. Research had found that many condor eggs had been rendered sterile by insecticides in the food chain. But, as they were on the 'Cites' endangered species list, in theory they were protected, and numbers were now thought to be increasing. With a life span of forty years and reintroduction programmes being put in place in parts of the Andes, there was hope. But how lucky we had been with our sighting.

'You should have seen them,' enthused Mig. 'They were just wonderful, you know.'

'What were they really like, though, in essence?' asked GT.

It was at this point (sadly) that the condor impression was born. Pete slowly took off his glasses and placed them on the table. He rose to his full six foot two inches, puffed out his chest, stuck his large beak regally in the air and, with startled, staring eyes, managed to ruffle his beard. His long arms stretched out horizontally with large fingers parted and he flew around the courtyard.

We should never have laughed; from then on, condor impressions abounded – but perhaps it was the spirit of condor, coming through Pete to keep watch over Mig.

Emily bid us goodbye. 'Good luck. I'll see you when you get back from Chimborazo.'

Her words left me somehow puzzled. I had never considered afterwards. Everything was geared up to the climb, to the summit and to getting there. I simply had not thought about afterwards. A flash of fear went through me. Was there to be no afterwards? Was this why I had not visualised it? Don't be so stupid, I told myself. We're all going to survive this. All will be well, and I buried the thought deep inside me. No doubts would stop me. I had come this far…

It was comforting to know that Lincoln had been nearly as far as the main summit and returned safely. At his tour office I gazed wide-eyed at the walls, thick with inspiring photos. There were brightly coloured parrots and butterflies showing off the lush green of the jungle, inviting an exploration by long dugout canoe; brown, barren iguana land with giant tortoises heading down to clear Galapagos waters; ice-cream topped volcanoes floating in purple skies; the dark, handsome face of an indigenous Indian...

We were met by Lincoln's young assistant, Carlos, a charming Ecuadorian who spoke good English. He was warm and welcoming, shook our hands vigorously and seemed pleased to be able to help us.

'I am so glad to be of service to such important tourists,' he beamed.

I told Carlos of our urgent need to reach as many peaks as we could and he came up with the idea of putting us in touch with a friend who had a Jeep.

'He'll be perfect. He maintains his own vehicle, loves going into the mountains, charges only 300,000 *sucres* per day and, yes, he is available for a few days.'

Gustavo would pick us up in the morning.

At last we were away from the worry of exorbitant taxi drivers, bewildering local knowledge and unfulfilled travel schemes.

Pete, in particular, was happy that proper plans could now be made. Poring over the guidebook, he concluded we should tackle Pichincha at 4,794 metres, Iliniza Norte at 5,126 metres and Cotopaxi at 5,897 metres. We would have to come back to Quito for nights in between.

Things were looking good. As if in confirmation, little synchronicities were happening. Along the Quito cobbled streets we passed two huge wooden doors littered with six-pointed stars; Mig discovered that he knew a friend of Michael Tobias; we met a young man who was about to start university with my son Scott; and I received an email via the South American Explorers Club from Uri Geller, which had come at the exact moment that I was writing one to him. That did not surprise me as Uri had always been a master of psychic serendipity – like the time he experimented with the method of a million or so people concentrating mind power on a set of numbers… It had been my only worthwhile lottery win ever.

I found time for some yoga and a long overdue meditation, which gave me not only some much-needed inner peace, but also an understanding about Uri. It was explained to me in the relaxed space deep within myself why Uri was involved with 'Climb For Tibet.' He has a very special energy, with which he has already done many wonderful things, but which is only now beginning to be put to its full intended use. He is to act as a transformer for the high, spiritual energy that is coming into the Earth and needs to be changed to a vibration that can be used at a physical level, and distributed around the world to promote peace and harmony.

This revelation explained why it was important to leave his gifts on the summit. He could then easily tune into them, as they carried his vibration. This would enable him to connect with the vibrations from the mountain and send them out into the world. He was a vital part of the process that was being organised... somewhere.

Feeling like a pawn in a game of chess whose players were unknown troubled me, but it also encouraged me just to let things happen and flow in the direction they seemed to want to go.

That evening we had the first serious rain since we had arrived. It came down oppressively.

I was tired, in spite of the quieter moments of the day, and both Pete and I were wound up from trying to sort out the film paraphernalia.

'Let's have a decent sleep and leave late for Pichincha,' I announced. 'After all, we have a four-wheel drive vehicle and there are no unknowns. Let's see when we wake up.'

'You know we have to start early when we're going for a mountain. It's only through being disciplined that we'll get the job done. We must be disciplined,' Pete said sharply.

That annoyed me. This was always a source of conflict in our relationship (and right now I didn't want to learn from it). I liked to let things float along and do what felt right in the moment. I hated the thought of my life being enclosed into boxes. Pete liked to have everything listed, planned and ordered. He hated leaving all the decisions to the last minute.

We compromised on not quite such an early start.

17 : Jaws of the volcano

Gustavo met us outside in the dusky morning street, before the sun had found its way through the close-knit buildings and the thick leaves of the maples. He looked around thirty years old and typically Ecuadorian – short and strongly built. Intelligent eyes sat in a round brown face, offset by a ready smile. Whether in the city or at the top of a mountain, he always wore boots, jeans and a dark-blue donkey jacket. A grey peaked cap, Chairman Mao-style, lived permanently on his head. We all liked him immediately and I felt a happy sense of a guardian angel come to take care of us.

His white Jeep looked loved. It was high off the ground with a short wheelbase and a huge roof rack onto which we spread our rucksacks. Green gingham-covered seats faced each other across the back of the vehicle. This was to be our trusty steed for the next few days.

We piled in and retraced the route through the city around to the west. Once on the dirt road we were bumped and jolted about, though the rain seemed to have settled the dust. We crossed over the pass, then down through the village of Lloa, and this time we had no problem in finding the Guagua Pichincha track. There was a contentment in having been this way before, but I missed the excitement of the unknown, and unexpected treasures for the eye. I often favour taking risks for the sake of novelty over what is safe and sure. This is not an ideal outlook for a mountaineer who wants to survive, but...there is so much world to see. As a child I must have been influenced by my brother Graham, who had always said 'boredom is a cardinal sin.'

Now, however, I had to try to concentrate on my Spanish, as communication was left up to me. I enjoyed trying to construct some sort of sense. Improvements happened fast, out of necessity. Gustavo was very patient and gesticulated a lot to help. Once we knew how to say 'far out!' – *salida lejano!* – I felt we were well on the way to international harmony – though I couldn't understand why Gustavo said his dog had lived in his house for a hundred years...

Suddenly the Jeep started bucking and diving over a rain-deepened rut and tipping dangerously towards a steep drop. The weight on the roof shifted to the left, accentuating the tilt. Mig, quick-thinking, leaned wildly out of the front door, horrified to see the right-hand wheels spinning off the ground. We balanced, swaying on a knife-edge. Very quickly and deliberately Gustavo made noises that suggested he would like us to exit ever so carefully from the back door. My Spanish interpretation had never been so good. Pete was the first to creep out and GT and I followed. The Jeep gently returned to all fours. Phew! Baptism by fire!

'Hey, I'll never forget that moment.' Mig's words came with a gush. 'Leaning out like that probably saved us all.'

We nodded with relief and clambered back in.

Gustavo set off looking quite unperturbed, as though nearly tipping up was a regular occurrence. Without further mishap he drove to about 4,000 metres, spat us out and went on up to the refuge hut. It was important for us to use the leg mode of transport to try to coax the body into acclimatisation. We snail-paced along. At least GT and I were ponderously slow and ploddy; Pete walked purposefully and steadily with long strides and Mig marched up as though he were hurrying to catch the no 11 bus at Piccadilly, twirling his stick as he went.

From the hut we turned to admire the wonderful views that stretched before us. Peeking out above heavy cloud were distant purple hills, with agriculture clinging to their sides, looking as if it had been painted on. Closer in, the olive green and pale brown of the sweeping *páramo* grasslands were guarded by an icy wind. Around us, glimpsed through gathering mists, was a lunar landscape with dark volcanic crags, lava scree and tuffaceous rocks, strewn as if catapulted from the belly of the Earth.

Today the refuge was open, so we took shelter inside it. Here Gustavo tried to tell us (I think) of the legend of the three Franciscan friars, who came up to this place in early colonial days, when ideas of climbing to the summit were riddled with fear. They were caught in a storm and found a cave to shelter in. The bravest of them went out to try to find a way down – and never returned. When the storm had abated, the other two searched and searched and, finally, overjoyed, spotted him on the high summit, kneeling in prayer. Delight turned to dismay when they discovered that he had been turned into a rock pillar, and would forever be praying to God on a peak close to heaven.

The building was as raw and cold as any cave would be at 4,500 metres. I borrowed Mig's lovely Free Tibet designer woolly hat.

The stark and bleak main room had a table and benches on which we sat to eat energy-giving sandwiches of a special sprouted bread I'd brought over from the UK. There was a sleeping room alongside, containing bare metal bunk beds. You would have to be very keen on rocks to want to stay here... There was very little else, apart from a poster showing a diagrammatic picture of a volcano erupting, with the title 'Los Volcanes son Peligrosos' – volcanoes are dangerous.

No bad thing to remind visitors that an active volcano could blow up at any moment. Guagua Pichincha had had a major eruption in 1660 that covered Quito in 40 centimetres of ash, and three smaller ones in the 1800s. It had also seen human turmoil in the form of a bloody battle fought on its lower slopes in 1822 when Ecuadorians had gained independence from Spain. Since 1981 the mountain had been rumbling.

It seems, I thought, that Mother Earth knows about the principle of impermanence... Probably she is shifting uneasily at the short-sighted human policies of 'take'. A balance upset will be corrected... I shivered – not just from the cold. Maybe part of me was sensing something... It would be just three months before Pichincha blew again.

There was one nice thing in the hut. It was a large visitor's book. It held names and addresses from all around the world, to which we added ourselves as 'Citizens of the Universe'. Mig wrote 'OM MANI PADME HUM' – and drew the beautiful Tibetan mantra of compassion.

'May all living beings lead a happy life' he prayed.

I wrote 'Harmony in Tibet is but one spoke of the wheel of Earth Peace.' My prayer was that our supplications would be one small step in the right direction to redress the balance... swaying on a knife-edge...

Outside visibility was vastly reduced. The cloud cover was low, and precipitation over a hundred per cent. We donned waterproofs, trying to cover up any bare flesh (though Yannick Penguin travelled nude as usual) and headed for the rim of the crater. The wind blew fiercely and I had to bend double over my ski sticks to move at all. Gustavo, wanting to fulfil expectations as a tour guide, beckoned me into the crater itself. Scarcely had I clambered over the loose ash and pumice of the ridge than the heat hit me. It came with the stench of heavy sulphurous gases. There was no wind. I felt nauseous and faint, and trapped in all my layers of clothes. I started to sweat. It was not hard to understand how some did not return from the jaws of the volcano...

Focusing carefully, I moved back up to the rim. Rather the other side of the ridge, the wild wind, the cold and the driving sleety rain, than the searing heat and unseen terrors of a boiling cauldron. OK; on this occasion I was happy to err on the side of boredom.

We all gained the murky summit pillar where Pete and I had stood before. Mig and I unfurled the Tibetan flag, taking care that it was not whipped out of our hands by the wind. Then the two of us sat, backs against a rock, in meditation...

With far away eyes I watched Gustavo on the summit... kneeling in prayer... Beside me I sensed Mig was asleep. Just for a moment across the mists of time there was no time...and I was the mountain...

My concentration was broken by Pete and GT arriving. 'We've just been to another summit, down and across that ridge over there. We think it's 4,794, that's 13 metres higher than here. You haven't been to the real summit.'

Only some of me wanted to get into the competitiveness of which summit was slightly higher. Most of me knew that it was far more important to have had a meditation with the mountain for a little while... But the egotistical part was dented. I rose to the bait of 'We got higher than you' with 'Bet you didn't. We don't know for sure about the heights, there's so much variation. You didn't take a reading with the altimeter. It was in Mig's pocket.'

But hang on... Did it matter? Inside me there was a little Egbert, with a huge head, a large mouth, arms that flailed about and spindly legs, which he used to jump up and down, shouting 'Me...! Me...! Me...! Of course it matters. I'm the best!'

Down, boy, down... Shut up... I want to be the best that I can be within myself...competing with myself...not at the expense of others.

But Egbert was all puffed up: ' Win...! Win...!'

Go away. It's enjoying the game that counts.

'I've got to be the one who's right, no matter what!'

Egbert... Go AWAY!

'Well, if you two have been to the highest point today, I guess you'll have to pay for supper,' I declared, as we gathered that evening at the vegetarian restaurant near the hostel. Maybe the drive for achievement could be put to good use. The main thing was that, apart from slight headaches and breathlessness, no one had really suffered from the altitude; a good indication that all would be well for Chimborazo.

'Basically, I can't wait to get there,' sighed Mig. 'All this acclimatisation takes so long...'

Pete was especially pleased that GT had gone so well. 'Archie, old boy... You were brilliant.'

'I say, Redhot...what a wondrous day!' GT replied. 'I really managed to find the rhythm of the mountain.'

We ordered lots of milkshakes. They were the Quito speciality, made with yoghurt and masses of fruit, and they were very cheap. We felt it was our duty to try them all – strawberry, papaya, mango, passion-fruit and banana – to figure out our favourites.

Mig decided on strawberry, and declared, 'You know, when I fulfil my ambition of having Tibetan noodle bars all over the world, I think I'll have these milkshakes in them.'

'Excellent!' I eagerly approved, visualising yummy, multicultural venues.

'But Mig, I thought your ambition was to repopulate Tibet,' teased Pete.

'Of course,' Mig replied. 'There is a lot of work to be done.' There was a twinkle in his eye, but he was deadly serious. As a direct result of the Chinese occupation, well over one million out of the six million Tibetans had been murdered or lost their lives. Never was an ambition so needed...

18 : The hellish hut

Gustavo was not picking us up until 8 am, so the morning start was gentle. I was excited that we were going up a new mountain at last. Pete gave me a long hug and I sensed his strength, which I knew was always there for me, no matter what our differences. It was a gift I treasured. A heartfelt hug harmonises vibrations and gives understanding, for tight in one another's aura there can be no pretence. We knew that we both burned with the same fire of making our 'Climb For Tibet' venture a success.

'Good acclimatisation is the single most important factor,' said Pete. 'Staying high at the hut tonight should really help our systems adapt.'

'Well,' I replied, 'my blood still feels pretty slow and lethargic.' I knew that even though we had had a couple of weeks at altitude, it takes five months for the new red blood corpuscles to increase by the desired fifty per cent for full acclimatisation. 'How's your blood doing?'

'Oh, zipping round as usual.'

'Typical… Why did I ask? You always do everything faster. Are you still taking the Diamox?'

'Yeah, I feel great, so it must help, though I do get pins and needles in my fingers occasionally. I've given some to GT and he's happy with it, but Mig won't take it. Western imperialistic drugs, he says!'

'I'll give him some of my homeopathic coca. He doesn't seem to be suffering at all, though, does he?'

'No, probably because of the amazing amount of water he drinks. By the way, you should check the colour of your pee. If it's yellow you're dehydrated. It should be clear. We must keep drinking all we can. There's meant to be a stream at the Iliniza hut, but we'd better take a lot of water up in case there's a problem.'

I groaned: water was always so heavy to carry. 'Maybe there'll be snow we can melt.'

The climb to Iliniza Norte's summit, at 5,126 metres, was meant to be a relatively easy scramble so at least we would not be taking all the other weighty stuff – harnesses, ice axes, crampons, climbing hardware and ropes – but we would have to carry sleeping bags and food, including lots of carbohydrate, which was especially important for a steady energy release. I noticed Pete sneaking a heap of chocolate bars into his rucksack. Hmm…we differed on our preferred type of carbohydrate.

Gustavo soon had the measure of our eating habits so he took us to the Machachi market to stock up on bananas. Mig went to buy, pushing his way between the dogs, firewood and cooking pots. It was a delight to feast our eyes on the yellows, oranges, browns, greens and reds of the different vegetables and fruits displayed, despite the teeming rain. Both stalls and people were covered in plastic sheeting, chunky ponchos and Panama hats, (which actually originated in Ecuador). This was the designated dry season but, it seemed the guidebook was right, any conditions could be expected at any time, particularly after the recent El Niño Pacific currents had caused exceptional storms and extremes of temperature. Anyway we were English, and it was good to have variable weather to talk about.

Even so, how we longed to be able to see the Avenue of the Volcanoes without their clinging cloud cover as we sped south down the Pan-American highway. It was about 40 kilometres (as the condor flies) from Quito to the turn-off west, where we followed a gentle river winding through fertile pastures, and on into the village of El Chaupi. We stopped here to stare at its beautiful little church, which was a whitewashed adobe barn with shield-shaped holes for windows and eight pillars stuck onto one end of the roof to hold up the haystack-shaped spire. It would have been sacrilege to visit by any means other than horseback; such was its air of bygone, sun-baked magic. This marked the point where we left the cobbled way that could possibly be called a road, and took a sandy volcanic-grey route that definitely could not be called a road. It soon became clear that the previous day's balancing trick had not been unusual, as we rolled along like a ship at sea, creaking and groaning, over ruts and holes and rocks.

'Nerve-wracking, isn't?' yelled Mig, who was excitedly riding shotgun on the back, clinging onto the roof, trying to weight the wheels back onto the ground as they rose and fell.

'More like body-wracking!' cried GT, being thrown about the inside of the Jeep, until inevitably we were told to get out and walk behind. He could then be seen padding along in bare feet, long red socks flapping from his trouser pockets, striking his fist in the air and shouting, 'I've paid good money for this!'

I wondered whether to mention that our guidebook had said to watch out in this area for particularly wild and territorial bulls, being bred for the bullring, but thought better of it. It said 'if encountered, move slowly and quietly.' Well, I thought, we can probably manage the 'slowly' bit.

But when GT and Pete went skipping off back down the track hand in hand, I decided the altitude had finally got to them.

The heavy showers had stopped and a watery sun pushed between scurrying clouds that swept the hilltops as we progressed upwards. The *páramo* stretched before us. Shrubby vegetation collected in the sheltered valleys while the rest was wide open grassland interspersed with compacted plants, some hairy, some waxy, all beautifully adapted to the harsh conditions. Tall, elegant grasses and lovely purple-petalled stars with bright cobalt bluebell-like friends clumped together, decorating our way, announcing that this kingdom of the wind, this abode of the condor, held its place in the heart of our Mother Earth.

At about 4,300 metres we had lunch. We sat on a little flat patch of grass in a thicket of small polylepis trees. These paperbarks, with characteristically gnarled and deep red trunks, have the distinction, along with the Himalayan pine, of being the world's highest altitude tree. The twisted tangle of their branches was home to fungi, mosses, lichens and other epiphytes, hanging and waving, giving an enticing enchanted effect, as if they were custodians of the mountain telling us, 'Come, wanderers, come… but advance at your peril.'

It was here we left the Jeep. Shouldering our rucksacks, we followed the now bewildering trail across a dry, rocky streambed and up towards a ridge, volcanic ash crunching at our feet. Our early eager steps were soon slowed.

'We should reach the hut within three hours,' I said to GT, gasping for air as I spoke.

'It may well take me six,' he replied, puffing hard, too; at last, someone whose pace I could keep up with. Many good conversations are born while walking up mountains. It keeps the mind happily off the agony of what the body is trying to accomplish, putting it into autopilot once the initial muscle complaints have died down.

So I asked, 'Why did you really want to join us on this expedition, GT?'

'Two reasons, really. The first was coming to Ecuador, in the footsteps of Edward Whymper, who's been a great hero of mine ever since I was a kid and read his *Scrambles Amongst the Alps*. After his controversial first ascent of the Matterhorn in 1865, when four of his team lost their lives when the rope snapped on the descent, he came to Ecuador, and in 1880 undertook what must have been the most successful mountaineering expedition ever. Along with Louis and Jean-Antoine Carrel from Italy, he made eight first ascents here, including the two highest, Cotopaxi and, of course, Chimborazo. Iliniza Sur was one of his conquests, but Iliniza Norte fell to an Ecuadorian, Martínez, in 1912.'

'I thought the Incas had been up to a lot of these summits to make sacrifices.'

'Yes, you're right, but the Incas didn't have a system of writing, so we can't be sure, except for the ones with bones and artefacts on of course. The mountains were certainly sacred to them. But imagine how brave the early European explorers must have been to attempt to climb to these peaks, which were shrouded in so much mystery and fear.'

'Yeah, and volcanic eruptions… What about your other reason?'

'Well, that's the spiritual side. It was the connection with Tibet that appealed to me…and Tibetan Buddhism, which I've been on the periphery of for most of my working life. I was privileged to know Marco Pallis and Richard Nicholson, two dedicated musicians who went to the Himalayas in the Thirties and came back as Tibetan Buddhists. When I used to go round for music sessions with them in London, it was like walking into a treasure trove of Tibetan painting and Buddhist culture. That fed my initial inspiration gathered from seminal books.'

We paused for breath where the ridge went down a little before becoming climbing steeply again. It had just been possible to talk in between puffing and panting, with a real slow, steady pace.

'And what about your family, GT? What do they think about you coming to climb in the Andes?'

'Oh, I don't think my two sons and their families worry too much now. I've been going off all my life and they accept it… And Chloe, now that she is eleven, is becoming keen on climbing herself… She's got the bug too, if you can call it that… But Debbie, yes, she probably worries…'

I moved on ahead, leaving GT to compose music in his head, as the trail became a two-up-one-back slog through loose volcanic scoria – pyroclastic fragments and heavy ash. The angle of incline was severe. Calf muscles cried out. It might have been easier to go up a mountain of jelly with marbles as icing. It demanded an intense focus, affirming 'I am strong… I am strong… I am strong,' though the interruptions for gulps of air seemed to make it impossible. Step, kick, slide, breathe… Step, kick, slide, breathe…

Step, kick, slide, breathe…

Somehow I was able to pull it into a rhythm, but there was a drifting, a distancing. And now the boots on my feet passing over the ground didn't seem to belong to me… I found myself moving into my mind…wonderfully…for a meditation in motion…

I am clearly visualising the star on the summit of Chimborazo. Its six points are held by the Council of Masters. There is an empty spot in the centre waiting for the presence of the crystal, so that the beacon of light may be lit. There is a grid of other beacons and the combined light will encompass the Earth. I am being told that there is something of supreme importance that I must know. It is this. The placement of the crystal can only be carried out if there is a holding in the heart of unconditional love. I must be aware.

Oh help! How? It sounds simple, but surely it's impossible… Surely?… Step, kick, slide, breathe… I can only have faith that whatever my soul has chosen to draw to itself, it is ready to cope with…and that there will be help available… Step, kick, slide, breathe… Step, kick, slide, breathe…

Through swirling mists I could see Pete and Mig reaching the top of the ridge. There was a saddle that came down to it between the two mountains, Iliniza Norte to the right – our route for tomorrow – and Iliniza Sur to the left, a difficult, technical climb. Once, during the Holocene period, possibly 10,000 years ago (just the other day in Earth terms), they had been one mountain, a stratovolcano, one beautiful, heaving cone of fire. Maybe they still carried the energy of being together as one. Maybe knowing that all life was originally forged as one was how to hold unconditional love…

The heavy cloud covered all things in the greying dusk. There was no sign of a sunset. Just…struggle to breathe…struggle to move…struggle to think… Drained and exhausted, I eventually gained the base of the saddle, where a gentle bowl revealed an orange building, the Refugio Nuevos Horizontes, at 4,765 metres.

Climbers used to the well-appointed huts of the European Alps would have called this a hell-hole. It consisted of four walls that were wet to the touch, six metal bunk beds and a high sleeping platform above the kitchen area, which contained a couple of gas burners and a sink. Two tables with benches sat on the concrete floor and some stools against a wall shelf. There was no water except what could be carried from the stream outside, provided it wasn't frozen, and no heating or light, even though the guidebook had said a generator would be available – at least we had head torches. I never did find the loo, though somewhere there was meant to be a hole in the ground with three protecting walls.

All this would have been fine, for it was shelter that we needed from the night and from the cold, but arriving as tired and hungry as we were, we were shocked to find that, although we had seen no one all day, the place was full of people. There were about twenty Ecuadorian teenage boys and girls noisily milling around, and we soon realised they had come up for a Saturday night party. A lot of booze had obviously already been consumed and a lot more was on the way. Even though I was used to a diet of teenagers, things looked bleak for getting any sleep or preparation for an early start to climb in the morning.

We scrounged a few very damp plastic mattresses and some floor space and waited for the chance to use a burner to cook some hot food. The settling gloom matched our darkening mood. I felt disjointed at not having a personal spot to place my rucksack and gear, which needed drying out, and out of sorts at the lack of peace and quiet that my gathering headache was asking for. In fact, I felt completely lousy. Both GT and Mig lay down, unable to move with pounding headaches, nausea and dizziness. Even Gustavo looked green around the edges. I passed around the homeopathic coca, remembering how I had felt at the Chimborazo hut.

Only Pete seemed his usual self, and chatted to an English couple, Martin and June, who had turned up for the climbing, but were similarly upset by the situation.

At last, after what seemed like four hours, but was probably nearer two, we were able to boil water for hot drinks and some meant-to-be-yummy packet supper. But by then Pete was the only one who felt like eating…pasta and Mars Bars.

We settled down for the worst night's sleep that any of us had ever had. The kids talked and giggled and chucked cans, some vomited, and some peed off the sleeping platform. Martin asked them to be quiet, with repeated and increasing irritation. He tried in English, in some sort of Spanish and even in French. Gustavo tried in real Ecuadorian. There was a general shemozzle.

I curled up and hid inside my sleeping bag. It was intensely cold, a deep damp cold that seemed to eat into my bones. Unfortunately, there was no space to lie next to Pete, who is usually a good hot-water bottle. My knees in particular, as the bits that stuck out the most, ached from the cold as I restlessly turned from side to side to try to get comfortable.

I remembered that in one of Shirley MacLaine's books she had described picturing a sun inside herself to create warmth, and then I thought of the little humming bird, the Andean hillstar, that reduces its heartbeat and goes into a state of torpor to survive an icy night. Maybe warmth is a matter of flipping the correct mind switch somewhere.

Soon my thoughts turned to the Tibetan monks who have mastery over their bodies and meditate in the deep snow, creating heat that is emitted in steam from their thin robes. I could almost imagine I was a monk…

I know the body is the messenger of the soul. It carries the spiritual expression… The annoyance and problems are a test… I concentrate on unconditional love… There is no sign of Egbert. He cannot cope with a love connection to others. He likes only separation…

Just for a moment I am incredibly, beautifully happy… I touch an inner peace… And I am warm…

19 : 5,000 metres high

I must have slept, for it was suddenly light and Pete was saying, 'There's been a couple of inches of snow. It's debatable whether we should climb or not, as we've got no equipment.'

The atmosphere in the hut was dank and smelly – an aftermath worth forgetting. Two of the youngsters approached GT and in broken English tried to apologise for their behaviour. Gracious as ever, he replied 'Oh, it was nothing...' and proceeded to become the best of friends with them.

Martin and June decided that with so little sleep and such bad conditions, they would go down.

We reluctantly gathered ourselves for the ascent. Mig was feeling groggy and less than enthusiastic. 'You know,' he said, holding his still aching head in his hands, and thinking of uncomfortable feet, 'I really don't want to do this.'

'You're going to do it,' rallied Pete. 'We're all going to do it. It's a training climb. It's important you gain some experience on snow.'

I always respected Pete's mountaineering judgement. We would go.

It didn't look good outside. Snow covered everything horizontal, it was still misty and there was a very cold wind. 8 am was already late for a mountaineering start, but the temperature was now slightly above freezing which meant there might not be much lethal verglass on the rocks. So Pete took a rucksack with rope, first-aid kit, water, food and camera, and the rest of us travelled as light as we could. That is not forgetting essentials – the crystal was safe in my fleece and Yannick just managed to sneak into the pocket of my waterproof at the last minute. Mig was not to be separated from his sacred stick.

We crossed the frozen stream and headed up to the saddle, which was the remains of the crater rim. For a while, unusual yellow and clay-like volcanic material was becoming exposed underfoot. After that it was like being in an old black and white movie – white cloud, black rock, white snow. With even poorer visibility we turned right up the southeast ridge, Gustavo looking overjoyed at being able to lead the way. The rocks were stable but large as we clambered over or between. Happily, the snow was not a problem, except that I suffered cold hands with swollen painful joints in spite of layers of gloves, but I gradually warmed to the climbing as we worked our way up. The ridge narrowed, and there were places where the run-out was steep. We were aware of this because GT dropped one of his ski sticks and we could hear it clattering down, far below us. The loss of it was annoying, as the sticks were proving so valuable on the easier general walking and particularly the descents. But however useful, it was distinctly more useful to have a body that did not need to take the risk of climbing down a steep slippery volcano side to search for the missing stick.

A huge vertical rock face loomed at us, barring the way. Traversing right, we found a series of ledges to gingerly follow above a steep drop. It was known as Paso de Muerte or 'death pass', but the ever-present cloud prevented us from seeing down into the 'death' bit. Safely across, we then moved into a gully full of loose material that had to be negotiated. Hopefully, it was still early enough in the day for us not to be threatened with rock fall. Here, Pete left his rucksack to pick up on the way down. He was unusually quiet. He was not panting, was he? Struggling for breath? Surely not? Even Egbert didn't believe it. It must have been an illusion.

Further gullies with loose rock led us around and up to the summit at 5,126 metres. We had made it – after a three-hour battle. There were no views... Just an iron cross, the definitive expressing of the mantra of compassion, 'OM MANI PADME HUM', a couple of photo poses and the warm hugs of a team achieving together.

It was an excellent success for Mig, as his first serious climb. He appeared to have managed with ease. For both Pete and myself, it was the highest we had ever been. GT said, 'I'm thrilled; in fact, when I was in the Tien Shan, I enjoyed wondrous summits like this...' And as for Gustavo, well, he was not your common or garden taxi driver, was he?

There were no takers for the great honour of being sacrificed at the top of the mountain so we headed down. By now much of the snow had melted and the rocks were no longer slippery, giving us some good scrambling. But I was in a sea of tiredness... down the gullies...across the ledges... Out onto the ridge... Drop to the hut... And down, down, down, on exhausted rubbery legs and shattered knees. Once at the Jeep the agony was not over. While Mig rode shot-gun again to try to counter-balance the almost impossible angles of the track, the rest of us had to cross seemingly mile after mile of rough grassland. There was walking when I felt like crawling, hot tears of weariness never far away, watching the little white Jeep in the distance, being tossed about like a tiny boat on storm-sculpted waters.

Yes, I thought, if being a tourist means travelling for pleasure, then at this moment we are definitely not tourists. Yet how much more satisfying is it to taste the courage of the early explorers like Whymper, to feel the winds of exploration and discovery that blew in their hair, and to travel with purpose. This way is to be participating, being inside looking out.

Now we became outsiders looking in as Gustavo took us home via the tourist route through the narrow, cobbled streets of the old colonial part of Quito, past squares with fine buildings, imposing churches and dilapidated history full of charm. Here, on a little bun-shaped hill, beset, we were told, by *bandidos*, we looked at an enormous statue of the Virgin of Quito. She was impressive, and carried a crown of stars on her head, eagles' wings, and a chained dragon on a globe at her feet. The significance was out of the book of Revelations in the Bible. What was it all about? I didn't know. As a tourist overlooking the sprawl of the city below us, with people going about their daily lives, I was just passing through. I was not involved. I wondered if I was a tourist on the Earth, just passing through. Was I a taker, or was I treading softly, with awareness? Monumental thoughts have a habit of drifting through when the body is tired... Thanks but I'd really rather think of nothing. Still, the thoughts persisted...

I cannot know what is happening everywhere. I cannot help everything at a practical level, except on a tiny scale. There are such huge problems in the world, like malnutrition and starving in the midst of plenty, and the drastic unsustainability of humanity's systems.

To some extent the Earth teaches us herself. For example, after the Chinese took over Tibet they clear-felled more than half the forests there to take the timber back to China. This eventually resulted in the silting up of their own rivers and the flooding of their cities downstream, with many of the rivers now so degraded that they no longer support fish life, or provide clean water. Examples of insensitivity to the Earth are all around us. At what cost to human life? What about our children's lives?

I am sure we can help. Problems can be solved from a spiritual perspective. As the physical is a manifestation of the spiritual, we can pray, we can keep our thoughts positive and compassionate, and we can give out unconditional love. It might not be easy to do, but it is powerful.

And now... now we had been asked to hold unconditional love on the summit...

I turned to the others as we drew up outside the hostel and spoke tentatively, 'We need to be in a state of unconditional love on the top of Chimborazo. My understanding is that the vibrational energy that we emit as catalysts could in some way affect the programming of the crystal whose function is to act as an amplifier for the light coming in.'

There was silence. I sensed a blocking. I had overstepped the mark. We were all on our own personal life journeys and I could not know or judge anyone else's. Nor had I the right to suggest what another should feel. What meant something to me in my terminology might mean something totally different to another. I regretted mentioning it.

'You know,' said Mig, 'it's time we all went and had a milkshake.'

'Wondrous idea!'

'Far out!'

The thought of actually having to walk the few metres to the vegetarian restaurant was not so popular, but then for a milkshake...

'First I must try to phone my kids,' said Pete, 'before it gets too late in the UK.' He spent a lot of time trying to send love down the wires to them. He knew that Claire and Graeme, at fifteen and fourteen years of age, were aware of what he was doing to help Tibet and the Earth, and that they were proud of his work. They wanted to talk to him whenever possible, and Caroline and Anna, at nine and four, needed to hear their father's voice regularly. He was worried, too, about the little one who was soon to have an operation.

Pete was certainly loving his children unconditionally.

It is a funny thing, this love business.

Were we unconditionally loving the children at the refugee school where our sponsor money was going? Of course: we expected nothing back.

Maybe I'll think of it as simply opening wide the doors of the heart...

Was GT loving unconditionally when he paid for Mig's expenses that came to more than he had planned...and for our milkshakes?

Was Mig loving unconditionally when he carved his Tibetan Buddhist mantra for the day's climb into his stick, opening up to the compassion spoken of by the Dalai Lama?

How was it when I checked with Mig that everything that we had planned to take to the summit was OK from the Tibetan point of view? For I so wanted it to be right for Tibet.

Gandhi had said that love was the currency of the spirit, a powerful energy, and that if we trust and honour it, then it would not let us down... Surely he must mean unconditional love, in the paradox that it will only come back to us if it is unconditional... around every corner, every minute... there, but for the looking...

I held the crystal in the palm of my hand. Still in awe that focusing on it gave me cold shivers, I felt mounting excitement. The time was drawing closer. Today we had all managed to reach over 5,000 metres. There would be no problem to 6,300 metres. We were going to make it.

I noticed the crystal had six sides. Of course. I looked at it end-on. It was a beautiful, perfectly faceted, hexagonal star.

The White Eagle Lodge leaflet, which I had brought with me on impulse, suggested visualising the six-pointed star. It said that it is a powerful focus symbol through which God's healing light comes and radiates to all beings. Also, that it denotes perfection, and stimulates the light within every human heart, the point of harmonisation between the inner and outer worlds.

Was the Master behind the work of the White Eagle Lodge involved in guiding us? Were all the different religions, sects and ways of looking at the finer side of life that we put into separate boxes in fact all part of one brilliant cosmic, pulsating rainbow that stretched across the heavens?

That night I slept heavily, and awoke still wandering in a dream.

20 - Wild windy country

I am lying down in the road. It is hard and rough and dirty. Cars, trucks, bicycles and all manner of traffic is rushing dangerously by, just missing my head. There is raucous shouting and jeering as crowds pass by. There are some who ignore me, some who laugh at me and some who even make a point of kicking me. All of this is incidental... The only thing that matters is that by using my body for protection I am caring for the child who is cradled in my arms...

The road becomes a river and I am floating...being drawn further and further...and further...

Suddenly I am standing aside and the river is a river of monks sweeping past me...hurrying... There is much to do. so busy...so busy. Maroon and saffron flapping. It is the entourage... They are slightly higher than I am... The Dalai Lama, in flowing robes, is turning and coming down to talk to me. He explains simply that we are a part of his work.

I did not want to open my eyes, nor did I want to enter the day. There was a lingering need to stay and savour the moment.

At breakfast Mig was wildly excited. 'Wow! Fantastic! This is a great blessing on our climb. Every Tibetan knows that to dream about His Holiness is the ultimate blessing on a project.' His face lit up and he positively glowed with happiness.

It was infectious. We all beamed, for this was a propitious sign to balance out all the nagging pressures, and I was thrilled that it meant so much to Mig.

It was in buoyant mood that we set off for our last training climb, Cotopaxi, claimed frequently as the world's highest active volcano (there are contenders on the Chile-Argentina border with higher peaks but lower volcanic activity). We were now used to the vigorous bouncing and bumping of our little Jeep over the Quito cobbles. It must even have had rhythm, as GT was inspired to expound great pearls of poetry: 'Let us swim in the oceans of the cosmos, on the tides of eternity...'

No doubt it was something to do with his latest composition.

Pete was concentrating on sewing wrist tags onto his waterproof over-gloves and sorting out the practicalities of the day. These included the impossibilities of the communications we had been trying to get right for days. Emails went to the wrong people, faxes acted as wake up calls in the middle of the night, phones were engaged and engaged, photocopying involved travelling to different offices... It was exasperating. Sometimes it seemed the old systems here were the best. I had been delighted to receive a lovely letter by post. Surprisingly, it had only taken a week to come. We were told that even by airmail it could take six months.

Why were we now driving past the airport when we thought that we had completed all the en-route city jobs and should be going south to the Pan-American highway? It seemed Gustavo had a surprise for us. (Maybe if my Spanish had been better it would not have been a surprise). He took us to his home. It was in a quiet, dusty street. Large metal gates opened into a small compound enclosed by tall, concrete walls. The house was a long, flat-roofed bungalow and there appeared to be some sort of a workshop business going on, judging by the fridges hanging about in varying states of repair. Gustavo's mum came out to welcome us. She was small, round and smiley, and wore a smart, bright pink overdress. The two of us had an instant affinity. As mothers we were both happy to chat away about our families and guess what the other was saying in a way that was so warm and affable that I wondered at the need for language. The communication was from different cultures, but of the similar joys, hopes and tears that were involved with caring for a family. It did not come from words, but from a sharing of the essence of ourselves. This gave me an insight into why the blocked energy of our recent correspondence problems may have been created...

Gustavo, she told us, was the youngest of eight children and she had many grandchildren. The family business was based here, indeed many hands were helping to raise the Jeep onto precariously balanced planks so that welding work on the leaf-springs of the suspension could be carried out. Brave wounds from the harshness of the Iliniza track were being repaired, assisted by the yapping encouragement of a little curly-haired dog that looked like a cross between a poodle and a sheep.

Would that heart wounds could be mended so easily, I thought, watching our self-assured Tibetan, in his old, borrowed thermal top and purple salopettes, talking elatedly about the dream.

Pete took some video footage and played it back to the wide-eyed family, enjoying the pleasure it gave. There, to the accompaniment of banging and sizzling, were the boys welding, GT looking dapper and explorer-like, Gustavo over the moon at being called our guide, and his mum with a knowing expression.

She served us apple juice on a tray with napkins and took us up on top of her house to see the wonderful view. Across the concrete, tin and red-tiled rooftops, we could follow a couple of planes landing and taking off into a clear blue sky and disappearing over tall, distant peaks, deep purple at the other side of the valley.

Gustavo then drove us out of Quito and south along the by-then-familiar, fertile, green Central Valley. To the right stretched the Cordillera Occidental mountain range, holding our recent scene of trial, the twin peaks of Iliniza. To the left lay the Cordillera Oriental range, with the dark emerald crater of Pasochoa, and Cotopaxi waiting demurely behind a tantalising veil of cloud.

The sun shone down on us, as it had five hundred years ago on the Inca peoples as they had constructed roads along this very same route, roads which were part of one of the greatest systems ever built. They stretched from here nearly 2,500 kilometres to the alluring, magical-sounding Machu Picchu, Cuzco and Lake Titicaca, and on a further 2,500 kilometres to Santiago. They were straight and uniform, crossing some near impossible terrain with carefully planted trees and canals alongside. Still, today, there is marvel and wonder at how the dovetailed blocks of stone, perfectly joined, were made without the use of mortar or steel to fashion them. The Incas would have had much to teach us, but history relates how the Spanish conquistadors invaded and set out to destroy this ancient and beautiful culture, and many of the roads were dismantled to provide stone for the houses of settlers. Perhaps in the fullness of time it will be seen that foundation rocks laid to ease the path along the road of life can be a gift of unconditional love for the next people…in spite of ruthlessness and devastation.

There was still much activity in the back of our moving Jeep. Mig covered his face and exposed arms in protection cream (in the absence of yak butter), as he had been experiencing sunburn for the first time ever, and we all filled up with as much as we could eat from the large food bag, knowing how appetite diminishes with altitude. Today we also carried extra luggage, as we had all the climbing equipment with us. Even Gustavo had thrown in an old grey canvas rucksack containing a helmet and short, battered ice axe. It seemed he had high hopes, though we still had no definite idea of what his mountaineering experience was, which was a little worrying.

I was busy with the tiny tape machine, recording some of the peace messages sent in by schoolchildren, with the idea that perhaps we could play them on the way up Chimborazo. They were from youngsters, aged 8 to 12, at Dunhurst in Hampshire. I had spoken to them about the climb and Tibet, and the wider issues of helping the Earth. They had each written a gem full of hope for the world and their future. So many touched our hearts, tempting tears. So many left us in no doubt of the special responsibility that we had been given to deliver these precious thoughts, pledges and prayers to the Watchtower of the Universe, that they may blow around on the winds and do their work... Children so often see things in a clearer way than adults. They seem to know that what they express from the heart will reach the heart of their Earth with love, that even just conceptualising messages can precipitate changes...and that they can make a difference:

I will care for everything. (Gussie Maier)

Treat every living thing with lots of respect. We should have world peace. If the Earth provides things for us, we should help the Earth in return. Don't use all of the world resources. Love all animals, whatever they look like. Treat animals nicely. (Issy Ehrlich)

May we have the strength to find peace in our hearts. (Harry Gillespie)

That we stop fighting and have world peace and we look after our planet Earth. (Giles Prowse)

I will not fight with my mum during the World Cup (Simon Jones)

Let all the hate in the world turn into love, and let there never be hurt in Tibet, and let the Dalai Lama be safe. (Ross Stewart)

Love the world, be at harmony and peace with it. Create your own shield of peace around you so you will not be angered by your fellow countrymen. Give out rays of love to the centre of the Earth. Live in harmony together, join hands and be forever family. (Catherine White)

I felt humbled by the simplicity and wisdom that poured forth from the tenderness of their years.

Within an hour and a half we had passed the road to Iliniza and were turning off east, near the NASA satellite tracking station, up towards the entrance gates and buildings of the Parque Nacional Cotopaxi. This park was Ecuador's pride and joy. It had been established in 1975, and assisted financially and technically by the World Wide Fund For Nature in 1983. Its purpose was the setting aside for posterity of a beautiful, unique piece of wild land that could be used in a protected way for education, research and recreation. It seemed to me it was the essence of what so many of the children were asking for in their messages – a part of the Earth that could be left in peace though still enjoyed by humankind in a state of harmony.

We paid our US$10 foreigners' entrance fee and drove through into an unexpected show of neat-and-tidiness, even to the extent of bump-free roads, which felt very strange. To begin with, we were in a well-cared-for, mature radiata pine plantation, which was part of a research programme testing climatic analogy in the northern and southern hemispheres. Considering that we were at 3,650 metres, the trees looked remarkably healthy, although the growth was slow, and diseased areas appeared as we started to ascend. With the depleted oxygen ruling all aspects of life, we did not expect to see many animals here, but were excited to find an experimental herd of llamas, all busily grazing among a pretty patch of grass sticks in the trees. How my dad will love to hear about this multi-land use project, I thought to myself, forgetting for a moment that he had passed on, and would not be there on my return home to regale with travel tales. He had been a forest economist and always loved to hear about different silvicultural happenings. In five minutes he would have worked out the balance of how many trees to the acre would keep the llamas happy, and vice versa.

We stopped to talk to a tiny baby at the side of the road. Its mother hovered proudly nearby, making little clicking noises that presumably meant 'come along now, dear, the dairy is open.' His rusty-brown body had a twitchy tail held horizontally on a thick, oily fleece. A long, chunky neck supported the pert little white face with sticky-up ears, expressing interest without fear, and a welcome-to-my-land. I was enchanted.

The llama, like many of the cleverly adapted residents of high altitude and other oxygen-deprived habitats, has an exceptionally large count of red blood corpuscles. These are rugby ball-shaped, instead of the normal roundness of a soccer ball. Both these factors give greater oxygen absorption through the increased surface area. Wouldn't it be good if we could emulate them, I mused. Perhaps the Tibetan lama already does...

The road meandered as it gained height, and took us out of the forest and up to an information centre built solidly out of stone. Here, the story of Cotopaxi was told. In Palaeozoic times two shifting tectonic plates had met, resulting in the creation of the Andean mountain range, and leaving dynamic volcanic activity, of which Cotopaxi is a fine example. She has had more than twenty-five eruptions in the past 400 years. The last major ones were in 1877, and had produced terrifying, catastrophic lahars, (rivers of lava, melted ice, rocks and mud), one of which had reached the Pacific coast nearly 250 kilometres away, travelling at 90 kilometres per hour, destroying everything in its path. Since then there had been minor eruptions around 1904 and a warming up when the snow on the summit melted in 1975. Today there is continuous fumarolic activity, steaming gently in the 750 metre diameter crater... She is resting.

Although the German geologist, Reiss, and the Colombian, Escobar, were believed to be the first to climb to the summit, in 1872, it says much for the daring of Whymper and his team, who spent the night in a tent on the rim of the crater in 1880, that their rubber groundsheet was melting from the heat...

The Inca, we read, worshipped this goddess of fire, and the spirit of water was much revered here, too. They also cultivated llama herds not only as beasts of burden (the male can carry 100lb loads and go for weeks without drinking), but also for religious purposes. With its exceptional ability to process oxygen and survive at altitude, the llama was considered sacred, and could be afforded the special honour of being sacrificed. It was important to keep the good will of the gods.

The modern-day sacrifices were stuffed. The animal statues, meant to be lifelike, looked right through us with sad, glassy eyes. There was brocket and white-tailed deer, paramo fox, skunk, llama, Andean duck, Andean gull, speckled teal and the black-chested buzzard eagle, but it was when I came to the stuffed condor, wings at the ready in mock take-off, that my stomach took a sickening heave. We had seen him in beautiful freedom. At least the puma and the spectacled bear were not represented.

Would a museum of stuffed humans bring similar interest? The Inca had, after all, put on show the sacred, mummified bodies of their former emperors. Maybe it would help the species to be identified? What about representatives from nations threatened with extinction?... I recalled the happy picture of Mig ash-running down from the summit of Pichincha, whooping in delight... A Tibetan in beautiful freedom...

The road took us onwards and up over a little hill. Suddenly we were presented with the set from an epic movie. I was quite unprepared for the beautiful freedom of the Earth that Cotopaxi portrayed. Before us lay a mountain of which dreams are made. It was a perfect cone of dazzling snow, reaching skywards like the top of a six-pointed star. Only one area of rock spoiled the total whiteness, as if to say, 'yes, I have a real heart.' White tresses of snow cascaded elegantly into the pinkish-brown rock-band, which in turn supported the layers of grey volcanic material and olive green grassland.

The harsh beauty did not stop there. Sweeping widely to the horizon in all directions were *páramo* plains with low shrubby vegetation in the sheltered parts, and our eyes led us down to a large expanse of rippling water, glinting and gleaming in the sunlight. It went by the name of Laguna Limpiopungo.

So lovely!

We seemed to have the whole of this stunning world to ourselves. Then, right on cue, along the shores of the lake came three wild horses galloping, driven by the wind, manes and tails flying... Yes, they always gallop in films, too.

'This is exactly how I imagine Tibet to be,' sighed Mig, quite moved. And all our hearts resonated with his longing to see his homeland as we crossed the plateau and started to climb up the other side.

From inside our little Jeep we knew this was the territory of the wind as we slowly jolted, inch by inch, over the ruts deeply carved across the road. Then Gustavo stopped in the lee of a mound of volcanic debris and, looking out for our best interests as always, indicated for us to put on all the clothes we had. At that moment we were not sure why, but there was a growing sense of mental preparation for the battle ahead to reach the hut. As the road twisted and turned with the increased gradient, patches of snow appeared, interspersed with bands of deep red material.

"This is like a lunar landscape," gasped GT.

It was a veritable desert, with great boulders and rocks of all sizes, pyroclastic bombs and lapilli that had been strewn about, carelessly scattered like seeds, by the spewing volcano. Clouds started to swirl menacingly, giving a feel of non-reality. But it was not until we reached 4,600 metres that we found out that we still had to penetrate the armour of the mountain. It was indeed the wind. We were met by one continuous, intense, gusting fury as we disembarked from a lurching Jeep. Gustavo tried a few different parking positions, but there was no let up. The vehicle was vulnerable. We rolled huge rocks and placed them around the wheels.

My immediate problem was with my eyes. The wind was picking up material and using it like sandpaper in clouds of fine dust that swept around my glasses and into my contact lenses. This was agonising. The answer was to find my goggles, which were in my rucksack, which was thrown from the roof of the Jeep. The wind snatched it, though it weighed at least 35 lbs, held it hovering for a second and then rolled it away across the stirred-up volcanic debris. I gave chase, thin air and painful eyes forgotten, and with a flying rugby tackle thwarted its escape. A greying Yannick penguin sat up, disgusted at having to eat dirt.

Now there was a whole new meaning to the word windproof, but I managed to organise my gear so that only my nose was exposed and we all set off on what should have been less than an hour's walk to the Refugio José Ribas, at 4,800 metres.

I had thought there could not be a worse hut walk-in than

the Iliniza one. I was wrong. This time we had the wind to contend with, which was dead against us, we carried a lot more weight and I found that my exertion to catch the rucksack had taken its toll. Breathing deeply, I adopted the slowest plod that I could without actually standing still. Walking upright was an invitation to be blown over, so it was a bent-over plod. I knew it was better to keep going steadily than to make the stops the body was clamouring for, so I managed for a while to move into mind awareness.

I remembered the time on a mountain on one of the Greek Islands, when the wind had been so fierce that I had lain down, fearful of being blown away. I had learned to harmonise my vibrations with the wind so I felt I was one with it, and my trembling had stilled. I had tried the same technique with the sea on a boat to calm seasickness, with some success. To work with a movement rather than fighting against it produces peace. So now I affirmed... My body is one with the wind... My mind is one with the wind... My spirit is one with the wind... I am one with the wind... I am one with God in the wind... I am one... I am... Gradually the battering became me and the struggle was together...

I sensed a welcome from the mountain with open maternal arms, like wings of compassion.

21 : Capricious Cotopaxi

'Oh wonderful and blessed Cotopaxi. We greet you and humbly ask for permission to dance upon your slopes for a while...'

She smiles on us...

'We have come to prepare for Chimborazo. Show us your strength...that we may learn...'

We are enveloped in an energy that is not only strong and beautiful, but is also joyful... All is well.

Grey, grey ash. Everything on the trail up was volcanic grey ash. From time to time I was aware of the darker tones of deeply

gouged, eroded valleys and peripheral patches of white snow...
and drifting mist...until... There were Pete's steadfast hands
pulling me up the last bit. He had already carried the hardware,
been back down a little way to take the food bag off Mig, who
had insisted on carrying the heavy weight of one of the ropes, too,
and accompanied GT, who carried the other rope. They had been
up there for a while. I was the last in. Now I was faced with the
happy sight of a steep yellow roof, sheltering a large hut, empty
of other people, with excellent facilities. Fantastic! Far out!
I might have thought differently, though, if I had known then
about the drama that had unfolded at this exact spot two years
previously. An avalanche of snow, broken off from the snout of
the glacier above, had buried the hut, and ten people had lost
their lives. Even without the restless movements of the Earth, it
was thought that global warming was causing Cotopaxi's glaciers
to recede at 2 metres per year. We were on the front line...yet
blissfully ignorant.

The others had settled into a spacious sleeping area with two-
tier sardine mattresses, next to an eating area containing an
enormous wooden table, which, like the wooden walls, I somehow
found comforting. There was a kitchen (fridge outside), a civilised
outhouse loo, and the luxury of lights that actually worked. We
were going to enjoy a couple of nights here, and happily paid the
fee of $10 per night to the only other person around, a friendly
warden from whom Mig had learned important information:
England was out of the World Cup.

Gustavo was worried about the Jeep, and after talking to the
warden, decided to go back down to try to find a sheltered spot
for it. We lent him ski sticks, head torch and gloves and watched
him bravely setting out into the gale and the falling darkness.

Mig had brought up a wonderful vegetable stew that he had
cooked in Quito, so we dined with great delight. It was the first

time that all of us had had a good appetite at this altitude. Our bodies were adapting.

Gustavo finally staggered in, looking wild-eyed and dishevelled. We did not have to understand Spanish to know that things were pretty bad out there. It appeared he had moved the Jeep, swaying dangerously, to the shelter of some sort of old building, but on the return he had lost one of my inner gloves, eaten in a flash by the wind. This was a severe loss, not only because cold hands could have serious consequences, but also as I had been particularly fond of them. Equipment that one is used to and likes is important on a mountain. Sometimes small things like this can make up the balance of whether one reaches a summit or not. This was attachment. Oh dear! Gustavo very sweetly kept saying how sorry he was. I felt bad that it mattered so much to me, for surely it was more important to share things…and where was the unconditional love now?

As I lay in my sleeping bag, the wind howled furiously. There was continuous loud banging and crashing. It was unimaginable to think of being outside in a feeble tent. Man is small…but all things are relative. In the circular light of my head torch, I watched a little dratong mouse scampering around, seemingly unafraid… Then I knew that we were being snugly held and rocked in the arms of Cotopaxi.

In the morning Gustavo told us the winds had been gusting to 159 kilometres per hour (not far short of 100 miles per hour). That's breezy. There was a weather recording station close by on an exposed knoll.

It was time to play with the climbing equipment. There was a huge amount for Mig to learn in a short time. Using the beds for anchor points, the table as the mountain and the benches for a crevasse, we showed him how to put on his harness, tie into the rope, belay, move together, pitch, abseil, prusik, use ice-screws, and deadman and crevasse rescue. It was the potted mountaineering-in-a-minute course. He absorbed it well – not too surprising how sharp the mind can become when it knows one's life or that of one's companion may depend on it.

We then dressed as if we had skin-exposure phobia and headed out into the real playground. The wind had abated somewhat, though we still had to shout to each other to be heard above the roar, and a blurry sun was doing its best to have some effect. Following the track across the brick-coloured slopes behind the hut we slowly worked our way up to the first substantial patch of snow. It was soft and covered in grit but served our purpose for Mig to practice walking with crampons on and try out the ice axe arrest. This method of rolling on top of the head of the axe so that it digs in and stops a slide is potentially life-saving. He enjoyed executing it, not knowing then just how much it was to be put to the test...

Our eyes followed what we could see of the track above us. It crossed the scree slope until it reached huge hanging ice seracs that marked the edge of the glacier. There had to be an easy way through and up, though we knew that, with many crevasses present, the route could change frequently. It was reputed to be a fairly straightforward climb up to the steep ascent of the crater rim and on up to the summit at 5,897 metres, taking up to nine hours. This was the most climbed mountain in the Andes, so why was nobody else around? It could not be just because of the wind, surely. Perhaps the shifting crevasses knew something we did not... But the exciting thought of reaching the summit dominated... And how would it be to lie on the crater lip and peer into the abyss, into this open wound in the Earth, as Whymper had done? We decided to turn back and save our energies for the night. We would aim to leave at 1 am, so the ascent and the descent could be safely completed before the snow became soft and dangerous.

It was a relief to be back in the hut and not feel like an old door being hit with a battering ram. The warden, when consulted, thought the wind might ease enough for it to be all right for climbing the next day, and that we were now into a period of eight days of forecasted good weather. Well, if this is good weather, I'd hate to see the bad, I thought, but at least it was dry. More than anything, his comment made my pulse quicken... as, even though mountains have their own microclimatic patterns, it could mean good weather for Chimborazo...

We sat round the boardroom table, still dressed in chunky jackets, warming hands around hot mugs of tea. It was important to keep up our liquid intake. Mig had offered to make us Tibetan tea and I had decided to give it another go. This time I did find it a little more acceptable.

There was much work to do, sorting out the peace messages, the weight of which I had been proud to carry up with love. They were so precious. They represented support and hope for Tibet and the Earth. They were a large part of the reason for which we were here, struggling against the hardships, revelling in the joys... and they inspired us. Everyone chose the ones they related to best and thought they would like to carry and speak out on Chimborazo. The high altitude boardroom resounded to the unexpected expressions of peace as the messages for the summit meeting were planned...

More climbers at varying stages of acclimatisation began to appear and occupy the other rooms in the eaves. Some were wandering about dazed, some were being sick. Two young men from Israel, looking decidedly pale, stopped to talk to us and hear about Tibet. Perhaps particularly because of the violence in their land, there was a feeling of empathy with their symbol of the star of David. Although the six-pointed star is used by different peoples from around the world, the commonality of its sacred geometry at a spiritual level is profound. It is even the Eastern symbol for the heart chakra, the body's centre for compassion.

Pete was particularly pleased that the Israelis took away forms to write us messages. His mother had run a guesthouse and as a child, he had spent many a night listening to tragic tales of atrocities to Jews told by a long-standing resident. He felt their struggle held many similarities with that of the Tibetans.

Gustavo, too, was trying to understand the Tibetan situation. With careful thought he wrote a peace message in Spanish and gave it to Mig. I enjoyed watching them communicate earnestly and with fun, each in their own language. Gustavo was typical of most of the Ecuadorians we had met in his friendly disposition towards foreigners. He spoke, drawing a map to help explain, of how Ecuador had suffered from Peru taking over much of its southern, oil-rich land. The Peruvians had been strong and warlike; Ecuador, the weaker brother, could do little about it, but had not wanted to fight. Maybe in the great scheme of things it was no accident that our climb should be in a country that held dear the concept of peace...

We organised our gear for the morning and, as dusk was falling around 6.30 pm, prepared to get some sleep. I went outside to the outhouse without full clothing on. The cold bit into me like a thousand swords, but the wind had dropped further and an orange sunset was painting the sky with raw beauty. Cloud formations were playing beneath us. I spotted a dragon and remembered Mig's forecast of luck. In the distance I could make out the twinkling lights of Quito. It seemed fairly clear. Behind, high Cotopaxi looked ready to receive us.

Back inside I discovered a new trick. We had boiled up the melted snow water for our water bottles, including purification tablets (which gave the delightful taste sensation of drinking from a swimming pool), but mine was still hot, so I used it as a sleeping bag companion. For some bizarre reason people tend to think that if you climb mountains you do not feel the cold. Well, I feel the cold. With this hot water bottle it would not take half the night to warm up, in spite of wearing near-full mountaineering kit. I felt too excited to sleep, but realised it was not because of the Cotopaxi climb. It was the nearness of Chimborazo... Sorry Cotopaxi, my heart has already been given away...

The rooster called us at midnight. This interesting alarm on my watch tended to cause both annoyance and amusement in climbing huts and on underground tube trains alike, but it had the desired effect of waking people up. Pete and GT headed outside to check the weather and persuaded me to go with them. The wind still roared, but the main problem was that we could no longer see the lights of Quito, for much to our surprise, a sleety rain was being buffeted around. This would mean snow higher up, so we reluctantly agreed to go back for a couple of hours' sleep. At 2 am the situation was worse. It was snowing. At this time of night the body is at its lowest ebb, and I really could not find the motivation to head out into a climb with considerably lowered safety elements, although I would have accepted Pete and GT's experience-backed decision either way. Though I try to think logically (or at least what Pete would call logically), my brain just does not seem to be made that way, and it has to feel right to go ahead. Pete and GT weighed up the situation, aware that gaining altitude was vital to our whole expedition, but knowing that the visibility would be lousy. This was critical as we did not know the route. Also the snow could have obliterated the tracks we needed to follow. Tipping the balance towards a no-go was the fact that Mig did not have his goggles with him. They would be vital for vision in these cold, windy and snowy conditions.

So we slept until it was light, and awoke frustrated that we had not been able to climb. This feeling was compounded by looking out of the window and seeing the usual clouds rushing by, indicating high winds, yes…but also a clear sunny day… But we had run out of time and could not stay another night. Today was 2 July. I realised it was my father's birthday, and in the whisper of an instant I was visualising myself in a corner of a pleasant English field beside his liquidamber tree, which was dedicated to his memory, and around which we had spread his ashes.

'Isn't the mind a beautiful thing,' I said. 'The physical state can't be that important. The body thinks it is in one place and the mind can fly to wherever you want it to be.'

'The mind is truly wondrous,' replied GT. 'But I still think we made the right decision not to take the physical body up Cotopaxi. Twelve hours or so of that wind would have been pretty bad. We probably would have been exhausted and left ourselves without the energy to tackle Chimborazo.'

'You may be right, Archie,' came in Pete. 'But it was the correct decision for safety, given the conditions. At least we've now had three nights at the huts at 4,800. Not doing Cotopaxi is disappointing… but that's mountaineering…'

'Certainly, Redhot,' affirmed GT. 'There's far more to it than just a summit. Mountains have always been the source of all my values, my alternative to church.'

'Yes,' said Pete. 'For my part, I find the mountains a great source of peace and tranquillity, an escape from the real world.'

Mig did not express any disappointment. He had seen rainbows, which were a good sign, and he was excited at having woken up with his message from the summit of Chimborazo on his mind. He just said, 'Guys, I think we all need a seriously good shower. I mean, look at us...'

Even those of us without wings flew down the mountain. We had a following wind. Still, I was left behind. I must have a body with a particularly un-going-downhill-type motion. So I sang 'Happy Birthday' to my dad and then, as if with a direct telephone line to my mind, I chatted with him.

'It's so beautiful that I'm doing exactly what I want to be doing with my life. I'm so excited that after all these years it's happening. I know I'm absolutely where I need to be. I feel so lucky.'

'I'm so proud of you for that.'

'I'm so proud of you too, Dad, and you know, I'll help my Paul, Scott and Mark to do exactly what they feel they must do at a heart level too.' His quiet confirmation that this was what he too felt to be right meant a lot to me. When he had been alive it had always been important to put financial security and social acceptance high on the list of priorities, as was the ethos of his generation.

I knew he was with me, and I was mindful of Gandhi's words about the freedom of love, but still I said, 'Dad, it'd be so nice to have a little sign...'

He laughed, 'You don't need a sign...'

Barely two minutes further on, I was stopped dead in my tracks. There, in all this vast area of desert, there, lying in the volcanic dust right in front of me, was my sign. It was a pine cone. No single item could have represented my father more. It was a moment of awe and wonderment, a moment of humble awareness, and I was filled with a peaceful joy. Who am I to question the workings of our world? Sometimes, to see the beauty...that is enough.

I found the boys changing a tyre on the Jeep and, still a little shaky, shared my experience with Pete. Then, away out of the wind, the snow and the dust, we recrossed the dramatic landscape and headed down into a greener world.

Gustavo decided we needed to relax. He took us to a beautiful old hacienda with a colonial air of days long past, tall archways and pillars, flowers and fountains, panpipes wafting through a lovely garden, a chapel with bells on and huge carved doors. The thick stone walls had been privy to many a strategy of history. Charles-Marie de La Condamine had stayed here, and along with Louis Godin had led the French Geodetic expedition from 1736 to 1744. Their brief had been to determine the true shape of the Earth. They had surveyed an arc of a degree of latitude here at the equator. Another team had taken similar measurements in Lapland in the Arctic. Thus it had been proven that the Earth was indeed an oblate spheroid. In the process La Condamine had bravely surveyed on Cotopaxi during an eruption, and had reached the height of 4,745 metres on Chimborazo, which was believed to be the highest mountain (above sea level) in the world for the next seventy years. The hacienda had also been the home of the explorer and naturalist Humboldt, who had attempted to climb Chimborazo in 1802, attaining 5,800 metres before he was stopped by a huge crevasse.

We of the 1998 peace climb team sat in the restaurant, and were served what we thought was going to be a typical Ecuadorian meal but turned out to be egg and chips, much to Pete's delight. Then we were entertained by the jolly sounds of guitar, flute, banjo and twangy voice. We were not quite dressed for the occasion but, hey, we bought some wine and nobody seemed to mind.

We drove out along a magnificent avenue of towering eucalyptus trees and turned to look back. There was a gift for us. The skyline was clear. For the first time we could see Cotopaxi without any cloud. Because we had not stood on her summit she remained mysterious to us, and we were left with a feeling of respect for her that felt good. Perhaps it was a bit like not wanting to finish a jigsaw puzzle for fear of losing an old friend.

Dear Cotopaxi, you welcomed us and held us to your bosom. You sorely tested our lungs and our ability to do anything in any way other than very very slowly. You cared for us by not letting us climb, that we would not squander our energy. Thank you. We have been blessed.

But, although we had all coped well, apart from some shortness of breath, we had not reached as high as we needed to go and we had not given our bodies the chance to adapt to the necessary altitude. In theory we were not yet ready for Chimborazo. We should wait and find some more time to acclimatise. That, however, was something we were just not prepared to do.

22 : Tell the world

The 3rd of July was a turmoil. The monsters of doubt and fear that needed to be slain would have to wait, as would the tuning into the greater purpose and contemplation on what we were about to tackle. It was preparation feet-on-the-ground time. We were so busy that even I had to use Pete's superior management game-plans system (list of things to do).

We rose early to greet the US filming contingent, the JMT Production Group. Michael, his friends and associates, Robert and the production's colleague from San Francisco, Bettina, were lively, intellectual and very aware of world issues. We all suddenly found ourselves having to talk intelligently (that is, even more so than normal), as we brought them up to date on all the happenings and plans. I found it a bit of a shock after the family-type, relaxed, fun conversations our team had fallen into, but we soon warmed to their kindness and excitement at what we were doing.

We also met the rest of the crew: Mateus the local cameraman, Atura the sound guy, Oswaldo the cook, and Louis, the driver. There were others with other roles to play, too. Everyone had different ideas on how it was all going to work. With such a circus around us, I felt it would be hard to keep focused on climbing in the right spirit, but if we wanted to tell the world about Tibet and the peace messages, we were going to have to put up with it.

At least Michael was a force to be reckoned with, and before long, he had us all running around, caught up in his infectious enthusiasm. 'Ah, gee! This is gonna be the greatest, guys.'

He did not tell us then that he was extremely superstitious about bad weather and avalanches, and nervous about Chimborazo's central rock walls, which were said to hold back huge amounts of unpredictable glacier. He had managed to climb so many peaks in the world without getting wiped out that he knew his instincts were well honed… Thankfully he reserved judgement.

We left him worrying about the hut generator and sorting out equipment details and headed for an important rendezvous with David at Safari. We had finally decided to hire two guides. Even though Pete and GT had never climbed with a guide and found it ethically abhorrent, I knew that they were sacrificing personal thoughts for the safety of the team. On the positive side was the extra safety needed for the cameraman, probably Michael, who, it was hoped would come with us. Most importantly, having a guide would mean we would have a radiophone with us. Ramiro and Fernando would join us at the Whymper hut the day after tomorrow. It was also arranged that an emergency bottle of oxygen and mask would be borrowed from the hospital.

Last minute as it was, I was desperate to have a cell phone with us. I had a long list of people I thought it would be wonderful to phone from the summit, headed by the Dalai Lama and Uri Geller, who needed to know the exact moment of our arrival.

Traipsing the city streets to buy, beg or borrow one brought no results – other than frustration and disappointment.

Meeting the others at the vegetarian restaurant and guzzling milkshakes cheered me up. The discussion returned to the possibility of a bivouac halfway up the mountain, which, of course, was what Whymper had done – but with porters to carry the equipment and the fuel for the fire. Both GT and I, being slower, thought it would increase our chances of reaching the summit with everyone together. Pete was so against it that we dropped the idea. He felt that carrying all the extra equipment for a night out would be crazy (even without the dried llama dung) and that the conditions would probably be too cold and windy for any sort of comfort or rest.

Mig finished his sixth milkshake and went off to look into renting better-fitting boots, and tracking down some Tibetan monks he had been told were in Quito, both of which proved illusory. Then he was to join Oswaldo to buy food for thirteen people for the next four days. We felt fairly safe sending him to represent our stomachs. You could not buy yak butter here.

My next job was to pick up a fax at the local hotel. Candy had sent the last few peace messages through, including a note from Uri saying he was praying for us. I wanted to let him know the most likely tune-in time if we couldn't track down a phone to take with us. Also I wanted to get in touch with my Paul.

As the time to leave for the mountain approached, thoughts of my children were tugging at my heartstrings... I couldn't help noticing a contented-looking indigenous Indian mother with giggling youngsters huddled together under a sheet of plastic, sheltering from the pouring rain, as I headed for the South American Explorers Club. There I found a note from Martin, whom we had met on Iliniza, saying he and a couple of friends had tried to climb Chimborazo. The weather had been so bad it

232

had been impossible to make an attempt, or even to think about setting off... Hmm... Have faith, girl... Faith...

A new phone had been put in at the club, for which I was able to buy international phone cards. Wonderful, here was a nearly self-controlling system at last. I tried both Paul and Uri repeatedly and unsuccessfully for fifteen minutes. Finally, I got through to Uri. 'Hi,' came his characteristically intense voice. 'I've just been speaking to Paul for the last quarter of an hour.' Wow! Was that synchronicity or what? Why, I wondered, did I ever doubt that Uri would know the exact moment when we were to stand on the point furthest from the centre of the Earth and place his things in the snow. Who needs telephones?

The discussion with Michael was not so easy. He was intensely focused on the natural world, passionately believing that it should be left as undisturbed as possible. He was a practitioner of Jainism, which is deeply embedded with the conviction that all life is sacred, so he felt it was not right to desecrate the top of a mountain by leaving anything there at all. As he was planning to come to the summit with us to film, I showed him the crystal. He dismissed it. I recoiled, as though part of me had been rejected, and regretted letting him touch it. This actually helped all of us to look closely at what we were doing. On reflection, we realised we believed strongly that to leave the crystal and other things buried in the snow, and the prayer flags, in keeping with age-old Tibetan tradition, was indeed the right thing to do. Because it was in tune with our belief systems, it was OK. Just as it was OK for Michael to think otherwise. We would agree to differ on this point, but I felt uneasy about it. Michael's ideas on the ecology of sacred space led him to believe any sort of human intervention was somehow inappropriate. But he did not dwell on it. There were more important issues to address, not least of which was the job of raising awareness for Tibet and expressing non-violence to assist world peace, the very essence of the project, and upon which we all concurred. 'Gee! My Gaad, it's gonna be amazing!' Michael concluded.

By now it was evening and we were treated to a lovely meal at El Magic Bean by Robert. We ate all the vegetables and beans our bodies could take, and filled our minds with US news. Clinton had been saying that to make friends with the Chinese was to make the world a safer place. Then at least the human rights problem and the nuclear threat could be aired.

'There are lots of Chinese nuclear missile bases in Tibet, which is hardly publicised...as well as dumps of toxic nuclear waste,' said Mig, emphatically. 'I have to believe that Tibet will be free one day, and then things will change. You know, a lot of my relatives and other Tibetans back in refugee settlements wake up early every day around five to listen to the Voice of America, which is broadcast in Tibetan, and they have so much hope... Their first priority is survival but they're so interested to hear any new news about Tibet... And the news inside Tibet is not at all good at the moment – the situation is just getting worse.'

Hope springs eternal, a distant feeling, like a flush of greenness when all that can be seen is brown winter branches, clothes that can be changed in the unending wheel of the seasons.

'Are there a lot of tears in Tibetan people's eyes?'

'Oh, yes, the situation is so saddening...but I keep telling them whenever I go back that we have a lot of support from the West... We have a lot of great organisations working with us towards our main goal, you know. But I don't suppose Clinton's visit will make much difference...'

'What will?'

'At the end of the day, this is my feeling: I don't think anything can set Tibet free, apart from the Chinese people.'

So we returned to the hostel pondering how we might reach

the Chinese people and touch their hearts. The Dalai Lama says the only way forward is with brotherhood, friendship and compassion. His shining example is like a star in the world and, as Gandhi had pointed out, the Chinese people can be thanked for exposing this light. We need to show appreciation, and work with them, not against them... The computer revolution means that, in theory, loving words can caress every human being in the twinkling of an eye. We can write our peace messages inspired by the Dalai Lama's ideals onto the worldwide web. If we can reach the point furthest from the centre of the Earth, then maybe that will draw attention to them, and maybe people will read them... Maybe, in spite of the restrictions, even some Chinese... If we can make it to that point...

The stresses of the day had left us tired and out of energy. Still, typically, it seemed to take Pete about five minutes to pack and go to sleep, and me the next three hours. Oh no, I thought. I am not only pathetically slow and tentative at climbing up and coming down, but also *so* slow at getting ready. Pete was always telling me that speed is safety... My weary mind was struggling with irrational worries and bogged down on what to take. Using the plastic bag method of compartmentalisation, everything had to be retrievable without having to tip up the rucksack. Climbing gear in one; wanted on climb; wanted at hut; summit things; peace messages; personal stuff that a girl needs on a mountain (face cream, eye makeup, hair-ties, spare underwear, notes from children, torn-in-half-to-save-weight books). Emergency food had to go in pockets... Keep an eye on the fact that everything has to be hauled up to the hut... Too often I come home from a mountain and discover I have carried up and down extraneous stuff like a pad of paper, a tube of toothpaste, old socks, old rocks, half a dozen lip salves or the next-door neighbour's keys.

But to prepare is to set the expectation free...

23 : To the Watchtower

The Americans were greeted at dawn on 4 July with our flurry of stuffing in breakfast, packing everything to vacate our rooms and stowing luggage in the cellar. For some unknown reason I was always able to quote the 1776 declaration:

> 'We, the representatives of the United States in Congress, assembled appealing to the supreme judge of the world for the rectitude of our intentions, solemnly publish and declare that we are and ought of right to be free and independent states.'

It was a good thought that today they would be championing the freedom of the Tibetan nation. Freedom from oppression would do for starters.

This morning I felt much better about having an extended team. The excitement of setting off on the adventure drove the adrenaline, and I enjoyed the sense of group-belonging and intent as we piled all our gear into a twenty-seater, not-falling-to-bits bus. This is it, I thought.

'Oh, guys,' called Michael, 'please take all your heavy gear off and put it back on again so that we can film it.'

Well, I enjoyed most aspects of it.

A handsome, smartly-dressed Ecuadorian seemed to be hovering around to wish us well on our journey... Wow! It was Gustavo, without his hat on. We all felt really sorry he was not coming with us, and presented him with a 'Climb For Tibet' T-shirt, with which he waved us goodbye.

Our luxury vehicle, with space and comfort and filming equipment, set us apart from the rough and tumble of the city. We were once again outsiders looking in. Maybe that is what making a film entails, but I felt slightly uneasy. Nevertheless, it was nice to be taken and not have to decipher the language and rush about any more. I could write up my diary, sort out peace messages and relax into my own mind.

I knew there was wider input which I did not understand, that we were being spiritually guided, and that we each had our own part to play. I tried to be open, knowing that was important. The crystal helped me. I clasped it tightly in my hand, feeling the power and sense of purpose it held. I was going to miss it. It had been with me constantly, in my pocket since the first couple of days, giving me comfort and strength, even though I knew it was not mine. I had simply been its guardian for a while. It had been entrusted to me...

'Oh special crystal, thank you for coming into our lives and touching them with wonder. We honour the important potential of your work. We express love for you and what you represent...' I am shown on the screen of my mind a hole in the snow, about the

*depth of an ice axe handle, and in it the position of the six-sided
shiny crystal end, pointing up...and out into the universe...*

'Wow! Oh gosh, what a stunning location!' I was brought back to
awareness by Michael's raptures over the filming opportunities.
There were lovely sights in all directions that made him want to
stop at every corner – beauty in the lusciousness and patterns of
the Earth, geological formations long-sculpted by wind, rain and
sun. But he was worried about the weather. It was distinctly grey
and drizzly – conditions bad for both filming and climbing.

'You'll see. It'll be perfect for us. It's been organised,' I said,
totally sure that all would indeed be well.

'Look over there! Look at that!' shouted Mig, right on cue. 'You
know, that's such a good omen.' Following his gaze to the west, we
saw the two peaks of Iliniza, momentarily cleared of cloud, with
the sun picking out the gleaming snow on the southern summit.
Reaching skywards as though directing us on our way was the arc
of a double rainbow...

Omens are important to a Tibetan. The Dalai Lama speaks of
an earthquake and the dramatic sign of a comet crossing a blood
red sky in 1949 at the time of the invasion by the Chinese army.
If natural systems are viewed separately from the workings of the
mind and spirit of mankind, then such omens make no sense. If,
however, all living things are viewed as an interconnected part
of one entity, then it is understandable that the weather should
respond to forces given out and needs may be met or disasters
unfold.

To our east passed Pasochoa. Behind was Cotopaxi, decked in cloud. I was quite pleased we could not see her. Somehow, I did not want the wrong mountain to look beautiful today. Mateus, who was the only one of the crew who could speak English, told us that apparently this season there was a very tricky final bit to the summit of Cotopaxi. The climb carried a sting in its tail in the form of a difficult crevasse that had opened up and required a swinging ladder to cross it. So, we had been spared that trial. We also learned that there had been an accident only the day before on Pichincha, even with Safari guides to hand. I hoped we had done the right thing by having guides. Here we were, setting out on our long-planned venture, about to be joined by two guides we did not know at all. Please, please, may they be sensitive to what we are doing, I prayed.

We passed along the fine palm-treed avenues of the valley holding Ambato, but this time climbed out heading west to approach Chimborazo from the other side. The Andes proudly displayed full colours for us. Magentas, purples and browns blended with sky tones caught on distant horizons. Deep forest green clung to the heights. Patchwork slopes blanketed almost unbelievable steepness with pale gold, lime and jade, while looking down on silver mists blowing like forgotten summer gossamer. The little plots providing food for a people's survival were scattered with lone trees clinging at jaunty angles as though for the fun of it. We took in the staggering beauty of the show and the immensity of the landscape, rolling and playing with our eyes. This was special magic, for we were entering the realm of the Watchtower of the Universe. Our mountain was guarded by some of the most stunning scenery on Earth. How privileged we were to be here.

We stopped to be greeted on the side of the road by a little biscuit-coloured mother donkey with a suckling foal. Thick, furry coats told their own tale of how conditions must often be. We were watched by a young man with a forked stick making stacks out of tall, cut grasses, helped by his pretty wife. In typical fashion, she wore a bowler hat over black, braided hair, and carried a little pink-bonneted baby. Two more shy, barefooted youngsters clung to her long skirts and peered at the frightening crowd of foreigners that we were. They were Quechuan Indians, direct descendants of the Inca. This was their land. We were trespassing, though we came in peace. Can the awful massacres by the foreigners of their history be forgotten? Can anything atone for it? We gave them a handful of money and a mass of cameras took their pictures, leaving them to the backbreaking work, the cold wind, the harsh struggle to grow the food they all needed and the simple joy in their friendship with the Earth.

As the road climbed, so did the excitement in the bus. It reverberated from seat to seat, rising to a crescendo as a huge mass of cloud appeared to our left, like the cloak of a high priest waiting for the sacrament to begin. We turned south off the paved road onto dirt. Now olive-grey dust blew up from the wheels of the bus in football-pitch-sized clouds, playing with our panorama. We knew we were so close. We could feel the presence – immense and powerful. My heart beat faster, partly in fear, partly in anticipation. Closer... Closer... Keep calm... Keep calm... After all, we had already made friends and prepared the way. All was as it should be. There was a job to do and...

'I see it!' shouted Mig, eagerly rushing up and down the bus. 'Look! Wow! It's steeper than Cotopaxi.' Across the near-barren sandy plain, interspersed with small shrubby olive-green vegetation, cloud was shifting and swirling, partially revealing the imposing white-topped mountain – our Chimborazo.

'Are you sure you want to do this?' grinned Michael. 'Hey, you guys, there's snow up there – a lot of it. Oh! Oh my Gaad! We need to stop and get a shot of the whole thing.'

Outside I greeted the mighty Watchtower, then glanced around. Pete, looking full of confidence and keen to get at it, was pointing out the route. 'Yeah, both huts are situated over that lump, and the line is more or less on a slant coming from that tongue of the glacier, right to left and up to where you see there's a rock triangle and then a rock band. The line comes through where the snow band is and comes up on to that left-hand ridge, which you take to the lower summit at 6,260. The higher summit that we want, at 6,310, is over the back by about a kilometre.'

'Welcome Chimborazo! We're here! We're here!' I couldn't contain my excitement any longer. 'We're going to be there! We're going to be there!'

GT was smiling as though he'd just conducted the best symphony of his life. 'It's wondrously impressive... It looks absolutely staggering.' He was caught up in sheer delight with everything that was happening.

Michael was dancing around, as I am sure all good film directors do, enthusiastically asking the crew to take every view in sight – the mountain, the climbers, the desert, the sky, even a group of vicuñas eating lichens that gave the illusion of lush meadows. 'Mig, what do you think? Are you scared at all?'

'No, to be honest, but I am sure it's going to be tough. I can definitely see myself struggling. I mean, it's looking more and more difficult, the more we see. The biggest thing is, I've got to reach the top...and complete my dreams.' I had to admire his courage. He really had little idea of what lay ahead, but he was determined to put himself in one hundred per cent, and I felt sure that, because of this, all would flow well for him.

'Tess,' Michael turned to me, 'what if you don't make the summit?'

I stared at him. He's obviously a great director, yes, he wears a cap bearing the word *ahimsa* (Sanskrit for non-violence), he's even sporting the obligatory pigtail…but to suggest not making it…? He probably did not believe me when I said, 'I've not really considered that.'

'But you must have…'

'No,' I replied simply. 'We're going to make it.' I wondered if he could smell the conflict in my heart as the fear attacked the excitement, as easily as I could smell the dust in the air. Having such a big team meant lots more support and less need to be frightened. There was a wonderful bond and commonality of purpose, but in a way the fear also isolated me, even from Pete. There were times when I felt I was standing alone because of it. I did not feel anyone else was afraid. I knew GT was worried about his acclimatisation, but that was all. Only I could face my own fear. It was a very personal thing. I suppose if I had been able to stand there shaking I would have scored big hugs and it might have gone away, but it was stiff upper lip, keep the lid on, lots to do… I needed time to myself to sort it, but that looked unlikely, so I pushed it down somewhere…to hide.

24 : Blessing

There was no let up to the desert. The dry plain stretched to the horizon in three directions. A few straggly grasses and sandblasted bushes hung on in the ubiquitous wilderness as we turned northeast through jostling cloud to join the zigzag route, which Pete and I had taken only two weeks before. It had been just a short moment in time, but now our bodies were better prepared and we came with our own army... The bus laboured under the strain of the steep slope, the dust and the rocks as it carried us into the great enveloping aura of Chimborazo.

At the Carrel hut the wind was cold but not fierce, the air was thin but not razor-sharp. Turning away from the mêlée of unloading people and equipment, I looked back down the way we had come and watched with awe an amazing sight. A huge covering of mist was tumbling and turning, billowing and rolling back, revealing the bed of grey desert sand. It was like the parting of the Red Sea. It was an auspicious sign... I knew, I just knew, that this was the beginning of our own perfect weather system. The chance of getting four days of good weather was very slight indeed, but so was the chance of a peace climb in the Andes happening on the Dalai Lama's birthday. All was well. A welcome had been extended to us.

The smiley warden, Antonio, greeted us with hugs. Sadly, he would not be coming up to the top hut, but he had arranged for a man with two skinny mules to ferry equipment. This was brilliant for all the food, the extra fuel for the generator to keep the camera batteries going, and also the gear of the unacclimatised bodies. The rest of us shouldered our heavy rucksacks and started plodding. Mig and GT slung a heavy rope apiece on top of their sacks, and Pete, with the group hardware, also carried my second sack on top of his. (Yes, even though this was 1998, it was wonderful being a cared-for female in a man's world.) Michael marched up alongside us, astoundingly, with a huge load and running a camera. Pete answered my surprised gaze with, 'He's stuffed himself full of Diamox. Let's hope he can keep it up.'

Scattered gravestones warned us of the impending memorial pyramid for the French climbers. It was a grim reminder. I had recently read the account of a mountaineer who had reached the place where the 1993 avalanche had struck, a steep slope just below the Veintimilla summit. There had been similar conditions to those during the disaster – fifty centimetres of fresh snow and strong sunshine. He had decided to turn back and had met a German guide who had suffered serious face injuries from a rockfall. Where was this rockfall area? Which ridge had the avalanche been on? From here we could not see the whole of the southwest face – just a large gap in the cloud, from whence shone a white light so bright it seemed like a peephole into heaven... Mesmerised, I sensed a strange glow of joy and a stirring of my heart. Maybe we'll find something special up there... At that moment, though, it looked completely unattainable – an altar too sacred to approach.

The gravestones had a sobering effect on Mig. 'Whoa! This is serious, isn't it?' It was the first time it had really hit him. He rushed on up to the Whymper hut at the elevation of 5,000 metres, scrunching heavy boots on the grey and brick-red volcanic track, clattering loose rocks as he went. I noticed from behind that he carried a second smaller stick on his sack alongside his special one. I did not have to ask what it was for...

Michael was full of admiration. 'Nobody goes at that speed at this altitude. He was positively running.'

What we did not know was that he had been told it was important to show respect to the spirit of the mountain, and he wanted to reach the hut quickly to do Tibetan prostrations, face down in the dirt in deference towards the revered heights. Then he would feel protected.

We moved on, conscious of the fast-approaching dusk. It must have been close to 6 pm. We wanted to do a blessing ceremony before the daylight died. As we approached the hut, a veil of magic seemed to have been drawn across our path. The peephole enlarged and we could see the entire Veintimilla summit shining for us, staggeringly, brilliantly, heralding the presence of the true summit hidden behind. The moment of our arrival and greeting had been timed impeccably, as though by divine guidance... Mig and I set up the Tibetan flag to the west of the hut, Pete and Michael manned the cameras.

The warm pink-brown rocks laid out a plush presentation carpet. There was an awesome physical silence charged with the gathering of energies that was taking place. An eerie mist, which was not a mist but more like phosphorescent ether, assembled around the top snows of the magnificent peak that glowed just like a light in a dream. Michael commented that in all his years as a film director he had never seen anything like it. It was unearthly. It was a melding of energies, like an emotive *haka* in preparation for a rugby match. It was a touching of souls. We, as climbers, coming before this highest of mountains, arising to the furthest point of our Earth, a summit so sanctified that most of the world knew little about it.

> *Oh, Great Chimborazo, Watchtower of the Universe, we greet you and humbly ask for permission to climb to your sacred summit. We ask for strength. We ask for oxygen. We ask for safety in our return. We climb as an expression of the light of Tibet, that the Earth may find peace.*

'OM MANI PADME HUM,' we prayed and Pete, GT, Mig and I, a warm, close team, stood with our hands in the air, together around the flag. The light fell from the mountain... And it was done – the hearts of our own guardian angels had resonated with the heart of the angel of the mountain. We knew not what was yet to come, but no amount of foreboding could take away the fact that we had been accepted and blessed.

Turning, I glanced downwards, only to be reminded of our altitude – as if there were any chance of forgetting, as if the lungs could forget. Under a paling, pink-tinged sky, the whole world was covered, past the cotton-wool horizon, with billions of churning, buffeting, white-horse clouds on a wild, unending sea. Only we were above it, only we were privileged to fly as if on the magic carpet of this lucid dream.

25 : A day on the edge

It felt good to be at the hut again. I loved the salmon-pink exterior and the solid feeling of shelter and safety. It was like an old friend. We settled into the long bunk room in the eves, laying out our sleeping bags and hanging up all the stuff like harnesses, helmets, ropes and penguins. There were a few other climbers around, to whom we chatted, and from whom we collected peace messages.

Eventually the mules arrived with the food, and Oswaldo was able to produce an excellent meal of soup and pasta for those of us who didn't feel like throwing it back up again. Eager and excited faces could be seen in the flickering candle light at the old wooden tables, which felt reassuringly real to the touch. We were joined by the mule driver, an indigenous Indian with a bright-red poncho and a battered hat covering most of his face. He stared, with a rather sad and bemused expression, at our peculiar foreign antics, such as filming everything in the dark, trying to filter perfectly good glacial water, and adding butter and salt to tea. With him was his eleven-year-old son, who clung to him silently.

'You'll never guess what I've discovered happened here today,' Said GT, obviously thrilled. 'The most wondrous and amazing thing: a baby was born.'

'Here?' I could think of a hundred thousand better places to have a baby.

'Yes. It was the mule driver's wife, apparently. Isn't that a beautiful symbol of renewal and rebirth to set the scene for our peace messages?'

Wow! Incredible... Maybe, I thought, that's the highest baby ever born, but then I remembered the Tibetan refugees...

We toasted the mule driver with lukewarm drinks in little plastic cups. He did not seem to be very happy. Such is life at 5,000 metres.

'So,' asked Michael, 'what do we reckon? Any danger of avalanches?'

'No, I don't think so,' replied Pete. 'In the Alps we have a risk of one to five. I would put it at less than two here. What we could see looked very glazed tonight. So it looks pretty good. Anything in the way of snow is going to be quite hard névé.'

'I would agree,' came in GT. 'I thought it looked very unlikely, and I didn't think the lower ice looked terribly problematical. I may eat my words but it looks fairly straightforward.'

'Yeah,' went on Pete, 'the only danger would perhaps be on the way down, when the snow gets soft in the afternoon.'

'Well, it's the unknowns that bother me,' I said. 'We don't know how steep it is. We don't know how we're going to react. We don't know how well acclimatised we are.'

'One of us does,' said GT.

'Two of us do,' joined in Michael. (It was amazing, really, that he was still vertical.) 'What about you, Mig?'

'Well, the closer we get the steeper it looks, and the more, what do you call it...risk-taking.'

'Terrifying perhaps?' suggested Michael.

'Yeah, but it's all such a new experience for me. I've never climbed on deep snow before. It's gotta be a belief in myself. There's no going back – in spite of problems like painful feet.' I knew, too, that he was battling an intense and severe headache behind his left ear and temple that would not go away. 'But then I think of the Tibetan refugees, thousands of them, trying to escape every year across the Himalayas, taking the risk with their lives... I mean, for us, we have all the equipment...' His father and heavily pregnant mother had escaped in this way in 1959. I knew his mother was worried by his mountain-climbing and protesting and had told him: 'Please, Migmar...cling to life.' But Mig was a fighter, as even his name portrays.

Names in Tibetan, commonly given by a high lama, are nearly always significant, such as Kunga – 'loved by all' – or Rangdrol – 'the self-liberated.' Sometimes they indicate character, such as Tagzhim – 'ferocious at home but timid outside' – or have purpose, such as to ward off evil spirits – Khyikyag (useful, but unfortunately also meaning 'dog-shit'). Migmar means 'Tuesday,' but as each day of the week is also ascribed to a heavenly body, it is associated with Mars – the planet of the warrior.

Migmar would always be the first if something needed doing for Tibet – within the constraints of the Dalai Lama's non-violence policy. I wondered how it would feel if my own land were threatened. My father used to say that fighting for your country brings out the best in you. Maybe it was a bit like mountaineering, when survival is at stake and you can't pretend to be anything you're not, and have to dig deep and find yourself; when you are forced into action, because doing nothing is not an option.

Now we had to try to sleep, but the dormitory was wildly busy. The Americans, with so little acclimatisation time, were suffering dangerous altitude sickness with vomiting, headaches and heart and breathing problems. Bettina seemed the worst hit, though Robert, trying to help, felt so lousy he could barely move. Various remedies were produced. The one that gave Bettina the most relief was Mig's Tibetan healing herbs, rolled into tiny burgundy-coloured balls known as *mhintro*. These are usually taken to help clear the system. Mig let me try them. They were bitter to the tongue, but gave warmth to the heart, for they were special. They had been blessed by the Dalai Lama. However, both Bettina and Robert knew the only safe answer for them was to go back down immediately it was daylight. Michael took still more Diamox, which helped him, and he eventually set off to walk across to the glacier in the dark. He was confronted by the prowling of a lone Andean wolf, looking for scraps. What else could there possibly be to eat? – unless climbers were on the menu. This barren land was completely devoid of plant and animal life.

I lay and listened to the howl of the wind rising and falling with crashings and distant rumblings, to the accompaniment of snorings, loo trips and gaspings for breath. For a time I felt as bad as I had when we had been here before, with extreme nausea, headache and the shakes. Thankfully it passed, but in spite of a hot bottle of water, Yannick to cuddle and Pete sleeping comfortingly beside me, I felt cold. It was more a cold from the inside. I tried to talk to the fear that was there. I was not really sure specifically what I was afraid of. It was a sort of Garden of Gethsemane feeling, a knowledge that there was a deep, dark, inky-black river that had to be gone through. After what seemed like hours of searching I finally found the point where I knew that all was well and I opened up with joy to the light and strength all around. The Council of Masters was there, with the star. What strength! – Wow! I became really warm.

The calm, cold light of the dawn of 5 July found us enjoying Oswaldo's breakfast mix of apples and bananas in yoghurt. Everyone looked bleary-eyed. Nobody had had much sleep. Only the four climbers looked in any fit state at all. The others were fighting severe nausea, dizziness, headaches and breathlessness. It seemed that in the planning to make a documentary, no account had been able to be taken of the time necessary to acclimatise. But the good-natured crew manfully struggled on, and came out to film us building our two stupas.

As we scrambled gently up behind the hut, our eyes were naturally drawn west, scrutinising the route we would be taking later on. It looked bleak and inhospitable. We could see three little figures with rucksacks making their way down steep ice painfully slowly. Somewhere up there in the frozen dark of night they had turned back. At the moment the southwest face was clear, but the visibility was not good. It was hard to make out the boundary between mountain and sky. There was no sunshine – just a flat, grey, lifeless chill.

Then, suddenly there was noise... What was it? It approached, coming nearer and nearer. Was it music? Over the brow of the track to the lower hut, came snaking along a procession full of beauty and colour. A crowd of maybe twenty-five; women dressed in bright-red shawls, long skirts and hats; men playing panpipes and flutes. At the back marched the drummer, leading a dancing, rhythmical beat. There was an air of celebration and gaiety. They stopped to drink from a glacial melt-water stream, and then, keeping to the chocolate-brown rocks, away from the snow and ice, gradually worked their way up to the highest possible edge of the hanging glacier to sing and pray. To our horror we realised they were close to the place where we could just make out some huge ice seracs had fallen in the night. From here, they looked insignificant, but we knew that up there they could swallow the whole party in the speed of a thought. However, the Inca descendants had total trust in their Watchtower of the Universe, whom they affectionately nicknamed Tayta, (meaning 'father' in their Quechuan native tongue). This mountain was their link between heaven and earth, the union of the spiritual and physical forces. Amazingly this was no different from the beautiful harmony and balance of the six-pointed star. I marvelled that this pilgrimage should coincide with ours. The draw of the might and power of Chimborazo was strong indeed.

To see such casualness in ascent was disconcerting as we struggled for breath and every movement was an effort. But our sense of commitment and purpose kept us together. We set to work conducting two stupa ceremonies. The stupa that Pete and I had built on our previous trip stood sentinel at the gateway as we repeated the process twice, forming a triangle, but with the soul energy input of all four of us. We read the Kuan Yin prayers of compassion, the Chinese words coming from Mig a little tentatively and from GT flamboyantly (in an Italian accent).

Each was rolled into a scroll, tied with pink ribbon, placed in a plastic bag and surrounded with a mindful construction of rocks. Then, in activation, we spoke peace messages, more peace messages, and still more peace messages... Powerful...moving...touching...and wondrous in their coming together in love for the Earth and Tibet. The way had been prepared. All was ready. Later our boots would pass through this gateway at the start of the climb, and we would know that these lights of compassion were shining forth to seek eternal healing.

Following the much-discussed plan for the day, we returned to the hut for a meal of soup and rice and the eagerly awaited arrival of the guides. Somewhere along the line there had been changes. So it was Pepé instead of Ramiro who had been given to us, and he and Fernando who walked in to join us as part of the 'Climb For Tibet' team that afternoon. They were both in their late twenties and typically nice-looking, sun-bronzed and friendly. Pepé was the spokesman, confident, intelligent and definite, with easily understandable English. We all immediately felt good about him.

'We have a lot of motivation for this climb,' he told us. 'When I read your papers I know it has something for the big mountains in the world and this is the contact with the Dalai Lama. The birthday of him is interesting, and also because it's a climb for the peace of the world. This is completely interesting for this reason.'

'How long will the climb take, do you think?'

'For me, the weather is completely clear, so we will walk between seven until ten hours today for the summit. It's definitely not windy. The conditions are very good.'

Fernando then spoke in Spanish and Mateus translated: 'He says it's a very special thing for them to climb with all these people and they will do their best to help them get to the top. For him, most of the highest mountains are in Tibet, and he likes it a lot, because it's like a dream for all the climbers and it's something special to be together here climbing for the same reason.'

Happily, wonderfully understanding guides had been organised, (though I could not quite relate to the word 'walk'). But there was something about Pepé that bothered me and I could not quite put my finger on it. He spoke in a really quick way, with a sort of hard, twangy, singsongy accent that reminded me of something. I was not sure what it was.

The plans were laid. We would sleep from 3 to 9 pm, eat breakfast and leave at 10 pm. We would take the Direct route up the Thielman glacier tongue, turn west up the steep ice ramp, and thread through the crevassed area, traversing to join the Normal route above the Castillo rocky outcrop. We would then follow up the southwest ridge to the Veintimilla and hence across to dawn on the summit around 6 am. We should arrive back at the hut well before 10 am, safely ahead of the snow becoming soft.

Michael would not be coming. It was very disappointing. He told us that he instinctively knew to forgo the ordeal and dangers, as his body was not sufficiently acclimatised, nor recovered from months of exhausting work. Also, his hired crampons and axe were not up to scratch. He would shoot from low on the ice.

So the teams were split, with Pete and myself in one, and GT and Mig in the other. This would be well-balanced, with experience and strength in each. Pepé, as the most experienced and English-speaking guide, would take GT and Mig, so Mig would have the most help possible. Pete and I would go with Fernando, as my Spanish was the least bad. We would be, as Mig pointed out, with a typical eye on the broader picture of life's metaphysical manifestations, six people representing the six points of the star.

Sleep was not going to come easily at three in the afternoon when the whole focus of life was rolled into this one day.

First there was the meticulous packing of the rucksacks.

Nothing important could be left out, as it might mean the difference between the summit or not, or, worse still, life or death. My problem was usually too much stuff: 'I think I'll take just one more jacket...'

'You haven't got any books in there, have you?' asked Pete, looking suspiciously at my sack. No, but I did agonise over whether to take Yannick or a spare ice-screw. Luckily, Yannick won. Accessibility of things was also important. If something was not easy to get at, it was not worth taking. So packets of guarana and coca, lip salves, penknives and nibbles such as dried apricots, nuts and seeds had to be in outside pockets. Camera with lots of spare film and water bottle had to be in the top of the sack. Searching and scrabbling around in the bottom of a large sack while balancing in the dark on a knife-edge ridge with companions waiting for you is not recommended. Today, though...today was unique and special and there were things more important...the precious things-for-the-summit bag, peace messages, little tape recorder, and, of course, the crystal. I made sure Mig had the prayer flags, which he had especially brought from India, and I gave him the Tibetan flag and two pictures to carry. One was of the Dalai Lama, the other of the young Panchen Lama, the second highest lama in Tibet, who had been kidnapped by the Chinese at the age of six in 1995. Then Pete checked through Mig's climbing kit and reminded him to take double water rations.

I lay trying to sleep, knowing it was impossible, worrying about what I had not packed. Anyway, how could I fall asleep with the point furthest from the centre of the Earth, the Watchtower of the Universe, the Great Inca God Chimborazo, waiting for our supplications... I knew I should drink all the water that I possibly could, but this eventually meant creeping up without disturbing the others, carefully negotiating the ladder, forcing boots on, heading out into the icy cold and finding the loo. This was sharing quarters with the noisy, fume-ridded generator, which was working overtime for the camera batteries, and was a sleep preventer in its own right. My headache worsened. Once outside, however, even without my contact lenses, I was able to take in a beautiful moonlit sky with an enigmatic glow coming from the direction of the Veintimilla. My thoughts were with the Inca Indian procession. Did they make the journey down safely?

For the six hours I waited, tossing and turning and envious of those snoring. Four times I heard the wind mount, stronger and stronger to wild gale force and then become stayed – as though by an unseen hand.

The 9 pm alarm call heralded, in readiness, a completely still and star-struck night.

26 : On the ascent

Could a day start the evening before? Well, with no sleep, I guess it had started twelve hours earlier. Or perhaps this day had started six months ago, when Pete and I had launched 'Climb For Tibet' – a dream which spoke of sorrow and pain, and showed a way forward in brotherhood and peace, a dream of changing the consciousness of the world. No, this day had started long before that, when I had put Chimborazo and Tibet together and said, 'OK, Tibet's people are too precious to lose, they are part of us, they are part of the Earth. They are like an almost extinct species. They need help, protection and love. We can learn from them. Their advanced spiritual knowledge can surely inspire and help humanity...' Maybe it had started at the moment my heart was touched by the Earth's cry for help...for we are destroying our own mother. Little children tell us they love the Earth. It is so simple, but we do not listen and carry on in greed... Or had it

been when I felt that pain in my heart for the Tibetan people...
perhaps carried through lifetimes with distant brown memories
of corridors of meditation... Anyway... anyhow...this day, to
express the highest ideals that there are, from the highest point
that there is, had finally come...

I arose lethargically, nursing a throbbing headache and sick
breathlessness. I desperately wanted to have had some sleep. I
would have liked to have had a hug with Pete, just a second of
closeness together that said 'keep safe, go well...' But somehow
that did not happen. Michael instructed us all to go back into
bed to be filmed getting up. That put me into an even blacker
mood of grumpiness. I had suffered the noise and fumes of the
generator for the past few hours. At least, I thought, that means
we will be able to have some lighting. The crew now decided to
turn it off as it upset the audio – but at the exact moment when
I needed some light to put in my contact lenses. I struggled in the
half-dark with my head torch, even angrier. That was when they
decided to interview us and start filming.

'Tess, what's the major thought going through your mind right
now?' asked Michael.

Was that before or after I had throttled him? Close to tears, I
told him I felt lousy.

'It's just nerves.'

Yeah... right. I was not good company. The stress of any climb
was enough, let alone this one. Being interviewed was definitely
not part of my preparation game-plan. I swallowed some capsules
of guarana that made me feel a little better, but I felt so sick I could
not force down much breakfast – just a spoonful or two of the
fruit yoghurt and a mouthful of granola. I would have preferred
my organic oats but it was too much effort to find them. I felt like
throwing up. Nerves...well, maybe, but mostly it was because I
was annoyed. I had no inner peace. I was annoyed with the film

crew, but more than anything else I was annoyed with myself for feeling so lousy for something so important.

The others seemed to be coping rather better, and sang a rousing and surprisingly harmonious round of 'Happy Birthday dear Dalai Lama.'

'Long live the Dalai Lama!' cried Mig, and my spirits rose a little.

'How do you say "Happy Birthday" in Tibetan?'

'Good question,' laughed Mig. 'We don't really celebrate other birthdays, but we do have these blessed coloured strings, known as *jendu*, which I would like you all to wear around your necks. I've also got some for the guides. They were given to me by my mother and have been blessed by a high lama. I've been saving them up. We usually wear them when danger threatens, but they'll give you a clear climb up and down. Their main power lasts about three days, so when they drop off you must burn them.'

'Thank you Miggie.' I was thrilled, and would treasure the blessed string he had given me. I was beginning to find more calm. 'I'm so proud that you are climbing with us.'

He smiled. 'You know, I think this is one of the happiest days of my life.'

'Thank you, my friend,' beamed Pete, receiving his string.

'May all your wishes come true.'

'And yours, too.'

Lastly, Mig turned to GT. 'I say, old boy...'

'Thanks... We're doing this together, we are.'

'All the way to the top.'

'Yeah. I've set off on many nights like this, but I feel this is the most exciting thing I've ever done. It's unique in my experience.'

Pete concurred. 'I've been climbing for about thirty-seven years, and doing the serious big stuff since about '75. But this is different – it's not just climbing a mountain. It's so much more meaningful. It's being done for a super cause, and it's a tremendous physical challenge, as well. I think the big thing that's going to hit me when we reach the summit is the fact we've achieved something for world peace, and especially for the Tibetan cause. We've really come together as a team of four, and we've come through a lot and gradually bonded together. It'll be the culmination of a lot of hard work – and a big success story once we reach the summit.'

'Yeah,' said Mig. 'It's going to be great for the awareness. You know there's still a lot of people who don't know about Tibet… or who have forgotten… This climb means a lot to me. I'm doing it not only for Tibet, but also for the peace of the world… It's so important.' He was a young man giving out a strong positive feeling that he could take on any challenge the mountain could throw at him. He trusted. He was not fearful, or even worried about what lay ahead, even though he had not slept either, and could not release the continuous intense head pain.

'Well said. We'll be thinking of the planet as a whole, won't we?' affirmed GT. Although lacking the boldness of youth, he gave out a sense of sure understanding of the ways of a mountain and the finer resources that would have to be found today. 'The other nice thing is that quite a lot of people are climbing too, on this very same day, for the cause. Perhaps they can't get very high physically, but are going to the highest point they can, for our purpose and the Dalai Lama. That in itself is very exciting.'

'The fact that so many are supporting us from all over the world does make an enormous difference,' I agreed. 'Hundreds and hundreds have sent us their own messages and given money for the Tibetan refugees and the Tibetan cause. We're not alone, we've got everyone behind us, and that gives us a tremendous impetus to make it, to do it all for them. All these people who've given us their thoughts and their love for the Earth and for Tibet – we will not let them down.'

'Yeah,' continued Pete. 'There's going to be this great sort of bond around the world. That's got to be really powerful...'

'Doesn't sound much like the usual the-reason-I-climb-is-to-get-to-the-top,' probed Michael.

'I think it's a lot more to do with learning about yourself,' I suggested. 'You push out your limits and go through fear, and you open up to clear thinking, which you don't get down below. You get a spiritual high, everything seems right and you find the answers to things. You're really living when you're climbing a mountain. You don't get many chances in life to rely on your companions to the extent that your lives depend on each other. You learn a lot very quickly.'

Sometimes prophetic words go by unnoticed...

'Enough talk. We've got a mountain to climb,' urged Pete. 'I just want to get up there and enjoy it. It looks good, it's a clear night. I just want to get to the summit and be on top of the world, with my three lovely friends...and the two guides, of course.'

Pepé had joined us and was quietly listening, looking fit and ready with a comforting air of confidence. With the interviews over, he checked we had sun-protection cream and water...and, yes, let's go. That was when it hit me. I knew what that strange feeling was that I had had earlier about him. A chill went through me. Oh, that was quite scary, for, fleetingly, a glance across his face and the way he spoke gave me the impression that...that he was Chinese. Don't be crazy, I told myself, but there it was again... the distinct sense of Chineseness. What awareness was I tuning

261

into…and in which time scale? Was it just my mind playing? No, it carried a taste of truth, but not in the present state…

Finding stuff in the dark… Over-trousers, inner boots, outer boots, gaiters, harness, waterproof, helmet, head torch, goggles, gloves, over-gloves… By the time I had everything on, and everyone had waited while I went to the loo yet again, I felt so bulky and awkward that I thought that I'd even have trouble waddling across a penguin colony… Yannick bobbed about in agreement, riding shotgun on the back of my rucksack.

A nearly full moon dominated the clear, deep black of the sky, shedding so much light that it blotted out the spangled touch of distant stardust, distracting us from the intense cold that bit sharply into our unmoving bodies. That was OK. It meant hard, safe snow. But we were not completely without cloud, for wispy diaphanous shapes danced on slivers of moon glint saying, 'this is all for fun…come and play…' while a tousled breeze caressed our faces. Where was the relentless wind now? Where were the savage skies? Flashes of lightning answered, far far beneath us, carving illumination through tumultuous storm cloud.

Mig picked up a little rock and licked it several times. 'Here, try it, Tess. My cousin, Sonam, who worked high in the Karakorum glaciers, told me that it helps you cope with altitude. It's because the stone belongs to the mountain, so is a way of connecting up at a vibrational level. It really works. It's to do with belief.' I tentatively tried while he carried out prostrations to the huge presence a thousand metres and more above us. I felt it looming over the little ants that were about to scurry across its buttress

slopes. Chimborazo... Oh great Chimborazo... We have come...
We hold dear your place in history... We walk in harmony with
your soul...

The silence was eerie, deep and awesome, as though it echoed
back the whole of space. There was no sound of a glacier wind,
no rockfall, no avalanche, no confusion from the world a long
way below. I heard just a throbbing heart with a crystal to guard
it. Then, around 10.30 pm, the jangle of man-made metal on
metal, clinking of karabiner on ice-screw, clank of descender on
karabiner, the brush of nylon waterproof on waterproof and the
crunch-thud of six pairs of boots...

We set off at a slow, easy pace. As we began to scramble up
the rocks, my mind jumped and juddered hither and thither.
Why did I have to feel so rotten? Would we be able to read the
messages? Where was the food I had stuffed in? How can I best
carry the over-gloves? My main problem was my eyes. I knew
that even the slightest wind brought dust into my contact lenses
and there was no means of taking them out to clean them safely
without losing them, and thus my eyesight. Sunglasses were too
dark, so I needed goggles, which would not fit properly over
my helmet with the head torch on as well. By holding my head
down at a certain angle I was able to maintain an uncomfortable
compromise, which was the start of a stiff neck which became
more and more painful as time progressed.

The gateway passed us by. Three silent monuments to
compassion, built to withstand the winds of time. May we
always open the gateway to compassion, I quickly prayed, but
my thoughts were needed in the physical to concentrate on the
irregular rocks over which we clambered.

Within half an hour we had reached the edge of the glacier
and the moon had disappeared behind cloud. The slope stretched
steeply away before us into the unknown. I focused on the present

moment. Sit on rock, crampons out of sack, point head torch at boot, fix on crampon, check safe and firm, test on the gravel-strewn névé ice on which we had stopped.

Then we roped up. Somehow the teams did not end up as planned. This change may have played a critical part in what was to unfold. I thought I heard Pepé say to Fernando in Spanish that he was going to take the *señora*, whom he had assessed as the weakest of the four. Thus it was that I found myself tied on to the rope behind Pepé, with Pete behind me, while GT was on Fernando's rope with Mig at the end.

I was actually very grateful. I felt unsteady and unsure, shaky and full of fear as we set off onto near-continuous steep ice at about 45°. I felt as though I had never been on crampons before. They felt ungainly and awkward. I could not stop thinking that just one little trip and it could endanger the lives of everyone. I could pull the three of us off. Every little thing needed to have one hundred per cent focus. I needed to control this fear. Pepé was wonderful. He gave me clear, simple instructions, which I followed to the letter.

Make sure the rope is just under tension. Keep the ten downward-facing points of the crampons on the ice. Climb up using the French method, that is, side-stepping up, but placing one foot over the other, which saves having to front-point, which is less safe and uses up calf muscles. Use one ski stick and the ice axe on the uphill side. Then, as we changed from a zig to a zag, he told me exactly when to change hands. Everyone had to wait as I changed over and sorted out the gloves, carefully and methodically. Every single step counted... Carefully... Steady... steady...

I felt I was going too slowly for Pete. He was so confident on ice... But I had to keep focused somehow. I tried to do affirmations... I am strong. I am safe... But it would not work. I could not afford the luxury of a mind that was not in total focus. Fleeting thoughts of alarm came. Were we below the menacing ice serac area? Was this the avalanche-prone bit? But I cast them aside. Please, Mind, do not wander... Looking up was uncomfortable, and anyway I was glad it was dark. I did not want to see the horrors of the steepness ahead. After a while I pushed up my goggles. If I kept my eyes down, the cold wind was just bearable. It improved the vision of the little pool of light in an ocean of blackness, an empty circle of cold white existence. I definitely did not want to look down while moving; therein lay terror. I tried very hard not to think of the going down. I needed to block it out, to be in the moment. It was too black to conceive. Ah...the gentle tug of the harness around my waist from the rope that connected me to Pete comforted my thoughts like a warm umbilical cord.

On and on through the timeless night... Extreme focus... Every step for humanity. The intense concentration forced me to find a rhythm, forced me to search for calm. It was truly a meditation. From time to time Pepé stopped, and then I looked down. It was so steep. I could feel the terror lurking just beneath the surface, but I knew I had faith, faith in Pepé, in the mountain, in Pete and in the spiritual and divine guidance of 'Climb For Tibet.' We could see the steady head-torch movement of the other three close behind us and Mig's little chemical light on the back of his sack. He and I had both decided we would carry the small amount of added weight to be able to shine extra light. We would get through this. We would. Because we were in front I had time to sneak some guarana capsules. I shovelled in all I could. I knew they were helping me. And I took coca pills whenever possible, although taking off gloves, reaching pockets and getting things out safely was not easy when concentrating on staying upright. Once when we were waiting for the others, GT shouted apologetically 'I'm sorry I'm so slow'. Slow? It was wonderful to have a stop for a couple of minutes. 'Of course you're not,' we shouted back.

Relentlessly the steepness continued. Somewhere we turned up the snow ramp into the long traverse, somewhere we must have passed through the crevassed area. Steadily, on and on and on... It was good not to have to worry about the route-finding but, I thought, probably Pete felt differently. Then, about three hours after we had started on the glacier, I detected a change in the energy coming up the rope behind me. I could feel Pete's weight gradually tugging. What was he up to? Here I was, stuck in the middle, with Pepé going the same pace, taking the rope ahead of me, but now I was getting pulled in two. Was all not well? Careful...careful... Don't trip... I tried to pull gently on the rope behind me to keep stable. Something must be wrong. I could not turn easily to shout down, but the dragging pulled me back and that caused Pepé to slow. Then, just as Pete was about to shout up the rope to stop, that was what we did. We were close to the southwest ridge at about 5,500 metres. There was a place where the gradient eased a little, and we could perch and take the weight off our feet for a while, despite the gathering wind.

'Are you OK?' I asked Pete, as he came up beside me.

'No.' He flopped down and sat with his head between his hands, breathing heavily. 'I feel really bad, Tess.'

I tried to comfort him. 'You'll get through it. Have a rest and by the time the others get here, you'll be fine. Keep going and all will be well. Come on, have something to eat.' I offered him apricots and nuts and Pepé offered him bread, but he just sat there shaking his head, feeling too sick to try, his breath coming in unnatural gulps. I was glad he drank water, but I was not too concerned, for I felt sure he would be all right soon. He always had such a positive outlook, and with all his strength and expectation, he would surely win the battle with altitude sickness. It would pass. Indeed, on Whymper's expedition it had also been the strongest who had suffered the most.

In a few minutes the others appeared. 'I'm too slow. I'm holding everyone up,' gasped GT.

'You're not. You're only about five minutes behind,' I insisted. Please don't be so negative, I thought. But he was not feeling at all well either. The altitude was attacking him unforgivingly. He was coughing and having real trouble breathing, with dizzy spells. He had been finding the going increasingly difficult and did not think he could give much more.

'How much further?' he asked. Hearing from Pepé that it was four hours to the Veintimilla, he knew then he could not do it. He had never had this feeling on a mountain before. Knowing that to keep going at all would mean a very much slower pace, which would seriously hold back the rest of the party, he selflessly said, 'I think it's right if I go down. It will give the team the best chance. Is this the most suitable place to turn around?'

No, no... We were all going to get there together... Please... This could not be happening. At that moment I could not guess at the enormity of his sacrifice. The climb meant so much to him...

We were now in an awkward situation. Pepé pointed out that if GT went down with Fernando while the rest of us went on as a rope of four, if subsequently someone else needed to go back, then the whole team would have to turn. I looked at Pete... I could see he had been influenced by Pepé's comments and was considering the only alternative... I did not want it to be a reality... Please, Pete. No. How can you let go? All that we have worked for together for so long, so much planning and drive, creation of the whole project, dedication, training, pushing everyone else... Please... No... No...

Pete was good at making decisions. GT's resolve had watered the seeds of his doubt. He did not flinch at the agony. Having been a mountain instructor for so many years he knew the safety aspect was the most important consideration. He felt he should be in control of himself on a mountain, enjoying the climbing, not being dragged up. He knew he was losing energy and having trouble breathing. He knew his body was not coping with the altitude and that it would become worse – a lot worse. This would put pressure on the team. He had been in the risk-assessment business for thirty years and now, now he would not jeopardise everyone else's safety. Mig and I seemed to be going all right. If he went down with GT it would give us a better chance.

'Tess,' he said, 'I am not prepared to die for this. There are other things in life. I have my children to support and I'm not going to chuck it all away.' There was good reason for his attitude. Ten years ago, while climbing on Helvelyn, he had watched his close friend Mark, an experienced climber, slip and fall to his death.

Pete was going to have to climb the biggest mountain of his life – that of turning back. The condor would fly no higher.

Should unconditional love be this painful? I was not sure I could give in this magnanimous way. Both men were stronger than I. Maybe the Incas were right about the honour of the sacrifice on the mountain.

Pete and Mig exchanged places on the ropes and I retied the knot to Mig's harness until I was happy with it. With great presence of mind Pete thrust the video camera at us.

'I'm sorry, Tess,' he said, a haunting voice in my ear...turned.... and then they were gone.

One warm tear just escaped onto a shivery cheek.

'I love you,' I shouted down the mountain into the abyss between tomorrow and eternity, but my words had been eaten by the night and were lost forever on the cold black wind.

27 : Heaven's gateway

In just a handful of minutes, in scarcely a moment of time, all had been decided. Our fates had been sealed and the hopes and dreams of GT and Pete had crashed. Not for a split second did I consider going back too. Even if the way forward had not been calling me so strongly, to go downwards for two hours in the dark on that steep ice, when one slip would mean everyone tumbling, held for me complete abject terror and dread.

I wondered, guiltily, if I should have tried harder to convince Pete to keep going, but I could not have questioned his discernment or tried to persuade him if he had felt his decision to be right. I could never judge what he needed to learn or where he needed to be for his own soul growth. In the mountains in particular, when life is at stake, it is important to listen to the sixth sense inside. I hoped he had done that. I thought of the time earlier this year when we had been training in the Alps, ski-mountaineering. We had been approaching the top of a near-vertical slope. He had followed his intuition to come and stand below me just before I had slipped. It would in all likelihood have been a fatal fall if he hadn't been there... Now he was not with me.

Our team had been such a warm, sturdy support system. To split this was a bitter blow, but now... Now it was all up to us. I would have to find ways to be strong, more so than ever. Having Mig, the inexperienced one, with me meant that I had to be more responsible for him, which changed my energy within and actually gave me strength. Egbert came briefly breezing in with a big smile on his face, singing 'I'm going to win, I'm going to win.' Yeah, yeah, Egbert, we're all in this together, but he gave me a boost of adrenaline. Also, the rest time had suited my body well and I had eaten all of Pepé's bread. It had been just plain integral bread, maybe left over from his bus journey up, but it had been exactly what I had needed. I had had no conflict, no choice to make. The others would hopefully soon be safe. I had to keep going now, not only for myself, but also for Mig and Tibet and all the many others who had supported us, but particularly now for GT and Pete – desperately now for them. We carried the essence of the whole... It was vital not to falter.

Still stunned by the change in circumstances, Mig was rubbing the back of his head where the pain had moved to and was drinking water in a camel-like fashion. 'Tess, we'll do it,' he said. 'You and Pete have put so much into creating "Climb For Tibet". I'm not going to let it be to no avail.' I felt really happy to have Mig with me. The desire to help Tibet gave us a strong common bond. I knew it meant everything to him. He knew it meant everything to me. There was a melding of heart energy in that great determined vision, and surprisingly things felt right. All would be well. But there was a lot of work to do first.

Pepé led on, and it was good to get the chilled body moving

again. It must have been about 2.30 am, although lack of sleep meant that time was irrelevant. It was more like a conscious dream through the night. There was no concept of being human with specific slumber times. Now Body, please listen, you're just a tool. I need you to carry me on and up. There seemed to be strength in my half-awareness. No, c'mon...focus... Every step counts... One step after the other... Take care to put the points of the crampons down flat to bite into the hard white stuff... strains the ankles... They'll recover... Calf muscles work, please... shoulders move precisely... I need each stick placement and each ice axe placement to be correct... Was it my imagination or was the slope easing slightly? It was my imagination.

Mig was going well, despite the annoyance of ill-fitting boots and the added weight of the spare rope. It seemed he had absorbed all the learning and fallen into an easy climbing technique, with all the vigour and fortitude of youth. But he did tend to want to rush along in no-11-bus-at-Piccadilly mode and then stop for a rest, rather than keeping a steady pace. I felt his genetic inheritance from the high altitude regions of Tibet was helping him. How fitting if this was to be the factor which tipped the balance, keeping him safe against all odds, allowing him to climb the mountain that was to help his troubled country.

Stopping was beginning to get difficult. The concentration of 'one foot over the other, breathe, ice axe up, breathe, stick up, breathe, back foot up, breathe, foot over the other, breathe, ice axe up' blended into a continuity of movement that seemed to be taken over by something other than myself. Mig described the phenomenon as someone else driving his body. To stop meant losing the driver, to gasp, to feel intensely nauseous and heady, to drift and then to have great trouble finding the reason and purpose to start again. Then I would remember something like speaking on camera in the hut, oh so long ago, saying 'We will not let them down, and that would spark the ignition. At times I would call to the driver... Please help me, please help... And I would feel wonderful assistance at a deep, high level of the spirit, lifting me up from the centre of the wheel of a spinning six-pointed star... And then I would float, steadily, not quite in my body, and yet the most grounded I had ever been, both at the same time. The seeming unreality of this sensation somehow drifted into accepted normality, and the edges became blurred. It reminded me of when Mig had practised moving his mind aside to allow healing energy to enter when his boots had first hurt...

Concentrate, Mind... On and on, up and up, with little awareness of the ridge or the dark night around. There was only the next step, and the next. The body was starting to cry out in weariness. This was a greater test than it had been designed for. How much more could it give? This is it. This is it. I can go no further. I am tired to the core. Exhaustion is no friend here in this steep, cold dread. Mind cannot hold the concentration any more. It is too much...too much... But I have no choice... C'mon... focus... The crystal.... Think on the crystal... Ah, peace. I am the carrier. It will act as a beacon of light, just as the Incas before us lit beacons on the summits of their watchtowers. It vibrates to the rhythm of humanity, expanding and magnifying thought a thousand times. It will channel high-frequency energy onto the physical Earth plane, via this special point that is spinning faster than anywhere else on Earth, a symbol of alignment with cosmic harmony. It will reach out into space further than anywhere else on Earth, the edge of our planet, like an arrow of light that can touch the stars. But its universal importance is truly to be part of the system to bring light to the crystal heart of humanity, to act as an amplifier for the purest, highest light... Divine energy...

Please help me... Please give me strength... I am God in strength. I am one in strength... Concentrate on each step... Oh, the effort is just too much... How can I keep this up? Oh dear God...this is hard. The angle that Pepé takes the route is too much for me. I need to zigzag more... It seems like vertical... I can't do it... I can't... I have no breath... There is no air... But a soft wind blew by and packed my lungs to capacity. Now, take it in. All the oxygen you need is here...

I had no concept of time. The hours went by, or were they days? The muscles were in agony, my neck excruciatingly painful, my eyes sore and tired, so tired. Climbing...climbing...climbing... My sack was part of me but heavy, though what do we carry that won't be the lightest that it can ever be up here? In truth we carry the expectations of GT and Pete. We carry hope for the Tibetan nation...the flag to unfurl as an expression of the Tibetan spirit. We carry the love and support of hundreds...a focus of dedicated energies. We are accompanied by the dreams of humanity for harmony on Earth. We are messengers for the beings of light. We shall not give up.

Pepé rarely spoke now, or if he did I was just not aware of it, but there was a moment when we were stopped, gasping for breath, and he passed us a sip of warm, strange-tasting liquid, which eased the parched throat. I knew I no longer had the energy to reach into my sack for the bottle of water. 'It's only twenty minutes till dawn, now,' he said. How could this eternal night end? Surely it will last forever...

That was when the cold hit us. A deep, biting cold that attacked our weakened and drained bodies. Mine started to shiver uncontrollably. I knew I had to take off my sack to find my duvet jacket, but I could not organise my thoughts into the right order to go through the motions. It was all a jumble. My teeth were chattering. Somehow I had to do it.

'Tess, have you got any water left?' asked Mig. Right... For him, yes, I could get into my sack. I found the bottle and dug out the jacket, managing at length to put it on, on top of everything else, so I was nearly as round as I was tall. The shivering subsided. Bless you, Pete for buying it for me...way back in another lifetime... It was snowing now, just gentle flakes – or were they gentle because they looked so pretty, dancing and frolicking to and fro in the round head-torch light. I played with them too inside the circle... catch me if you can... Each individual flake was a friend, special and magic, for in their symmetry every one was a six-pointed star. Maybe that's why there's a higher vibration on a mountain... It's because of the lovely snowflakes... 'Tess, c'mon... We must go.'

'Go? Go where?'

'C'mon!'

Oh, the agony of moving again...though not quite so sick... The joy of motion...not so dizzy. But why is all so white now? There's a sort of hazy grey white everywhere. The night had gone and left us to our fate. Dawn came. When did that happen? The dawn of 6 July... Ah, yes...and with it the steepness eased... Thank goodness. It's taken away the terror of falling, though it's still down there. I can't do it...but I can ignore things I don't like. I won't think of it now.

The rope yanked behind me and I fell to my knees in the snow. Ah, now it's soft... the hard snow had left us behind too... But I don't like this stopping again... The world spins too much... My head is in some sort of clamp... There's something funny happening inside it... It feels like it's on fire...

'Oouhrgh!' I looked down the rope to see Mig vomiting, his

face wracked in pain. I wanted to go to help him, but my body would not respond to the request. I knew that if I could find some guarana, then I would feel better, but I was too confused to remember where it was and there was too little energy to try... Maybe something to eat? No way – nausea too much... Churning stomach...

There was a voice. Pepé was trying to get through the haze... 'Head torch off... Sunglasses on.' Yeah, I can do this... I can...and I'll take my helmet off too... Ah, the freedom of being able to move my neck better and to see around. It did not gain much. The blackness had been replaced by whiteness. The slope fell away to the right. We must be somewhere on the ridge, but visibility was only a few metres across snow to an unending wall of cloud.

Mig moved up to where I was. 'C'mon, Miggie,' I encouraged. 'We've got to do this. We're going to do this.' We urged each other on, each seeing in the eyes of the other the reflection of the agony that the body was going through, the throbbing head, the confusion, the disorientation, the struggle for breath, the feeling like there was a rock sitting on the chest. Above all, though, it was the feeling in my head that bothered me. Something was trying to get out of it...

We staggered up. 'C'mon, do it for the Dalai Lama.' The mind is a weird thing. It can lead the body beyond the limits of what seems possible. One thought can stir great resources of energy. It can push and push. We knew that we both burned with the same passion. There was no way that we would give up.

For a time I became quite lucid and spoke to Pepé's quiet strong presence. He was so steadfast for us. Surely our snail's pace must be frustrating him. 'It doesn't matter how, but we have to get to the summit, the real summit. We are going to get there, whatever it takes.' Maybe he was frightened by my conviction, maybe impressed, but it must have been unusual. Was he aware of the depth of importance of it all? I believed that at some level he was. He was the one who had been especially sent to guide us and show us the way.

Now there seemed to be a rough track in the snow that we were following, though we met no one else in the whole of our white, white world. It continued snowing, but not too heavily. In fact it was useful, as it kept things cold, the easier for the movement, the better for the safety, and the low visibility was perfect. I did not want to see any views. We had a job to do and I trusted that every detail of the weather was just what we needed.

We continued ever upwards, plodding upwards, carried by the intense determination that was overriding all things. I could feel spiritual help all around, like a gathering of souls at a party – guides, father, grandmother...but all seemed to bow towards the Council of Masters. This was their show.

Onwards, always onwards, while the moments of clarity were lost in a sea of confusion and pain. Inside my head was a deep, high feeling which I was having trouble understanding, though I could relate to the Incas practising the ancient rites of trepanning, that is, cutting away part of the skull to ease the pressures of the brain. It was a bit like wanting to vomit but through the head. It was stuck in a triangle and was pushing to get out. Let it out... Let it out... Aiheeeee... would my head explode? There was not enough space left inside. Relax... It subsided for a while.

Then I knew.

The awareness had crept up on me, while something else was controlling my body, working my legs. It came somewhere between the dawn and the rest of forever. My brain, that vast computer in my head controlled by the mind, was expanding and swelling. I was into the stage of Acute Mountain Sickness that was Cerebral Oedema. OK, everyone gets it, I tried to pretend, but I knew that was not so, and I knew that it was serious, deadly serious. Fear took hold, and with the fear, a realisation. I would have to go down. Joke! We're going to the top.

We stopped again for Mig to be sick, and then again, and again. He had nothing left inside him. He was hunched over and wretched. I gave him the last water that we had and he idly poked his finger through the ice that had collected around the lip of the bottle. Each time one of us was close to the impossible, to the giving up, the other would say, 'C'mon, we can do it.' We fed off each other's fluctuating energy. 'Do it for the Dalai Lama.' And we would move again. One of us always had to be strong, and the mind would always rationalise something.

Mig used his prayers to his guru, which gave him persistent strength, and his heart was being lifted by the thought of condor wings... But he never wavered in his belief that he would do it. He was scared, scared of going home to his friends and saying that he had not done it. It was so much tougher than he had thought it was going to be, but there was no way he could go home without having done it. Above all, though, above everything else, he had a country to free, and this climb held a stepping stone towards that goal. It was something he could do. He would not fail.

His desperate tiredness and exhaustion was taking its toll. He was beginning to hear voices in his head. They came and went in the confusion of his mind that was busy with a life review. There were images of every part of his twenty-one years, friends, good things, special times...as continuous as the mountain slope, which seemed to go on and on and on...

Surely we must be nearing the Veintimilla... That must be it ... No... That must be it... No... False summit after false summit came and went...on and on... But at least the mind could wander away from the confines of the body. Behind it all was the shining star of belief that carried him...that carried me....

Weird, weird... Brain trying to get out, trying to explode...

expand, expand... Then suddenly I would be gone – where to, I do not know. I would miss chunks of time altogether. I felt like I was hallucinating, but could not remember what I was seeing. I would shake my head and say 'I am awake... I am awake,' while drifting in and out of awareness...

As my physical condition deteriorated, the angle of the slope continued to ease. This was a blessing, but lurking around was a growing fear of how we would get down later if we kept going. We were going on long after the planned time, when we should by now be going down. The snow would become soft and dangerous. Sometimes the light was so bright behind the whiteout cloud that I knew the heat of the sun would be working on the place where Pepé had said was risky for avalanches. Trust, girl, trust... But would we get down if we kept going? Don't think of going down... It will take care of itself... Still, I was frightened.

I seemed to be brain-dead... There was a floating feeling... Thoughts would not work properly. It was too painful to stop. I felt too sick...but I felt sick anyway, and it was as if I was not here... I was so tired, so very tired, and my brain felt so swollen... Leg after leg after leg... Oh, please help me, please help me... I called...but this time there came a different reply: 'Not so...we will help you no more. You must give every ounce of your life... everything...so that there is nothing left, nothing of yourself, no individuality... No longer child, mother, sister, lover... In the knowledge of the giving of your life, there is a letting go, a humility. Only in this way can there be an arrival at the summit, on your knees, giving out the vibrational energy that is needed... that of unconditional love.'

What? I did not understand, beyond the thought that there was no help.

But there was one thing that was completely and utterly clear from that moment. I would not make it down. I was not going to make it down. If I kept going I was going to die up here... I did have the choice. I could turn right now, but if I kept going, then the fluids in my brain would expand further, and then I would die. Amid all the confusion of my mind this point was crystal-clear. That was my total truth. To me it was a reality.

I knew immediately that I was not prepared to turn back. There was too much at stake... All that I had worked for and dreamed of. To continue was fulfilling my life's purpose and if I was to die in this beautiful and glorious moment then...so be it. I was doing what I had to do. What about my loved ones?... My children...my children... That is another lifetime. I am here now. There is only now. There is no other... And anyway they are with me, they are part of me, for with love there is no separation. Somewhere in the far reaches of my memory there stirred a lilting voice: 'If your heart believes that you are doing the right thing...if you truly believe that you will continue to exist...it is the spirit which is most important... Sometimes you can afford to give up the body...'

There was no choice to be made, for I would keep going and give everything. If this frame of mind was what was asked of me to try to reach the summit then I would give it. Four times I asked myself if this was right. Four times, unfalteringly came the reply: we keep going...

I am filled with unimaginable joy. I am rising. My soul is soaring. I am held on all sides by countless wings of light that emanate from loving heart chakras. They whisper on silent winds. There is a dazzling, pure golden brilliance that washes me, that enfolds me, that pours at me... And I respond, for I am one and the same. I am all things and all things are me. I am love and all things are love. I yearn to be here forever and the yearning is... for there is only now forever... And I have come home. This is perfection...

I see colours flying from the heart, colours of shimmering light...the dance of purples and silver, reds and pink... I feel it...the determination and the unconditional love... A sea of rainbows... Joy and excitement... Show me... Show me more... Oh! I am touched by this lovely display expressed from our hearts, and see the wonderment of joy from this, the abode beyond the body. I am filled with insight and thankfulness.

Mig, in his joy of commitment, shows much white with rainbow edges, that play and waft and whirl in tints and tinges of previously unknown hues... Oh, how beautifully... Pepé is as though not human... Rather, our own energy and resolution that is leading us, but as a guide of energies more than a leading. His quiet strength is pink with yellows and browns at the side... And his tones are of compassion... Yes, Chinese...but it is also that of all peoples, for it is reaching out to the energies and dyes of humanity, melded and mixed...blended with a brilliant white divine viscosity...painted across the Earth... That I see... That we are... From all parts of the world colours are gushing, flowing and cascading...and I watch entranced from this highest of places.

The body is taken over by the mind, and the mind is being taken over by the spirit, touching the robes of divinity... And with it, deep inside, comes wonderful crystal clarity and understanding of all things. There is no longer any need to ask anything.

There is complete and utter peace.

Suddenly, I was in body awareness... Please... Oh please... Let me stay in that state of ecstasy and bliss... I don't want to leave.

I wanted to lie down in the snow and die. I wanted to take all my clothes off and happily go to sleep. I knew I felt funny. I knew that I should be going down quickly. I told Pepé and Mig that I felt funny, but I knew too that it was my responsibility, and I knew that I had asked Pepé to keep us going whatever. But was I lying down? Or was I moving? Or was it the snow that moved?

Then I knew that I still climbed, for the eyes differentiated. We took a sharp turn left, looking down at ice-forms in a deep *bergschrund* of wondrous, swimming, blue-green beauty, and then a curving slope up softening snow to the final slopes of the Veintimilla. It opened out to a broad volcanic dome. The visibility had widened, but we could not see further than the edges of the dome. There was a sense of other people having been here before.

We staggered to the middle and fell into a heap. My body lay motionless like a rag-doll abandoned. Mig was still vomiting raw stomach fluids. We became cold and then colder still within seconds. My thoughts took so long to put together that I could not manage more than simply... We had to go on. But I was in no state to move an inch in any direction.

Pepé counselled us. We should go down. It's safest to go down. Very often climbers turn back at this summit. It is 9 am. This is late, because the snow will become treacherously loose on the steeper, lower slopes. Our own condition is becoming rapidly worse. It is completely right to go down now.

28 : Flags a-flying

The Veintimilla was a prize well won. We had penetrated right through to Chimborazo's final shield of protection.

'Let's call this the real summit,' Mig suggested, but looking up into his drawn face I could see behind the glazing of his eyes that it was not what he wanted. A fire still flickered there somewhere, waiting for a fine wind of resolution to rekindle the flames.

But we both knew that the other was at the end of their tether, that we had reached that point physically many hours ago.

'I can't go on,' he said.

'Yes you can,' I said.

'I'm going to take all my clothes off and I'm going to die,' I said.

'No you're not,' he said. 'I'm not carrying your dead body down. Tell you what, you stay here and I'll take the crystal across to the summit for us.'

Wow! To say that when he had not one single ounce of energy

left… Now I knew why I always called him the Snow Lion Heart. His heart was so very very big. I was so close to accepting his offer. I was going to put my head down, never to raise it again. It was OK. I was drifting into a hallucinating dream, in a state of not caring. I teetered on the edge. Then a voice in me said, 'If you lie still in this cold for a minute or two longer you will die anyway. Better to find a last bit of energy that must be here somewhere and move across to the summit. At least you will have got there, though there is no way that you will get back down after that.'

Somewhere there was a way out of this deep state of torpor. 'Miggie, we'll do it for the Dalai Lama.'

There was one more final incentive. 'Tess, when we get down I'll buy you a milkshake. You can have banana and I'm going to go for strawberry.'

We would go the final road.

With a superhuman effort born of importance to someone else rather than self, I found the energy to sit up and say 'Miggie, you must take the responsibility for your own life in deciding to keep going. It reduces the chances of getting down safely.'

But Migmar was representing the lives of all the Tibetan people, who had given so much more than us. They had suffered so much more. This…this was nothing compared to the Himalayas, escaping with no food, no clothing, no drink. We had proper mountaineering gear, we had boots and crampons, while they… they had pictures of frozen dead children… He was not about to give up. Between us we would do it.

So, at Pepé's insistence, we ditched the rucksacks and every bit of weight possible. If anyone was later to doubt my sanity, they would know… for I left Yannick behind at 6,260 metres, on this, the western summit of Chimborazo. Mig took the flag, the prayer flags and the sticks. I pressed play on the tape recorder and Gandiva's sounds of Tibetan gongs reverberated out for a moment of time, as I gathered the things-for-the-summit bag. The crystal stirred in my heart pocket.

We now had to go due east for one kilometre, but first...first for a little way we staggered DOWN, which was a mixed-up sensation. Then, Pepé turned anxiously to look back and halted dead in his tracks. It had stopped snowing and there seemed to be a gap in the cover behind us where there was a large black cloud, just like those painted by children, hovering close to us as if with malign intent. I saw real fear in Pepé's eyes. 'I'm not happy,' he confirmed. 'A friend of mine died recently, right here, when a similar cloud appeared and he was struck by lightening.' Wow! Pepé was learning too. Mountaintops seem to be good places for soul growth. Then whiteout mercifully took over, hiding the black cloud. So the cloud was Pepé's, and I thought no more about it, except that his arrival at the summit would indeed be in the energy of unconditional love... After all, I had already seen the colour of his energy.

Our main problem now was wading through soft, knee-deep – often thigh-deep – snow. This was where Whymper had reported being in it up to his neck. We struggled to stay in the huge footprints Pepé was making for us. He must have been really tired too, but he did not show it. He left things along the way, Hansel-and-Gretel-like, to find the way back in the whiteout. Thankfully I only had to give up one of my sticks. I needed the other to hold me upright. As before, things seemed more possible when moving, in spite of the almost laughably hard conditions, and I marvelled that I was still going.

Then we had to go UP. Oh dear God, if I can only do this last 'up', I will never ask for anything again. How can this body do it? The mind is so strong, so clever, it does not care if it is in the desert or a forest or up at 6,000 metres, it carries the body to places impossible, in golden dreams. It is strong. It is king...

and yet flying above the mind is more than this. The spirit is supremely powerful, with neither the confines of time or space, nor conceivable limits...

Those in spirit, and more in tune with the divine, watched us coming. 'Tess, you know,' said Mig, with wonder seeping from his tired voice, 'I feel energised by the blessings of Churchill and Gandhi.' How lovely... It was understandable that they would not want to miss this for the world. They would see not so much the supreme physical effort, as that which we gave out, the sacrifice which we had made. They would then know that we had given our all and that we came humbly and asking for freedom from oppression in Tibet and for the peace of the world. This was as it should be. There was no other way to come to this sacred ground. It had to be in unconditional love... and this was what I had come to learn.

Suddenly Pepé stopped. This was it. We were almost surprised. 'Well, if you can find a higher spot,' he said, 'let me know.' Higher spot? This was the furthest point from the centre of the Earth – 6,310 metres above sea level – and we were on it... But where was the summit? The gradient was a bit like that of a football pitch... Where? My heart was beginning to fill up and overflow into tears. Pepé waved at the space in front of us. There was only untouched snow. With the eyes we could see no further than the distance to the next person on the rope; after that sky and snow, snow and sky were all one huge canvas of whiteness. But with the soul we could see round the circle of eternity. There was only this moment, no past, no future, no cause, no reason... There was total oneness of all things...and joy, such joy, such beauty and completeness. Nothing else mattered but this. I sensed the spirit of immortality.

Somehow Pepé had the video camera... 'Please, just press the red button and keep pressing,' I entreated him, while Mig stood with his green sacred stick – the stick that was a carrier of compassion – and showed us the way. 'It's just that spot there.' He said as it flew from his hands to mark the place. 'We're there… Oh, God… We've made it.' His voice quavered in the passion of the moment. It had been twelve hours – twelve life times – since we had set out from the shelter of the hut. Truly the mountain we had climbed had been within ourselves.

I took six final laborious steps through the soft snow, trailing the rope that connected me to Mig, and collapsed to my knees… and then to my face. I felt neither the stinging burn of the cold, nor the rasping snatch of my lungs, for it was the facing of myself that had been the most painful. I had moved into the understanding and certain knowledge of the greater sense of self, which no amount of thinking could explain or describe; only experience can know it. Being one with all things was no longer just a belief; it was a deeply felt experience. It was knowing. In total trust of the universe, and in the letting go of my separate existence, I had been given the prize of the knowledge of my own truth. That was liberation. That was freedom.

Humbly we come… We are indeed one spirit, Chimborazo.

On our knees, Mig and I embraced. It was a long, long embrace, born of toil and hardship, of battle and undiminished determination. As we clung to each other, I allowed the tears to fall from my long-dehydrated body, gasping for the oxygen needed, and my chest heaved in pent-up emotion and relief. Suddenly, all the pains of the fire in my brain, the exhaustion and the agony were lost in one huge surge of power and energy that entered us from we knew not where.

Mig took off his gloves to unfurl the Tibetan flag – a sweet moment of devotion – and we held it up between us to speak out our messages…blue, red and yellow, bright and vibrant against the spinning white of all colours.

'We ask for humanity to listen to the Dalai Lama of Tibet, whose shining example...' I broke down in wracking sobs as the snow dripped from my clothes onto the flag and the brittle icicles of my exposed hair stroked my cheek. ' ...A way forward in peace and brotherhood...for a free Tibet and our Earth in harmony.'

The snow lions on the flag reflected the strength of their brother as he pulled his maroon balaclava away from his mouth to speak, bursting from his heart. 'I... I'm going to do everything I can, dear Tibet and its people, to free you, and to heal you, within this life...and if that doesn't become possible, I want to come back in my next life to heal and to free you... Happy Birthday, Dalai Lama...'

'Happy Birthday, Dalai Lama.' I echoed, as he continued, 'And may your examples set the world free...of violence.'

'OM MANI PADME HUM,' we prayed, and his face crumpled into a wide smile. 'Tess, we did it... I gave up, down there... I thought we couldn't do it...' And he fell onto his back, his arms punching the thin air that clasped cruelly at his lungs. Through tears of exhaustion he cried from the depths of his being, 'PEACE ON EARTH! PEACE ON EARTH! PEACE ON EARTH!'

The snow lapped at his body.

'Don't get cold, Mig.'

'I don't feel the cold.'

'Here, look.' I drew from my heart pocket our crystal – 'ours' for the last time – and offered it to him to touch. 'Give it a kiss, Mig.' Then I held it high. 'It will be a light to shine throughout the world...filled with divine energy...and will bring world peace... We deliver it.'

'Tess, this has got to be it...' Mig's excitement sharpened our focus. There was a deep, almost blue hole that presented itself to us. It was about the size of an ice axe handle. I placed the crystal carefully in.

'It's upright... Fill the hole with snow so it will never blow away, and will bring peace for always and always.'

Our souls danced in harmony with the colours that were given off... There was an ethereal sense of the Council of Masters upholding a radiant star of light all around us...and it was done.

We were a Tibetan, an Englishwoman and an Ecuadorian, gathered, representing many by the intention of their peace messages, in the name of universal love.

Beside the resting place of the crystal another hole waited, and into it we laid Uri's little book of positive ways forward, and the spoon bent with the power of world peace coming down. We wrapped them in snow, like gifts to the spirit of the mountain, as, across the globe, the turn of the Earth showed teatime in an English country house. Uri was there with his family, close in their love for each other, tuning in to the place where we were. All was unfolding...

Then Mig opened Bill's ring, so beautifully and lovingly made out of copper, vibrating with the 'OM'. The message inside was an ancient Chinese proverb... 'When you reach the top of a mountain... keep climbing...' The wisdom it held brushed past us silently as Mig filled the container with snow to fulfil the prayer of coming down safely. Oh, Wow! Oh, Wow! I was allowed to think beyond this moment for the first time. There was a chance of getting down. The magic of the ring was sustained.

The cold warned of minutes too long, as with fumbling hands I opened the birdseed packet from Lawley. The energy of love for the birds of Tibet symbolised new life after death...as the seeds scattered... And Tarka's fur represented the simple power of love as Mig read Candy's message. We knew that we had neither the time nor the stamina to read more from here, except just the special one from His Holiness. We both had copies somewhere on us, but the boost of energy was beginning to drain and neither of us could find it. We were content knowing that there is more wisdom in the unseen...

Hurriedly now, I stuffed a film cartridge with snow to take for GT and Pete, while Mig opened out the prayer flags. 'The whole "Climb For Tibet" team dedicates these prayer flags to the Tibetan people, in and out of Tibet, and especially to this mountain, this beautiful mountain, and to the whole world.'

'May there be peace on Earth.'

'May there be peace on Earth.' Mig's hands moved up and down to emphasise each word he spoke. 'These prayer flags are... probably... I'm sure... I'm sure...the highest prayer flags in the world... They must be... They will fly from the highest point on Earth... Oh, Tess... we've gotta put them up.' He tied them securely to his faithful stick, which had for so long been at his side, imbued with compassion – the twin soul of unconditional love. Its life purpose was about to find fulfilment. I tied the other end to the smaller stick and he staggered back to spread out the flags. 'It doesn't matter if they touch the snow... The mantras written here, on the representations of the five elements, will always be blown by the wind on top of Chimborazo, the highest mountain in the world. Basically, the wind will whistle and will speak out the prayers and mantras on all these elements and blow them around the Earth.' We pushed the sticks deep into the snow... support for the power of the messages.

'Long may they fly from the point furthest from the centre of the Earth...and may they bring down Earth Peace.' Just as we put the prayer flags up, the incredible stillness and calm that we had been experiencing changed. A steady breeze blew... I had never doubted the weather angel...

If you had been watching our planet from space that day, you would have seen the colours flying from a bright star at her highest point... The blues, whites, reds, greens and yellows, blowing, again and again...messages from the mountain...spinning into a whiteness and purity ablaze with light... They were carried by the wind-horse, whose job it was to encompass and embrace the Earth with blessings of peace and harmony. As she turned, they would have an uninterrupted journey... for there was no place higher...

29 : A light for peace

For long years of legend it had been said that Chimborazo, Watchtower of the Universe, held treasure. At the beginning of 1880, as Whymper's party set off to climb, the local officials had said, 'We understand, *señores*, that it is necessary for you to say you intend to climb Chimborazo, although everyone knows such a thing is impossible… But we know very well that you intend to discover the treasure that is buried there.' Yes, indeed, today we had found treasure, but we had had to look in our hearts.

I had experienced the strength of the mind, fed by belief. It had pushed the body way beyond what it was capable of, carried on wings of compassion. In the knowledge of death and the opening of the gateway to the divine I had found supreme joy and deep peace. I had perceived the interconnected oneness of all things. I had beheld detachment, for I had undergone the ultimate letting go – that of my life…as seen through the veil of being only in the present moment... And, this day, I understood unconditional love. My treasure was these gifts wrapped in this sense of the spirit of eternity. For years, maybe lifetimes, I had been trying to learn these things. Now, as if through a rite of initiation, I had a new direction. My purpose would be to share these understandings. For this I would survive, though part of me desperately wanted not to leave. I was thrust back into life awareness. I fell back into selfness.

This self brought with it the weight of accountability. What happened to it mattered. Up until then I was always going to do what I was going to do, come what may. I had never felt that I was in the hands of Pepé. He had been there as the route guide, for safety, to record with the camera, and somehow, in a way that I did not quite understand, to bring a sense of the compassion of the Chinese. He had been a strong, gentle, angelic-like presence, a guide in the true sense of the word. Now, we had done what we had come to do and I was happy to feel that I could hand responsibility over to him with a 'Let's go. Please...somehow... get us down.' Down? The concept was strange and new, as though it was an idea in the future, something I had to grasp onto before it drifted away...

It must have been around 11 am, though I had no sense of time, as with one brief last glance at the forever picture of the fluttering prayer flags, I turned into the white wilderness. Every movement took an unimaginable effort, for the instructions from mind to body did not always make much sense. The lucidity of the summit actions had disappeared. The fire in my brain seemed to have rekindled and was burning brightly, eating me away, cell by cell. I did not dare shut my eyes. I knew I had to stay in body awareness, though the fire was so heavy that my head felt like a ball of lead. Step by slow step we retraced our way into the white mists of the ascent, picking up the trail markers, each foot wearily lifted into the deep holes, one after the other. My totally drained body responded only to the urgency of life...life...life.

At the Veintimilla we could not risk stopping longer than to gather our rucksacks through a nauseous, deadening haze. Even being reunited with Yannick, sacrificial fodder, abandoned here and cast away at this critical moment of his penguin career, failed to make an impact on my awareness. There was just one thought: down... down... For every slow drag of the boot through the soft snow would mean less pain in my head.

Mig, still doubled up vomiting, led the shuffle in a reversal of the rope positions. Never had we left the comfort of our connecting umbilical cord, but exhaustion was in control. We floundered and fell like dazed toy puppets, somehow aware that while the gradient was gentle it was all right to do so. Even Pepé stumbled in tiredness. Crampons started balling up, creating high-heel shoe effects as the snow gathered in lumps, to be whacked off by ice axe or stick. At least that roused us, for sleep was stealing its way in. I shook my head repeatedly... 'I am awake... I am awake... I am awake... But where had those last minutes gone? The body kept moving, though consciousness was not there. Can't stop... can't stop... Too much agony... Too hard to get up again...

But warmth gradually crept in, as the white cloud became brighter, like an almost dazzling cloak enveloping us, and we had to stop to stash our outer jackets. This allowed an awareness of the extreme pain from the neck to drift in...and the mouth, almost too parched to speak. I had no desire for food, nor the energy to find it...but water... Oh, I'd sell my soul for just a sip... Stuffing mouthfuls of snow only seemed to make matters worse. Dehydration competed with all-out weariness, leaving no room for fear, either of thoughts of the steepness to come, or of the possibility of soft snow avalanching.

We inched slowly downwards, and mercifully, as the ridge

gradient increased, air richer in oxygen began to enter our lungs and the cloud cover, both of mountain and of mind, began to lift and drift. I felt happy that the visibility widened, though it included only more bright snow and extended whiteness. No longer did I need to be isolated on an energy level, floating in space. Here the world could come in if it wanted to. I quietly prayed for our safe return, and visualised us all back at the hut. Then – the picture that lit my way – I saw myself hugging Pete... Ah!.. That, now, was all I wanted. Surely we must be nearly there... Surely he would be coming up to meet us soon...

The cloud lifted further and it became hotter and brighter still as we reached even steeper ground. I tried to force every tired cell, every shattered sinew to focus...focus... Place the crampon points carefully... Don't trip...don't trip... Can I do this without stumbling?...

'Ice axe arrest time, Miggie,' I cautioned.

Pepé belayed us as we went down, with no more than his ice axe loosely in the snow. I did not fancy anyone's chances if Mig and I were to slip at the same time, or if one was to pull the other off. There would be little Pepé could do, unless we all rolled onto our axes and arrested. Somehow, in spite of the dangers, though, I had none of the fear that had previously built up to such a level of dread. I was simply too tired and drifted too often into a dream state... I was full of a gentle peace... Anyway the soft snow was thankfully so much easier than the hard névé ice of the night. I barely noticed the steepness increasing, our way disappearing over the edge. It gave a sense at last of the Earth somewhere beneath our feet, far far below, as though we could fly down there at a moment's notice, condor-like, on easy soaring wings in reckless abandon.

'It is necessary to speed up here,' Pepé's insistent voice came, so we turned inwards and front-pointed backwards, using the claw of the ice axe and one hand to steady ourselves, increasing the pace. Was this the avalanche risk area of which he had warned?

Meanwhile, at 5,000 metres, outside the Whymper hut, binoculars were searching…searching… Eyes were tired of the brightness reflecting back a mountain face, desolate and always devoid of three expected figures.

After the turn-around, GT and Pete had made a quick, experience-motivated descent over the tricky terrain, soon recovering their equilibrium, and arriving back before dawn. They had slept a little and talked to Michael. Then they had waited. GT had delighted in building a special fourth stupa, in which he had placed his Debbie's precious gift of lapis lazuli, her Buddhist message of transience, affirming that all things move on, and his Chloe's lovely painting of the mountain of peace. It had helped him reach a truce within himself for this, his mountain of peace, in spite of the frustration of not being able to continue the climb. He was concerned for the safety of the team, but for Pete the waiting was a nightmare. He worried deeply. He deliberated on the probable positioning on the mountain. He paced up and down. He paced up and down again and again…and then again. The weather looked OK. The sun was shining. They could see nearly half way up the ridge, before a dense topping of cloud blocked the view further. By 9 am there should have been a sighting of the return… at least by 10 am…definitely by 11… but Chimborazo lay still, silent… and empty…

At 1.30 pm the day was warm and a handful of others arrived at the hut, including a couple of Norwegians looking at the possibility of climbing and a couple of Frenchmen, just curious... There were friendly conversations and Oswaldo cooked a meal, but Pete had no stomach for normality. He was frustrated and angry with himself at the way things had turned out. Not withstanding his intense desire for the team to reach the summit and for all to be safe, his head was swirling in an overriding black cloud of anxiety. I was up there somewhere. Something must have happened... The guides' radiophones did not seem to work, so what was going on? The risks of mountaineering played havoc with his mind, filling it with 'what ifs'... Fear seeped into his heart... I was hours overdue... He was not there to protect me... He was a man of action and yet all he could do was wait... Dammit, I was still teaching him patience...

They organised a search party; Fernando would take Oswaldo with him. The sun was dipping lower in the sky when they left at about 3 pm, carrying water and ropes. The mountain face was still completely devoid of any sign of life. Visibility was even now remarkably clear to the middle of the ridge, for the sky was gentle. It was as though all was in abeyance...watching and waiting... waiting and watching...

But at around 3.30 pm, as he clutched the binoculars with weary arms, Pete suddenly spotted the small, dark dots, descending slowly, moving in and out of the cloud on the ridge... but he saw only two, and his blood ran cold. The guide would have been OK. Mig was young and strong. So something must have happened to me... An empty eternity stretched out ahead of him. Seconds became hours...minutes became days...

I fell. In a daze, my dragging, pointy feet on jelly legs tripped and I tumbled downwards. The falling, gathering momentum did nothing for my sleeping mind. It was in relaxation. Surely I should be turning over and forcing my ice axe in?.. Phwam! The rope went taut and my harness bit into my waist. I dug in my crampons and the claw of the ice axe, brushed the snow from my nose and glasses with a wet glove and looked upwards. The rope was tight to Mig. He was lying on his ice axe with a big smile on his face.

'Hey... It works!'

'Thanks Miggie. You're a star.' We had been descending close together whilst Pepé was far above us. He had lengthened the rope between himself and us, adding the spare rope that Mig had been carrying all the way, so he could give us a long belay at the times when we were not moving together. Mig's quick reaction had saved us... Good training guys...

Looking round, we realised we had reached the limit of the dispersing cloud. The veil was being drawn back, revealing a sun shining brightly and a world awaiting us. We were perched just down from the ridge, taking on an extensive, white, smooth-looking descent, which dropped steeply away. There was a sense of trying to escape from a huge cake, tiptoeing down lashings of dripping icing. Well, yes, it had been a fitting birthday celebration for His Holiness. The 'Climb For Tibet' team had lit his candles with fire from their hearts... Long may the light of his ideals shine...

'There're the huts!' Mig pointed excitedly. Nestled far below among tiny dark chocolate rocks we could see both of them, tin roofs reflecting silver but warm to our colour-starved eyes, before gazing further and beyond to where grey and white took over again in the distant curvature of the cotton-wool horizon. Being able to see the way down now gave us false relief, making us feel as if we were nearly down. The seracs, crevasses, bumps and dips barely registered. Why aren't Pete and GT up here to meet us? my feeble mind enquired, not taking on board that it would be a strenuous climb of five hours on hard ice – considerably more in these soft, risky conditions. We continued down them, our way becoming hotter, the snow stickier, the lips dryer and the skin frying. Sweat was dripping inside our heavy clothes, losing precious moisture.

I tried to rid my crampons of the balling-up snow and slipped again...then again and again. Each time, Mig held me quickly. It would have been funny if it were not so serious. There was such a feeling of non-reality to the exhaustion state. I just felt weak all over. Then it was Mig who was falling... Oh, no!... But before gravity and speed could take over he rolled and arrested himself. He had been practising. Pepé took no part and made no comment, but when he was close I could see the weariness in the grey of his face and read the urgency of getting us down before we cracked up completely. Three more times Mig tripped and fell, threatening to pull all of us off into oblivion and three more times he stopped himself...as though his ice axe held the magic of condor claws...

Where was the rest of the team? My mind, once so steadfast, now floundered and gave up. I wanted Pete to tell me what to do, to take me home. Surely, if we were nearing the end of the story, my prince should appear and carry me off on his tall white charger... I needed his strong arms around me...

Time floated as we weaved steeply between ice-carved and wind-blown forms, now peacefully bathing in the sun. Then we came close to a tumbled area of fresh avalanche material, which floated into my awareness in a detached way allowing no apprehension. Here a shout alerted us to climbers approaching from below. There were two of them. It must be Pete and GT.

Thank goodness… We were now following a track of footprints that made the going easier. Nearer and nearer the figures came towards the track, but in disappointment I realised I did not recognise them. They must be passing climbers. The fact that this was not the time of day to go climbing eluded me. Where is our team? Pepé spoke to them in Spanish, then they moved past me on the track to where Mig was pleading with them and they gave him a bottle of water. Turning, I saw what I needed so desperately, but could not reach back the arm's length that was necessary. I simply could not manage that one step back. The body would not respond to the instruction. I pleaded too, but with rambling, rasping words, and then liquid gold was poured down the desert of my parched throat to bring back life to withered flowers…

I gratefully allowed hands to help me down to a flatter stance, where I was surprised to recognise that they belonged to Fernando and Oswaldo. They set up a long rope for prusiking down the next steep pitch, while I asked Mig to belay me on our rope into a crevasse for some privacy to answer a call of nature. Yellow pee? More like orange gone off the scale, but it was the first time that I had been since leaving the hut nineteen hours ago. A record for me… We took jackets off, immediately regretting it, for we became chilled in an instant, but with no time for loitering we were rushed quickly down the protected prusik rope, falling off many times. My thoughts shouted… I can't take any more… I can't go any further…but there were still feet to move… Surely… surely…we're so close…so close…

The sky was decorated with glowing pink tinges turning the light to evening magic as we approached the meeting of the glacier tongue with the rocks. Here a muddy stew took over from the soft snow and there… There was a welcoming mêlée of people. Mig unroped and rushed ahead, shouting, 'We made it! We made it!' and fell over in the mud. I followed and slipped, landing in the mud too. There was laughter and talking, sounds of 'well done' and cameras, but I only wanted one thing. Suddenly it was there…at last. My eyes were filling with tears. Strong arms were around me…and Pete was hugging me. It was a hug I had waited for for so very, very long; a hug which said 'This is the end of the supreme effort needed… All is well now.' I sobbed uncontrollably, in an emotional, exhausted letting go, and the hug spun around and around, enfolding me in love…and the knowledge that we were now safe.

Pete carried me the rest of the way down to the hut on his back. GT carried my rucksack. We paused so I could drink, cupping my hands, from a glacial melt-water stream. It tasted better than the finest champagne that I could ever dream of. It was an instinctive acceptance of the gift of the miracle of life from the mighty Watchtower. I did not know then that Michael had filmed the Inca descendants on their pilgrimage, fulfilling the same ritual in this exact same spot – for this was the partaking of the sacramental life-blood of Chimborazo.

The way led us out through the portals of the stupa park, now four stupas for the four hearts of the 'Climb For Tibet' team, beating with the memory of the expression of compassion. The whole park carried the energy. Just as the whole team, with the wonderful sensitive assistance of Pepé, had placed the prayer flags on the summit. For GT, and especially for Pete, there was the coping with the blackest, grungiest of disappointments, for they had taken a different road. They too had had the battle of facing themselves. But because of them, the team had made it. Every part had been essential to make the whole happen…like a jigsaw puzzle. Is this not what life on Earth is about? Many do not have opportunities to reach summits, but we each have a vital part to play – however unsung – and every energy affects the energy of the whole.

Dusk fell suddenly as we reached the hut on this day of our primordial pilgrimage. At nearly twenty hours, we thought it must have been one of the slowest climbs to the summit and back without bivouacking ever recorded... Then I learned that Pepé had previously guided the brave mountaineer Norman Croucher. It had taken three days...but then, he has no legs... I felt very humble.

Surprisingly, I found I could not eat, though I had had nothing since the bread at 2 am, but it was no surprise to surrender to the blessings of sleep...

I am riding pillion on a magnificent grey horse. The flowing mane and tail are of pure, almost translucent white. We are galloping so fast and hard that the hooves scarcely touch the Earth and I know not if we are flying. My hands clasp around the waist of the rider to save me from falling, but I do not want to touch the sacrosanct robes...for the rider is the Dalai Lama...

I awoke with tears on my jacket pillow and the haunting dream seeping through my being.

It was time to read out the peace messages to the Earth, from the mountain-stage. Sunshine smiled down on us that uniquely clear fourth day. Mig tied a purple sash around his Tibetan national costume, a rock-coloured *chuba*, worn over purple climbing salopettes, and proudly held high the Tibetan flag which had recently seen so much service. He looked every inch the warrior for peace that he had proved himself to be. The dedication and purpose of I-have-a-country-to-free drove him on, but as for the climbing, well, he did have some reservations: 'I shall NEVER do any more climbing!'

He displayed the picture of the Dalai Lama that he had carried with such love and then passed it on to the Norwegians. They were planning to climb Everest from the Tibetan side and would take it with them. The inspiration would continue to travel the world...

We started to express all the messages by speaking them out:

The best solution to any problem is Love (Paul Burrows)

May love, compassion and peace shine throughout the world, but especially in Tibet (Zara Fleming)

On and on into the day, we spoke out every prayer, every promise, every wish, every hope...and the mountain reverberated with the beautiful words of compassion for all life, non-violence and universal responsibility... And the peace energy came together and multiplied a thousand-fold, and then incalculable times more... It arose, guided by a six-pointed star, through the crystal beacon at the furthest point of the Earth...and was sent out... shining...to the far corners of the planet...

Then we started the long journey home to become part of that world again. Far below, in tall, windswept tussock grassland we stopped to say farewell to the spirit of the mountain. The four of us stood in the 'Climb For Tibet' formation, raised palms together...

Oh, Chimborazo...we leave your eminent and all-powerful sacred presence. Thank you for letting us bathe in your aura and return safely. Thank you for being the place of light shining always for Earth Peace... We shall continue to hold the vision and the focus. We shall continue to spread the messages... It is done... OM MANI PADME HUM...

And the mantra of compassion rang out to touch the crystal heart beheld in distant summit snows...

Quito greeted us with a languid gaiety. It seemed different. No, it was probably I who had changed. Was it that in my quest for inner peace I had touched a different reality? Here, now, I was just playing a game, the purpose of which was to learn and to grow. It was to be enjoyed, not to become bogged down in... As a representation of this, a wart that had been on my finger for years had completely disappeared... For the body manifests changes in its own way. My mouth which had been badly burned by the snow reflection, was swollen both inside and out. For four weeks talking would be uncomfortable, eating painful and kissing impossible...

As the 'Climb For Tibet' team gathered at the hostel for the last time before dispersing, there was a sense of much work still to be done. Pete and I were to take all the messages and reread them from the Matterhorn in Switzerland, which had been dedicated to world peace, while also delivering a friend's ashes to that mountain. Then we would present the messages to Jiang Zemin, president of the Chinese people, on his forthcoming visit to Britain, read them gently at the vigil outside the Chinese Embassy, and display them on our website to be available for all.

And there was the collecting in of the sponsor monies, half of which Mig was to take to the Khanyara refugee camp.

'You know...' Mig said, 'it was a real unbelievable struggle on the mountain...but the thing that was running through my mind over and over again was the agony of those Tibetan refugees escaping across the Himalayas...'

'Certainly, when you think of all that physical effort and pain that we've been through, in a sense it's a kind of symbol for what's happening in Tibet,' GT said.

Yes, indeed... And I knew...that the burden of the body was the pathway to release the wings of the soul...

There was, however, still unfinished business to attend to... 'C'mon, Tess...' urged Mig, 'I'm going to buy you a milkshake.'

Peace messages

O Excellent Earth, our only home, so wise and beautiful and mysterious, forgive us all: and help us to deliver Tibet from oppression and the rest of the world from indifference. May freedom rule with the moon and compassion shine through even the brightest day.

I send peace and love and health to everybody around the world. May all nuclear weapons be neutralised and disarmed soon.

As I stand on the highest point of the planet, the Earth below looks pristine, idyllic. At a distance, many things look different from how they really are. So my dearest wish is that the destruction of nature, the cruelty, suffering, violence, hunger and disease which darken so many corners of the world and affect both humans and animals can be brought to an end: and that with compassion and kindness to all creatures, the world will really be a beautiful place – from far and near.

Stay loose but hang in there to help free Tibet.

Peace and tranquillity are of an essence, but most of all I feel we must endeavour to seek true happiness and that is through ultimate freedom of the mind, body and spirit. Seek within yourself for the answers and the result will be startlingly good. – You are free and full of love.

I pray that the people of China peacefully and soon allow the freedom of the Tibetan people.

We are just tiny specks of dust on a mountain's side. Never must we forget the humility of life, to respect and cherish Nature – She is always consistent and will always remain steadfast. We on the other hand will come and go like the wind. Surely PEACE is the only answer in our world. Surely protecting Nature is our only answer. Why then do so many want to abuse the gifts of life? On top of the mountain, may these messages be heard, loud and clear in all corners of the world. May the Universe rise up and once and for all fight for Peace, Love in our hearts and Harmony always.

There is no more pressing cause to climb for today than Tibet. So climb high and with high hopes – for the courage of its people and the resilience of its environment and culture. I shall be with you in spirit on July 6th .

Love will heal the planet and bring peace to all beings.

Light to all beings, compassion to all beings, joy to all beings, love to all beings.

King David wrote " May the Lord bring down peace from the mountains and from the hills justice." I have said Mass for Peace on the summit of Chimborazo. I pray that your climb will be successful and that all your prayers, as you make that pilgrimage, will be answered.

May the whole world come together in the understanding that in diversity lies mankind's strength. Love the things that are beautiful.

May the peace of the mountains spread to the hearts of the world.

May God's Healing Angels lift you even higher than the heights you have just scaled, and may your prayers and those of His Holiness for the future of your beloved Tibet be truly fulfilled.

All we are saying is give peace a chance.

We're shining from our hearts, we're setting ourselves free!

We are children of the Universe. May we grow to learn the consequences of our actions and become one with the Earth. Thanks to Divine Oneness for each new day and this forgiving planet. I rejoice in the beauty of life.

On behalf of the European Parliament's Intergroup on Tibet, I send you our good wishes for a safe journey. We will continue our efforts on behalf of the people of Tibet, and your epic climb will serve as a reminder to us politicians to redouble our endeavours from the comfort of our offices! Good luck.

Man is the most dangerous animal on Earth, destroying as he does everything around him through greed and ignorance. He does not own this still beautiful world. He shares it with all living creatures and if he does not get this message very soon, not only will the tiger and rhino be extinct, but man himself will be on a suicide course and tomorrow will be too late.

May your climbing the mountain be successful in drawing attention to the mountains of inhumanity which beset the Tibetan people.

May all beings be one in universal compassion. May Tibet and His Holiness continue to be a light for this dark world. May the peace and unity and respect between the world's religions be also a fruit of the work of peaceful compassion.

Goodness and justice will prevail.

It must start with me. When a critical mass of people realise that all is ONE, and determine to live according to the human values of Truth, Right Conduct, Peace, Love and Non-Violence, only then will peace reign and Mother Earth be healed.

May all beings be at peace, now and for ever.

Love the world, respect the world and the world will be a happier place.

All the people should be free to determine their own future – Free the Tibetan spirit.

Freedom for all Tibetans.

May all the good that is in Tibet live on.

I, and many others, support His Holiness the Dalai Lama, and love His people. (To them) – have courage, remain persistent in what you want. Do not despair – we will support you, and we love you. (To the mountain itself) – Take great care of your people, and of yourself. You are unique and precious. We respect you. With love and affectionate best wishes.

May all the beings throughout the world experience happiness, peace, and freedom. May all living beings be free from suffering and may they find everlasting happiness. May there be peace and happiness on this planet.

I hope and pray for religious freedom for Tibetan people both in Tibet and India and pray that all religious restrictions and bans be lifted.

Peace for all.

Om Mani Peme Hung.

Freedom for all.

Peace for the World.

The Truth of Tibet is like a child. It cannot be denied. It will always be. And, will someday be set free.

May peace and compassion overrule oppression and cruelty throughout the world.

Harmony for Tibet and our once beautiful planet.

Peace in our hearts.

A little love can cure the world's pain, so may love grow and spread.

If the inhabitants of planet Earth fail to grasp the fragility of humanity's moment in space and time, then we will never reach the stars. I wish you the very best of luck. Take care.

Hello world! I love you.

At the furthest point from the centre of the world, comes the resounding message from the heart of humanity: live with and not against; co-operate and not compete; love and do not hate; turn towards and not away; walk with and not ahead nor behind; share and not possess; and then we may find a way towards living at one with ourselves and our Earth. There are no shadows on mountaintops.

A wish for peace, tolerance and lack of fear between all people.

Source of my Being, help me to live in Peace

And save my home, the planet Earth.

May the world be blessed in peace.

May the deep and profound spirit of Tibetan Buddhism bathe all life on Earth with joy.

May we all have the strength to climb whatever mountain may be before us and find a clear view of the right path.

Man's spirit burns ever so brightly – Humanity's greatest endeavour is to keep it in view.

Peace must be the only way forward. Let's all try to understand, love and care for each other and work together to heal ourselves and the world and save the people of Tibet.

All disagreements can be resolved in harmony.

For the children of Tibet, love, lots of love and sport.

Let there be peace in the world.

Long live the Dalai Lama.

May all beings be at Peace – now and forever.

Heaven arms with gentleness those whom it would not see destroyed.

From the highest mountain, may the smallest voice be heard.

Love – love – love.

Free Tibet – Free the world of ignorance – Open our hearts and our minds – Value simplicity and love.

I will love the Earth whatever happens.

Let us take responsibility for the world in which we live. Its life is in our hands and we must accept this duty and bring peace to all.

I will try to communicate more with my fellow humans and bring peace to our world.

Dear Earth – I don't want war, I want peace everywhere. I don't want nuclear tests, I don't want hatred. I want love and respect for the Earth everywhere, no pain, no hatred, no killings – just love and peace.

To be friends with each other.

I go forward, you go backwards and somewhere we should meet. This meeting shall bring the world together in peace and freedom.

I hope for the Tibetans' spirits to rise as high as their mountains, and that freedom can be found by compassionate measures – no cruelty, just respect.

We should respect the Earth that we live on and the elements it gives to us.

Let there be peace between the Tibetans and Chinese. Let all the love and kindness within every being on the Earth unite to stop the destruction of the Earth and the harm caused to all mankind.

You can always climb higher within.

May God speak to all of us and show us the way forward. May He soften the hearts and minds of the Chinese leadership, both in Beijing and Lhasa.

Tibet will be free.

If enough of us think peace, then there will be peace.

May the long-time sun shine upon you and all that surround you, and the pure light within you guide your way home.

Phew, we made it! Good luck to you all and safe return.

Love one another and the Earth our mother.

I will see the good in everybody.

I will live peacefully and pray for all the people in Tibet. I will do my best to look after my family and friends and try not to harm the environment as best I can.

Love always prevails. It is the light of everyone's soul. Protect those you cherish in non-violent ways.

Peace on Earth – goodwill to all mankind.

Let peace overcome war.

May we reach out to all beings with compassionate hearts and let peace blossom.

Hedowch – Peace to Tibet and peace to the people of China.

Respect and care for all citizens of our planet Earth.

For the orchestra of life to play beautiful music everyone must work together as part of the whole.

For the children of Tibet – love and peace.

Listen in the quiet of your minds and with your hearts. There is no need to fear. All is well.

I will be less negative towards others and more forgiving to my friends and family. I will be more tolerant.

I will be kind to everyone I meet and know. I will help to send out the message of world peace as I think it is important that we all preserve our Earth.

We live in a troubled world, but strength, as in the Tibetans, will see us through.

Peace to the children of Tibet and everything on Earth.

I will always try to resolve disputes peacefully.

I will respect all living things of the Earth.

Let the world be a happier and more friendly place.

This is a peace message for hope for the Tibetan refugees – And I hope for world peace – And I send my love to the children of Tibet – Love, peace and happiness.

I will honour and respect the feelings of any other human being, no matter what walk of life they come from.

Let us be mindful of the power of a loving heart.

The children of the world want to live in peace with others and the natural beauty which we must take care of and love.

I will not fight with my brother.

Inner peace brings outer peace.

May you be free in Tibet again.

That wrongs be righted and all be free under the sky.

Love will heal the planet and bring peace to all beings.

May all beings be free from suffering and the causes of suffering.

There is no power in all creation greater than love.

Be happy and don't worry. Peace and happiness is much more important than how much land you own. Enjoy life as it comes to you.

Love, respect, peace and tranquillity always throughout the world.

Let love rule.

Love is like a rainbow. It comes in many different colours and feelings, and in all shapes and sizes. If you can find the pot of gold at the end of it, you will find peace within yourself, and will therefore be able to share that peace with others – keep looking, for what may not seem apparent at first will become obvious once you have found your inner light. Peace to all my brothers and sisters of the Earth.

The Earth is our mother. We must take care of her. Her sacred ground we tread upon with every step we take. The Earth is our mother, we must take care of her.

Of all the teachings we receive this one is the most important. Nothing belongs to you of what there is, of what you take you must share.

I hope my message can be shined down upon the Earth from its highest point, and that my thoughts will help to bring peace in not only Tibet but the other places in need of support. SMILE WORLD.

Hippy rubbish and preaching to mountain wildlife will achieve very little. What's needed is action, action that will make a difference. I pledge to make a difference.

I wish you continuing harmony with the human race and the further progression of survival for all the species that inhabit you!

Man must now nurture the Earth as it first nurtured us.

I will have love and peace. I will not be judgemental of others. I will not be selfish. I will not succumb to consumerism.

Peace will be sustained if we consider everyone as equal and not hurt anyone or anything. Once that is achieved then we can all live in peace.

I will honour and respect the feelings of any other human being, no matter what walk of life they come from. Mother Earth was once a peaceful place. I hope that we can make her happy once again by working together.

I would like to see a world containing only those who don't work for personal profit, but with their first thought for others and the environment. Tibet is just one of the many gems in our world, and should be as free as any of the birds which fly our skies. I hope for eternal peace all over the world.

Respect one's neighbours. Respect their religions and beliefs. Settle arguments through peaceful means and the world will be a happier place.

Preserve today's plants and wildlife so future generations can see the beauty we see today.

I will treat the Earth with the respect it deserves, the animals, the plants and everything and everyone in it.

You can all do what you want because you are all amazingly beautiful.

Love Mother Earth like you would your own mother and love your own mother like you should love yourself.

Think peace. Believe peace. And let's keep the peace.

Respect, love and be kind to the world and all the people in it. Stop the cruelty, oppression, greed, selfishness and inequality that presently seem to rule the Earth. Choose good leaders to carry the world into peace and away from violence and wasted and unkind actions. Carry love with you and do productive things each day. Bless my mother who holds the very spirit of a wonderful person.

Care for animals as you care for your good friends.

Calm the torrent, cease the tempest, live the life, keep the peace, restore the liberty, feed the hungry, help the sick, give the freedom, comfort the oppressed, use the gift, accept the different, nurture the young, stop the fighting not by fighting, live life in happiness.

I know that it will take us all time to realise the extent and the long term aspects of our abuse, but please do not despair of us. Many of us are truly sorry and strive to improve our society for the Earth's sake, so please don't give up – we need you. This need to preserve you will hopefully unite us in peace and harmony, regardless of our different beliefs.

In the idea of every lie there is the seed of truth waiting to blossom.

I will respect my share of the Earth and the animals and plants that go with it always, so give the Earth a chance.

Let us take responsibility for the world in which we live. It's life is in our hands and we must accept this duty and bring peace to all.

You have one mind – use it. You have one heart – listen to it. You have one body – respect it. You have one life – live it.

As there is the word peace in every language, so there should be the will to make it happen, for the sake of everyone on Earth now and in the future. PEACE. Frieden(Gr.), Pokoj(Polish), Pax(Latin), Mir(Croat), Shalom(Jewish), Paix(French), Shanti(Hindi).

I will not judge people by class or religion and I will treat everyone as an individual. In doing this the world will be a happier more peaceful place to be.

I will not have fights with friends and family. I will love nature. I will look after and respect the countryside.

Take care people.

May all beings be at peace, now and for ever

May the roof of the world be restored and may the Dalai Lama continue to flourish towards universal awakening.

SMILE…

Climb For Tibet
A cry from the highest mountain

We invite you to tune in with us for peace on the sixth day of every month at 6pm (UK time). This is an important focus, visualising the 'Climb For Tibet' six-pointed star fired up from the North and South Poles, the Himalayas, the Andes, the Pacific and Africa, encompassing the Earth and all her beings in the light of peace. Wherever you are physically, a mind that is quiet and focused makes a powerful contribution. Do join us.

With love and respect

The 'Climb For Tibet' team

You can also send us a peace message for our next event or contact us via our website: **climbfortibet.org**

Together we make a difference.

Acknowledgements

I would like to send warm and heartfelt thanks to all of my family and friends who have given me their help, support and encouragement, and have stood by my need to give the writing top priority during the growth of this book. With special thanks to:

His Holiness the Dalai Lama for his inspiration and universal love. The other patrons – Joanna Lumley, Uri Geller, Doug Scott, Ivy Smith and Princess Helena Moutafian and for their belief in 'Climb For Tibet'.

All those who gave of themselves by sending peace messages and sponsorship to 'Climb For Tibet'.

All whose names walk across these pages in the unfolding of the story, especially Mig, GT and Pete – a team forged in caring.

Lawley and my three sons for their unending love and support and all that they teach me – not least the arduous task of how to press the right buttons on the computer without panicking. Paul for sharing his higher truth and for feeding me, Scott for translations and dependable priority assistance even when under university pressures, and Mark for the continuous use of his room, which houses the computer and his technical know-how – aided by two little black and white cats whose job it was to sit on all the papers with love.

My 'Climb For Tibet' partner, Pete, for all things – including painstakingly transcribing all the tapes and peace messages, and always being there for me with love and strength at every twist and turn and every tired-out writing moment… and for not giving up on me.

Dan and his team at Eye Books for the glorious vision of how to share heart journeys, and for believing in me and giving me guidance, and especially Clio, for in-tune editing and making everything beautiful.

The illustrators Robert Beer, Mig, Paul and Scott whose combined beautiful efforts had no definite edges as to which picture belonged to whom – sketching for the greater good of the whole.

Yannick's godmother, Filly, and the Duffy family for literary advice.

Those in spirit who held my hand.

Chris at Samye Ling for reminding me to write with love.

Andean Adventures for kindly letting us use their photo of Mount Chimborazo on the cover of this book. Recommended tour operators, exploring beautiful Ecuador for trekking, climbing, bicycling etc. **andeannadventures.com, andeannadventures@gmail.com**

Special acknowledgement

The author would like to honour the Ascended Spirit Master Advarr, whose light of spirit soul, it is now understood, was motivation for her own soul to undertake this journey.

Master Advarr, alongside many Masters from Spirit, works ceaselessly through individuals on Earth for the world expansion of light and a higher consciousness of divine energy. They wish this to be known. Master Advarr's guidance is channelled through Ivy Smith, for whose loving dedication special thanks are due.

The author would like to warmly acknowledge this introduction from Dorothy Forster, the inspired reviver of 'The Big Ben Silent Minute' and Peace Prayer (**thesilentminute.org.uk**), which is a lovely expression of this pathway of Spirit light.

*Source of my being, help me to live in peace and save my home, the
planet Earth.*

Other books by Tess Burrows

Cold Hands Warm Heart

Old-age pensioners Tess and Pete journey across the coldest, driest, windiest place on Earth, with the intent of reaching the South Pole to read out peace messages collected from people from around the world. Their mission was to promote peace on Earth, and Tess charts their highs and lows as they haul themselves and their kit across the Antarctic continent in pursuit of it.

£9.99

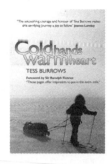

Touch the Sky

We share in Tess' experience of the vibrancy and colour of Africa as the gutsy and compassionate grandmother takes on Kilimanjaro, the highest mountain on the continent. For this peace climb, as a metaphor for people pulling together, she drags with her a tyre filled with peace messages, but can she make it to the top of a mountain that defeats sixty per cent of those who attempt it?

£9.99

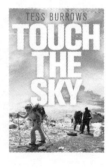

Soft Courage

Yannick, the soft-toy penguin who accompanies Tess Burrows on all her extreme adventures, tells us about them from his particular perspective. He has absorbed some of the Buddhist teachings that have inspired Tess herself, and his own inner journey unfolds during his extensive travels with Tess. In his simple way, Yannick reminds us of the things that matter most.

£9.99

~~About~~ out The Author

~~Tess~~ was born in Southern England in 1948. Educated ~~at~~ School, she gained a degree in ecological science from Edinburgh University and moved to Australia to grow trees.

In 1984 she returned as the mother of three young boys.

It was not until 1987 that she started climbing, and after a number of unusual events raising funds for charity, knew that she could help the Earth – and make a difference.

By 1998 it was time to help Tibet and world peace.

In mountaineering terms she was not an experienced or even a good climber, nor did she have the strength of youth...but it was a dream whose time had come...

Now, in 2018, Tess is proud to have four grandchildren, with another on the way. This further fires her passion to heal the Earth, so the work of carrying peace messages to far, high places continues.

She is also the author of four books, with another on the way. The new book is inspired by her walk across the Himalayas.

Dreams beget dreams...

See more about Tess and her projects and leave peace messages on her website **tessburrows.org**

Be Awesome!